Lala Lajpat Rai

Lala Lajpat Rai

Dr. C.P. Raj
Dr. Ved Prakash

AMIGA PRESS. INC
Delhi -110051

AMIGA PRESS. INC
H.O :- 28-A, Indra Park, Chander Nagar
Delhi :- 110051 (India)
Tel :- 011-22504028, +91-98736-57000
Email :- amigapress@gmail.com
amigaeditorial@gmail.com
Website :- www.amigapress@co.in

This edition is published by Amiga Press.Inc

ISBN : 978-93-84533-23-6

First Published 2018

PRINTED : Replika Press Pvt. Ltd.

Preface

Lala Lajpat Rai (1865-1928) was an Indian author and politician who is chiefly remembered as a leader in the Indian fight for freedom from the British Raj. He was popularly known as Punjab Kesari (The Caesar of Punjab). He was also the founder of Punjab National Bank and Lakshmi Insurance Company.

The non-cooperation movement failed. Therefore there was a lull in political activities. In 1927 the British Government wanted a report on political reforms in India and on amending the Government of India Act. So it appointed a commission. The commission consisted of Sir John Simon and six other members. All of them were members of the British Parliament. There was not a single Indian as member. It was composed solely of White people. The commission was an insult to Indians. These White men were to shape the future of India. The people of India rose as one man against this step. Under Lalaji's leadership, it was resolved to boycott the Simon Commission.

Lajpat Rai moved a resolution in the Central Legislative Assembly in February 1928. "The present constitution of the Commission and its terms of reference are unworthy of acceptance by this House; therefore, this House advises the Government that it should have nothing to do with the Commission."

He made an impassioned speech on that occasion. There were several English men and government officers in the Legislative Assembly. It was known that they would vote against the resolution. Lalaji appealed to the Indian members thus: "Let the members understand that they are slaves in the eyes of the British Government and of the world. When they vote on the resolution let them remember that in 1919, because of a single epidemic, six crores of people died in our country. Let them remember that in this country ten crores of people do not have even one meal a day."

What right did the British Parliament have to frame a constitution for India? That was Lalaji's fearless question. Only Indians had the right to decide about their future. They were determined about it. The report of Motilal Nehru and his colleagues was ready. It had protested against the British attitude. Lalaji toured the whole of India to give publicity to the Nehru report. He asserted: "Those who oppose the report are the enemies of Swaraj and enemies of India."

Lala Lajpat Rai was a voracious reader and everything he read left a great imprint on his mind. He was deeply impressed by the ideals of patriotism and nationalism outlined by Italian revolutionary leader Giuseppe Mazzini. Inspired by Mazzini, Lalaji became indoctrinated into the revolutionary way of attaining freedom. He, together with other prominent leaders like Bipin Chandra Pal, Aurobindo Ghosh from Bengal, and Bal Gangadhar Tilak from Maharashtra, began to see the negative aspects of moderate politics advocated by many leaders of the Indian National Congress. They voiced their strong opposition to the Congress' demand for gradual progress to dominion status and began voicing the need for complete independence or 'Purna Swaraj'. In personal views he was a great believer in inter-faith harmony, but he did not think right of the trend by Congress leaders to sacrifice Hindu interests to appease the Muslim section of the party. Lala was one of the few leaders who realized the difficulties of a united anti-colonial struggle and a possible source of religious conflict between the Hindus and Muslims of the country. His proposal for "a clear partition of India into a Muslim India and non-Muslim India" on December14, 1923, in The Tribune, met with major controversy.

The book tries to cover the life and works of Lala Lajpat Rai in a comprehensive way.

—*Editor*

Contents

1

Biography

"People once awakened, and awakened rightly, cannot he put down "

— Lala Lajpat Rai.

A great national leader who came to be called the 'Lion of Punjab.' Worked tire-lessly to improve education, to promote unity among Hindus and to reform society. His clarion call and glorious life inspired the nation. The Lathis of the servants of British imperialism cruelly cut his life short. It was the evening of October 30, 1928. Standing on the platform at a crowded public meeting in Lahore City, a person known as the 'Lion of Punjab, 'said in an inspiring voice:

"Every blow on our bodies this afternoon is like a nail driven into the coffin of British imperialism." Terrible blows had battered the chest and the body of the great man who made that stirring speech. The humiliation inflicted by the high-handedness of the British was more painful than the wounds.

On the morning of the seventeenth day after this, the great revolutionary died. Onward along the path he had trodden his followers marched towards freedom. The great leader cut down by the high-handedness of the then imperialist Punjab Government was Lala Lajpat Rai.

AN INTELLIGENT STUDENT

The great patriot Lala Lajpat Rai was born on 28th January 1865 in Dhudika village of Ferozepur District of Punjab Province, His father Lala Radha Kishan was an Urdu teacher in a government school. He belonged to the family of Agarwals, a family noted for its love of freedom and self-respect. Although illiterate, Lajpat Rai's mother Gulab Devi was an ideal Hindu woman. It was from her that Lalaji imbibed patriotic sentiments.

Lalaji was a very intelligent pupil. He won scholarships. Poverty and sickness stood in the way of his higher education. He passed the Entrance Examination of the Calcutta University in the first class in 1880. The same year he also passed the Entrance Examination of Punjab University. Afterwards he joined the Lahore Government College. At the same time he studied law.

Because of the poverty of the family his education was interrupted for two years.

The Dawn of Ideals

The two years spent in Lahore were important in Lalaji's life. As he read the history of the past glory of India and the biographies of her great sons, the boy shed tears. The love of freedom and the keen desire to serve the country took root in him at that time. During those days the Arya Samaj founded by Swami Dayananda

Saraswati was dynamic in social service. It was a time when enthusiastic Punjabi youths were attracted by the progressive ideals and reformist plans of the Arya Samaj. Lalaji was then hardly sixteen. When he joined the Arya Samaj in 1882 his life of social service began. Patriotism was kindled. The idea took root in his mind that the chains of Indian slavery should be broken.

The Lawyer

Having passed the first examination in law in 1883 Lala could practice as a muktiar (a minor lawyer). He had also to bear the burden of running the family. Eighteen-year-old Lalaji practiced in the revenue court of Jagrav town. After passing the Pleaders' Examination he came to Hissar in South Punjab and commenced practice as a lawyer. He had no thought of making money in his profession and settling down comfortably. He wanted to devote his life to the service of his country. He wanted to read the biography of Mazzini, the brave revolu-tionary of Italy. He could not get a copy of the book in India. Lie wrote to a friend in England and got it. Mazzini's bravery, magnanimity and patriotism thrilled him.

THE BEGINNING OF PUBLIC SERVICE

His life of six years in Hissar became the apprenticeship for public service. After the death of Swami Dayananda, Lalaji with his associates toiled to develop the Anglo-Vedic College. The three tenets of Arya Samaj are the reformation of society, the advancement of Hindu Dharma and educational progress. Lalaji earned a thousand rupees a month. He kept aside a part of his earnings to keep his father above want and arranged for the interest on it to be paid to his father. on tenth of his income was earmarked for work for the nation. The greater part of that sum was being used for Arya Samaj activities.

When the Lieutenant Governor visited Hissar, Lalaji pleaded that the Welcome Address to be presented to him should be in Urdu. To satisfy the British officer a speech had already been prepared in English. Lalaji's suggestion madeeveryone nervous. But without a trace of fear, he presented the Address in Urdu and there by invited the wrath of the British.

Most of his time was given to Arya Samaj activities. Working ceaselessly he set up branches of the Arya Samaj. He built up educational institutions. But he was not partial towards any community. He was elected unopposed to the Municipal Council from a constituency where there were a number of Muslims.

To The Political Sphere

In 1888, still a lawyer, he entered politics. The Indian National Congress was fighting for the country's freedom. Realizing the dire need for freedom, Lalaji joined the Congress as a freedom fighter. Sir Syed Ahmed who was in the Congress had just then left it.

He had begun to argue that Muslims should not join the Congress and that they should support the government. Lala wrote bitter open letters to him in the Urdu weekly Koh-i-noor'. The letters earned high praise in political circles. The same year in the Congress session at Allahabad, when Lalaji arrived with eighty delegates from Punjab, he received a tumultuous welcome. his heroic speech in Urdu there had a great effect on the Congress leaders. Lala was a young man of 23 years. His fame spread quickly in Congress.

In Lahore

The small town of Hissar proved inadequate for his growing social work. After qualifying to practice as an advocate in the Punjab High Court, he settled down in Lahore in 1892. The Congress session of 1893 was held at Lahore. The first Indian to become a member of the British Parliament, Dadabhai Naoroji, was the president of the session. Lalaji served as an enthusiastic volunteer.

Lalaji worked like a bee. There was no time for rest. When he was immersed in Congress work there was a split in the Arya Samaj. Lalaji gave a new shape to the D.A.V. College and stood by it.

Lightning In His Pen

Lalaji was not merely an outstanding politician but also an able writer. The biographies he wrote in Urdu are memorable.

He wrote the biographies of the patriots Mazzini and Garibaldi who unified Italy. He also wrote outstanding books about Indian great men Shivaji, Sri Krishna and Dayananda Saraswati. The books on Mazzini and Shivaji contained passages, which encouraged people to fight for freedom. So the government even thought of arresting Lalaji.

THE SERVANT OF THE SUFFERING

The sense of service shown by Lalaji and his devoted endeavor to help the poor, the downtrodden and those in difficulties bestowed lustre on his multifarious exertions. A terrible famine struck the Central Provinces in 1896.

The draught shook people. No one can forget the part played by Lalaji at the time.

Orphans and the destitute were at the mercy of the Christian missionaries and were being converted to Christianity. Lalaji began a movement to help the orphans. He saved 250 orphan children from Jabalpur, Bilaspur and other districts, brought them to Punjab and admitted them to the orphanages of the Arya Samaj.

He realized that he did not have sufficient time for both social service and legal practice; so in 1898 he reduced his legal practice. In 1899 a worse famine struck Punjab, Rajasthan, Kathiawad and Central Provinces. Again Lalaji led the movement by the Arya Samaj to save helpless children.

It was a trying time for him. He organized an extraordinary movement. Not only were 2,000 helpless persons saved but they were also provided with food, clothing, education and employment. In this movement sometimes there were clashes with Christian missionaries.

Government set up a famine relief commission in 1901 and got Lalaji's views. His account of famine conditions and his views led to a change in the government's attitude to the destitute. Hindus and people of other religions were able to establish orphanages for destitute children of their folds.

In 1905 an occasion arose for Lalaji to dive deper into another matter. There was an earthquake in Kangra district resulting in enormous loss of life and property. The Arya Samaj of Lahore set up a relief committee, As its secretary Lalaji toured Punjab province extensively and collected money for the committee. His service to the people at that time was unforgettable.

VISIT TO ENGLAND

The same year general elections were being held in England, the Indian National Congress decided to send two represen-tatives to acquaint the public with conditions in India. Lajpat Rai and Gopal Krishna Gokhale were the two represen-tatives. When they returned from their visit to England, thousands of people welcomed them at the Lahore railway station. Students unhitched the horses and they pulled the carriage.

During his tour of England Lalaji told the people they're about the conditions in India during the British rule. More than this, his reading of the situation was important.

It become clear to him that Indians alone could mould their future and for that purpose, the government should be in their hands. He resolved that India should undertake the fight for freedom, the use of articles made in India and boycott of foreign goods. He put forth these views at the 1907 Congress session held in Surat City.

GOVERNMENT'S WRATH

1907 witnessed a high-water mark in the adventurous life of Lalaji. That was a time of revolution when the winds of change were blowing across the country; new ideas and a new zest moved the people. There were riots in Lahore and Rawalpindi.

In Meerut preparations were being made to observe the iftieth anniversary of the first fight for freedom (1857). Peasants were upset on account of the proposal of the government to increase the water rates in Punjab. It was a grievous crime in the eyes of the government that Lalaji and certain lawyers addition to this, there were disturbances, supported the ryots.

Sir Densil lbbotson was the Lieutenant Governor of Punjab. He wrote to Lord Morley, then the minister in the British cabinet who was in charge of Indian affairs: "It appears that some leaders like Lalaji have sworn to drive the British out of India. An attempt is being made to kindle hatred Against Englishmen and break the government administrative machinery."

Those were days when there was a sense of fear in official circles. A poor Indian was murdered. A factual report appeared in newspapers. An attempt was made to foist the guilt on a Punjabi journalist.

The people of Punjab protested against the mischief of the government. In addition to this, there were disturbances, because of unjust laws like the Colonial Settlement Act and Land Mortgage Amendment Act and because of increase in the tax on land and water rates. Sir Densil was perturbed. Without any reason he deported Lalaji and with him Ajit Singh (a relative of the great patriot Bhagat Singh) to Mandalay in Burma.

People all over the country opposed the unjust action of the government. Tilak wrote in the newspaper 'Kesari'-"if the British rulers act like the Russian Czars, the people of India will have to react as the people of Russia did." Government had to bow to the vigorous protests of the people and the legal profession; it had no choice. Government realized that the deportation order was improper and illegal; it brought Lalaji to Lahore on November 18 and set him free.

Lalaji was considered one of the famous trinity of the Congress radicals. The three great men were Lala Lajpat Rai of Punjab, Bal Gangadhar Tilak of Maharashtra and Bipin Chandra Pal of Bengal.

The country affectionately called them Lal, Bai and Pal. There was a split between the radicals and the moderates in the Congress organization. Lalaji found that it was not possible to bring about an agreement between the two factions; he therefore kept out of the Congress for a few years.

In 1911 he re-entered the Lahore Municipal Council. When he stood for election to the Municipal Council his popularity was immense. Even the deaf, the dumb and disabled' people turned up to vote for him. A dumb voter brought a photograph of Lalaji to indicate that he would vote for Lalaji.

IN OTHER COUNTRIES

Lalaji re-entered Congress in 1912

He left for England in April 1914 with the Congress delegation as a representative of Punjab. He had planned to be there for six months. But because of the outbreak of the First World War, he had to change his plans. It did not seem wise to return then. It was likely the British would keep him in detention for a long period. Lalaji went from England to America. His visit to America was a voluntary exile. In America he made a number of speeches about India and conditions of life in this country. He wrote a number of books. As part of the effort to develop the Indian agitation he established the Indian Home Rule League in New York.

How could there be dearth of work for the Indian hero in America? He set up the 'India Information Bureau'. He started a journal 'Young India' and gave a fillip to the movement. He himself edited the paper. The paper expounded the Indian culture and xplained in detail the necessity for Indian freedom. It attracted the attention of everybody. The circulation increased. Through this paper it became possible for not only Indians but also Americans and people of other countries to understand the aims and objects of Lalaji and to sympathize with India's aims. The movement gained support.

While in America he wrote two books: 'Arya Samaj' and 'England's, Debt to India.' His life in America was not bed of roses. He himself cooked his food. He earned money for his living by writing books and articles. Germany was then at war with England. The German Government attempted to take advantage of the dissatisfaction of the Indians by enticing Lalaji. But he refused to be tempted.

While in America, Lalaji found time to visit Japan. In both the countries he made friendship and won the sympathy of influential people. He conducted himself in such a way that both countries came to trust him. Thus he made a name for himself. At the end of the great War in 1919 he wanted to return to India. The British Government would not give him a passport. In India in Jalianwalla Bagh of Amritsar, British soldiers fired on helpless Indians at a public meeting. Lajpat Rai got news of the dreadful massacre even when he was in New York. He was eager to join his countrymen. He got the passport at the end of the year. In December 1919 Lalaji came from New York to London. There he met the famous author Bernard Shaw and some socialist friends. Then he came to Paris.

THE NON-COOPERATION MOVEMENT

Lalaji thus brought about a revolution in the attitudes of the people of England and America towards India. He returned in February 1920. Lokamanya Tilak, Jinnah and Shrimati Annie Besant accorded a heroic welcome to him. Welcome Addresses were presented to him in Bombay, Delhi and Lahore. He was elected as the president of the special session of the Congress held in September 1920.

Next year Mahatma Gandhi started the Non-cooperation Movement. The movement gained momentum in the country. Lalaji jumped into the agitation with his bosom friend, the revolutionary Ajit Singh. In response to Lalaji's stirring call, the whole of Punjab Province joined the movement. The agitation shook the firm foundations of the government. Government schools and colleges were boycotted. Work in courts and offices came to a halt. The people were firmly united against imperialism. Lalaji himself started a national school in Lahore. Tilak opened a political science institution. Thus enthusiastic youths found guidance. Lalaji undertook a whirlwind tour of Punjab for ten days for that purpose and collected nine lakh rupees. Full of reverence for him, people contributed money enthusiastically.

In Prison

Lajpat Rai's organizing ability and heroic speeches were inspiring. Government was finding it difficult to face the intense Non-cooperation Movement growing day by day. All over the country there were agitation and hartals and the rulers were shaken. Lalaji became a dangerousperson in the eyes of the government.In December 1921 Lalaji was arrested. The other leaders of the movement, Motilal Nehru and Chittaranjan Das were also imprisoned. Lalaji was sentenced to 18 months' rigorous imprisonment. Because of the people's protest and the pleadings by lawyers he was released after two months. It was one o' clock in the night when he was released. When he came to the door he was arrested again. He was tried for another offence and was sentenced to rigorous imprisonment for two years.

While in jail he fell ill and his health deteriorated. When the public learnt this vigorous agitation was started throughout the country for his release. Government released him. Lalaji went to Solan to improve his health.

ORGANIZING THE HINDUS

As soon as his health improved Lalaji become active again. He joined the 'Swaraj Party' of Motilal Nehru. He was elected to the Central Legislative Assembly. By that time the Hindu Muslim unity move shaped by Mahatma Gandhi had failed.

Lalaji had to turn his attention to communal problems. He was himself influenced by the Arya Samaj and was a staunch supporter of the Hindu dharma. But he was aware of the need for Hindu Muslim unity in the fight for Swaraj. The Non-Cooperation movement was crumbling and ill feeling between different communities was reaching dangerous proportions. In the 1924 Hindu-Muslim riots Hindus suffered much in Kohat of North-West Frontier Province. In two days of riots not only were 150 Hindus killed but also 400 persons had also to be shifted to Rawalpindi. Mahatma Gandhi undertook a fast. There was a conference to bring about friendship among the followers of different religions and a national council was set up. But the problem was not solved. The Kohat tragedy pained and disappointed Lalaji. He had to stand by the helpless Hindu community. To counteract associations formed by the Muslims, Lalaji tirelessly fostered movements for 'Purification of Hinduism 'and 'Organization of Hinduism'. As long ago as 'in 1924 Lalaji expressed the fear that Muslims might want a division of India and demand a separate state for themselves. This shows his far-sightedness.

He presided over the Hindu Mahasabha held at Calcutta in 1925. The speech he made about Hindu dharma and the necessity to uphold it woke up the Hindus. In 1926 Lalaji participated in the International Labor Conference held at Geneva as a representative of workers in India. He also took part in similar conferences held in Britain and France.

"Unhappy India"

Lalaji went to Europe in 1927 to improve his health. Katherine Mayo, a foreign journalist, visited India. She wrote a book called 'Mother India'. It was about Indian civilization, culture and life. She saw only sheer ignorance and filth in India and nothing good or decent. It gave a totally misleading picture of India. In an article Gandhiji protested and called it a 'gutter inspector's report'. The book Mayo wrote was published when Lalaji was in London. The book created uproar in India and Britain. People who were opposed to the freedom of India had given money for the publication of the book. Lalaji read it. He could not keep quiet. Soon after his return to India the first thing he did was to write a book 'Unhappy India.' He gave a fitting reply to the false propaganda of Miss Mayo.

THE SIMON COMMISSION

The non-cooperation movement failed. Therefore there was a lull in political activities. In 1927 the British Government wanted a report on political reforms in India and on amending the Government of India Act. So it appointed a commission. The commission consisted of Sir John Simon and six other members. All of them were members of the British Parliament. There was not a single Indian as member. It was composed solely of White people. The commission was an insult to Indians. These White men were to shape the future of India. The people of India rose as one man against this step. Under Lalaji's leadership, it was resolved to boycott the Simon Commission.

Lajpat Rai moved a resolution in the Central Legislative Assembly in February 1928. "The present constitution of the Commission and its terms of reference are unworthy of acceptance by this House; therefore, this House advises the Government that it should have nothing to do with the Commission."

He made an impassioned speech on that occasion. There were several English men and government officers in the Legislative Assembly. It was known that they would vote against the resolution. Lalaji appealed to the Indian members thus: "Let the members understand that they are slaves in the eyes of the British Government and of the world. When they vote on the resolution let them remember that in 1919, because of a single epidemic, six crores of people died in our country. Let them remember that in this country ten crores of people do not have even one meal a day."

What right did the British Parliament have to frame a constitution for India? That was Lalaji's fearless question. Only Indians had the right to decide about their future. They were determined about it. The report of Motilal Nehru and his colleagues was ready. It had protested against the British attitude. Lalaji toured the whole of India to give publicity to the Nehru report. He asserted: "Those who oppose the report are the enemies of Swaraj and enemies of India."

Imperialism Strikes

The 30th of October 1928 was an evil day in India's political history. The Simon Commission was expected to arrive in Lahore on that day. The rulers had taken precautions to prevent a public protest. Prohibitory orders were enforced. Lalaji was ill that day. Still he led the procession to protest against the. Commission.

When the Simon Commission arrived, on one side there where traitors to welcome them. On another side the revolutionaries demonstrated against the Commission. In the protest march youths staged a tremendous show. A hartal was observed that day; there was a sea of black flags. Thousands and thousands of hearts and voices shouted "Simon, go back!" The lion of Punjab, Lala Lajpat Rai, led the procession. When the trains reached the station, the cry "Simon, go back!" hit the sky. Police security arrangements crumbled. The crowd was so thick that movement was impossible. The Police charged with their Lathis (stout sticks).

The blood of innocent people began to flow. Lalaji's friends Sukhdev, Yashpal, Bhagavati Charan and others surrounded him, in order to protect him. Police officer Scot saw Lalaji and his bodyguards.

He ordered the Police to beat thebodyguards. A Police officer named Sanders came forward to do the job. The Police Lathis rained blows on Lalaji-on the head and all over the body. Lala realized this incident would lead to conflict and a bloodbath. He told the huge crowd of revolutionaryyouths: "Leave this place." The crowd dispersed.

The same evening there was a mammoth public meeting. The despicable action of the Police was severely condemned and the Simon Commission was boycotted. Police Deputy Superintendent Neal was present at the meeting. Lalaji turned to Neal and said in English so that he could understand him: "The blows, which fell on me today, are the last nails driven into the coffin of British Imperialism."

One word from Lajpat Rai to the youths would have been enough; they would have let loose rivers of blood. But Lalaji practiced non-violence strictly. The country had to restrain its anger. In the very week of the incident Lalaji attended the All-India Congress Committee and all-party meetings. He grew weak and returned to Lahore.

Lalaji fell ill and died of a heart attack on 17th November 1928. The whole of India knew that his death was a result of the lathi blows. A deliberate murder by the Police!

More than a lakh of people took up in his funeral procession.

INDUSTRIAL AND ECONOMICAL THINKING OF LALA LAJPAT RAI

There can be no denial of the fact, that the industrial and economical future of our country mainly depends upon the introduction and successful working of the Joint Stock system. Gifted with vast natural resources, which can produce any amount of raw materials and with an enormous and ever increasing population which is always in want of employment, India could achieve wonders in the line of manufacturing industries, only, if it had the necessary capital and the still more necessary skill at its command. Of artistic skill it has plenty.

What it lacks is the power and capacity of calling in the assistance of modern Science, and modern appliances in the refining of its arts, and the production of larger quantities, at lesser cost, of its articles of art. Precious little has up to this time been done in the way of enabling qualified Indians to acquire this skill. Beyond providing some facilities for acquiring an elementary and mainly theoretical knowledge of modern sciences in connection with the

Arts Colleges, the Government has done practically nothing in the way enabling or encouraging Indian youths to acquire mechanical skill with a view to the industrial development of the country. It was not perhaps to the interest of the British to take steps which might have eventually closed the Indian markets to English goods. If so, they probably did not foresee that the doctrine of free trade might drive even the English goods out of Indian markets in favour of that placed in their natural resources and in their populations than the British Isles. Thus their neglect has not only injured India, but brought no permanent benefit to Great Britain. Is it not a fact that English goods are being driven out of markets by the cheaper productions of Germany, United States, France and Japan? But in the absence of Government initiative in the matter, we, Indians, too have not done much to provide facilities for the acquisition of mechanical skill by our youths, because of want of foresight and of power of organisation in us.

Instead of putting the horse before the cart we have been all this time busy in making the cart go with the horse behind. Instead of applying most of our humble resources in equipping our countrymen with mechanical skill in order to enable them to stop the exploitation of this country by foreigners, we have been spending lacs upon fruitless agitation for political enfranchisement. It never occurred to us that in these days of science and machinery a nation poor in economics and skill could never be politically great or free. Thank God that after a lot of dissipation of energies we have been awakened to a sense of our duty in this direction and on all sides there is a demand for technical training and Industrial education. But few of those who cry for technical education and are even prepared to incur some amount of expenditure and sacrifice for the same know what technical education is, and how it can be introduced in this country.

The movement therefore is suffering for want of expert knowledge and no amount of agitation or enthusiasm can make up for that unless the latter is accompanied by earnest efforts to provide means to Indian youths to acquire this knowledge. Many an industry can be made to flourish if we had only technical knowledge to work it up. The first thing therefore to do is to send Indian youths to Europe and America to be trained as experts. Let each province send one youth every year to learn all that is required to start and successfully work up a particular industry. Japan has done the same through its Government, because there the Government represents the country. In India the case is different and the country will have to do this by itself what in Japan has been done by its Government.

Capital is the second important factor in the development of industries. Individual wealth is powerless before the accumulated wealth of millionaires who have joined together on the joint stock principles. Rich citizens can no doubt do a lot by investing their riches in manufactories and industries which can be run by them with their own resources. But Joint Stock enterprise must be met by similar combinations and these combinations, to be successful must be organised on sound principles and with perfect confidence in those who are at the helm of the affairs. This confidence can only be begotten by the promoters themselves being men of substance, having substantial risks in the enterprise and of acknowledged integrity and honesty of purpose. Joint Stock enterprise in India is yet an infant of very tender age, it is a foreign plant that has yet to grow and take root before it fructifies and as such it requires great care and caution to watch its growth and secure it a fruitful crop. The friends of Industrial development need about the conscious and indolent the people of this country are.

Our lacking in enterprise is mainly due to want of faith in each other and unwillingness to co-operate for common good. It is therefore of the greatest importance that the business of company promoting in this country should be entirely above suspicion. There seems to be no room for encouraging individual speculations under the sense of company-promoting. The English company-promoter, of whom we have of late read so much in British Journals, must not be allowed to abuse the confidence of those Indians who are disposed to give a fair trial to joint stock system and who if once deceived are not likely to enter the lists again. But equally vigilant must we be against the Indian company-promoter, if there are any, who may be disposed to copy their British co-adjustors and make a profession of company-promoting at the cost of those who might be willing to invest a portion or the whole of their hard earned savings, in business or businesses which is or are likely to be of profit to themselves as well as to the country at large.

The Indian shareholder is generally a sleeping partner and prone to leave the business to those, relying upon whose name and fame, he signed his application for shares. He is no good for control or check and therefore gives a carte-haunch to the managers. If he is proved to have been unfortunate in placing his confidence all that he shall do will be to curse his stars and nothing, further. He will not move an inch to see that those who have played fast and loose with his money, receive their deserts and thus deter others from similar acts of treachery and bad faith. Much less is he to be moved by: considerations of public good or the good of the country.

Under these circumstances the friends of industrial development cannot be too vigilant against this class of company-promoters. In England itself a cry has already been raised to the effect that the existing laws do not sufficiently protect the shareholder from the devices of a cunning and sharp director. A writer in the Contemporary Review of June 1901, while reviewing the causes of the economic decay of Great Britain pens the dirge on the Company Laws of England. Says he, "Our company law is a most excellent law in favour of cunning company-promoters, financiers, stock-brokers and of everyone who wishes to rob the nation of its accumulated saving. "After giving a table of figures showing the amounts of capital involved in companies liquidated from 1892 to 1899 as ranging between 34 millions sterling and 77 millions he quotes the following remarks of the

InspectorGeneral of Companies in liquidation: "It appears that the total number of abortive and liquidating companies during 1899, were in proportion to the new companies registered, 6 percent as against 56 per cent during the previous year. "To explain it still more he is believed to have further said, "About 57 per cent of the Capitttl belongs to the more or less solvent class while the remaining three-fourths in number or 63 per cent of capital wanted represent the insolvent class, "The italics are ours. Upon this data the writer bases the following pregnant remarks of his own—"Whilst the thrifty part of our population has been robbed within a few years of several hundred pounds earned by millions of British toilers during a life-time of patient labour, promoters who perpetrated these enormous frauds on the nation, nor their satellites have been imprisoned with hard labour.

The new Company Law is not designed to protect the unsuspecting public but to protect the company-promoter and his associates. It is a law in favour of the strong against the weak. In consequence of this immunity from punishment for fraud, in consequence of the growing difficulty of making an honest living by productive industry and in consequence of the ease by which company frauds may be perpetrated under the shelter of our company law then popularity of promoting swindling companies is on the increase."The Indian Company Law is much the same as the English, in fact, almost a copy of it, and the rapidity with which companies here too are being floated and then wound up or sold at considerable loss to the shareholders raises an apprehension in our mind lest in a few years the state of affairs here might justify the same strictness as we have quoted above about the class of professional-company-promoters in England. Let us hope at any rate that the occasion for such a complaint may not arise soon, although signs are already visible which excite our worst fears.

Lajpat Rai.

FAMINE ORPHANS AND WIVES

That the last two famines have told very heavily upon the numerical strength of the Hindus is a fact which does not require to be established by any great array of facts and figures. The tracts mostly affected by these famines were mainly Hindu and consequently it was amongst the latter that the suffering was the most acute and the effects extremely disastrous. In these tracts the community not only lost lacs by death, but an immensely large number have so seriously deteriorated in physique, that though not totally incapable of bearing children, the offspring which they might bring forth must be small in number and extremely weakly in body. Besides actual losses by death many a family has been deprived of the means of continuity of line by the survival of women doomed to life-long widowhood. Even men who have survived their wives are not seen to be remarried.

Add to this the loss by conversion to other religions, which have been sufficiently numerous to cause a gap which will not be easily filled up. However true it may be that people whom sheer want of food and drink forced to accept the protection of other religions in these periods of dire calamity can hardly be called converts but it is a fact all the same that they are lost to Hinduism. The Hindu is conservative to the core, and loves his religion and nationality, above every thing else. To him the loss of religion is worse than death itself, but what is he to do when starvation and other privations following in the train of grinding poverty root out the very idea of religion from his mind. It was only in extreme agony, that they sacrificed their beliefs, to the necessity of keeping body and soul together. The choice lay between two agonies — one of starvation, the other of loss of every sentiment and connection that was dear and sacred — and it is no wonder that many succumbed to the second, though only after they had last stage of suffering beyond which there was only the awning abyss of annihilation.

Many must have willingly preferred death to the acceptance of relief at such a heavy cost, but how can we blame even those who, fearing the pangs of slow dissolution, exchanged life or religion. Be what it may, it is a fact that in these calamitous scarcities which have held the country in their squeezing grip for the last five years consecutively, a very large number of men and women have been lost to Hinduism, which, otherwise would have been a source of strength and power generally as well as a source of increase to its numbers. Then again numerous families have been ruined and have practically (at least from a Hindu point of view) ended, by their young ones having been taken away to long distances from their homes, and kept in charge of organisation which are beyond the reach of their parents and relatives, if any living.

These children though living, are for all purposes dead to their parents, their relatives, their caste and their community. We are talking not of orphans only but even of those who either deserted by their parents in the vicissitudes of famine or who strayed away from their homes either in search of food or in search of absent parents who had already left for labour, and who while thus straying were collected and relieved, as they say, by benevolent philanthropists belonging to other denominations. These children were principally the victims of that short sighted policy, which in the first instance, allowed very large number of relief seekers to accumulate on large works distant from their homes and their villages, and then allowed philanthropy to take charge of other people's children during the pendency of the famine, either from the Government poor-houses, and Government orphanages by the authority of Government Officers or from the streets etc., when they were straying in search of food or relatives.

In plain words the truth is that the various missions engaged in the work of famine relief purchased so many converts to their faith at an awfully cheaper price per head than it ordinarily costs them to evangelize one non-Christian soul in India in years of normal rainfall. It is an open secret that even ordinary methods of sale and purchase were resorted to. Children, boys and girls, were sold and purchased at a few annas, or a few pices per head.

Don't you be thinking, gentle reader, that these are imaginary statements. We know what we state and we can prove it, if necessary, to the hilt. Why, quotations from Christian papers themselves, will bear out the truth of our statement. What, then does it amount to ? Briefly told it amounts to this, that a Christian Government, with its anti-slavery laws, allowed the missionaries of its own faith, to take charge of deserted children, in many cases with parents living, and in some cases to purchase them of parents themselves, with the ostensible object of converting them to Christianity in lieu of supporting them with food and water, in the time of famine. Ah I but for fallen Hinduism, the state of things should have been the reverse.

A Hindu would gladly feed and clothe any number of the poor of other religions, in times of famine, or no famine and would never think of taking advantage of other people's misfortunes and troubles and poverty. By the help of others he has to pay for it dearly. Neither a Muhammadan, nor a Christian will feed him except at the price of his religion. Even in this famine, if well-to-do Hindus had used some discrimination in the distribution of their charities they could have saved thousands of their people and their little ones from being sent out of the bosom of Hinduism forever. Rich Hindus swelled the lists of famine Charitable Funds, a decent portion of which was spent through the Christian Missionary who used it in the Christian interest as effectively as he could.

Broad-mindedness and charity to the poor, without any distinction of creed and caste is a noble trait of character of which Hinduism might be proud, in the abstract, but in this world of sects and creeds and in these days of struggle and competition between creed and creed, it does not pay. If over-rich, superfluously rich, resourceful Christianity cannot stand it how can poverty-stricken, slavery ridden, helpless. Hinduism afford to indulge in it. But we have digressed It was not our object to read a sermon to the Hindus. We meant to state facts and to comment upon them a little.

To resume, in Rajputana alone, Hinduism lost seventy thousand of these unfortunate children, who were collected by Christian Mission of various denominations and dispatched to distant places in various parts of India. The Arya Samajists took charge of about a 1,000 and sailed them to the Punjab. There were some married girls amongst the latter who had been deserted by their husbands and who would have joined the seventy thousand mentioned above, but for their timely rescue by the Arya Samajists. The latter are now searching their husbands and using all possible means of restoring them to their families, but those whom the Christians took away, are gone for good, whether married, or unmarried, orphan or no orphan.

The Arya Samajists removed these children to the Punjab because they could not maintain them on the spot. They depended entirely upon local support in their own province which they could not have got but by the removal of the children to the land of five rivers. No amount of descriptive rhetoric, short of the actual sight of misery, would have moved out people to the necessity of taxing their scanty means.

The removal of the famine stricken children to the various districts in the Punjab was an effective appeal which touched more successfully the heart of every Hindu who could save even a little out of his own necessities. Then the question of maintaining and training them after the famine, was another difficulty in the way of providing relief on the spot. In the case of orphans at least, it was out of the question to give them temporary relief during the pendency of the famine, unless the relieving agencies were prepared to make permanent arrangements for bringing them up as useful members of society who could, in the course of time, earn their own livelihood.

Of course all these ends could be achieved even in Rajaputana, if the Arya Samajists could command the same amount of funded help as was at the back of Christian Missions. Failing this, mere necessity forced them to remove the children to their province. But there was no difficulty in the way of the Pain. England, America or other parts of Europe. To him Rajaputna was as good as the Punjab, Bengal, Madras, Bombay, or any other place in India, still there might be some justification for those missions who had their permanent or orphanages and buildings at the places to which they removed the famine stricken children of Rajaputana or the Central Provinces. But what possible justification could there be for the transfer of these children to distant places by those missions who had to keep them in hired buildings ?

At Lahore, itself, two of the mission orphanages, one containing more than a 100 boys an A the other more than a 100 girls are located in hired buildings. Is it not, then, reasonable to infer, that besides the avowed facilities of management and economy, there was another object too, which induced our philanthropic Missionaries to remove these children to places distant from their homes ? What ever be the object, however, there can be no denial of the fact that this action of theirs has resulted in the complete loss of those children to their families and homes, at least of such who have parents or other relatives living and willing to take them back. And this has taken place under the policy of neutrality followed by the Government. The truth is, that with these of recurring famines, which have become an almost permanent feature of this ill-fated country, this system of orphan relief is a standing menace to Hinduism, and it is therefore with great satisfaction that we have read the recommendations of the last Famine Commission on this subject.

Our gratification enhances still more when we remember that in 1898 even a strong ruler like Sir Antony MacDonnell failed to carry into practice the principles now so clearly enunciated in this report, in 1895 Sir Antony allowed Christian missons to remove Hindu orphans of the N.-W. P. and Oudh to distant parts of India, while he had practically refused the same privileoe to the Arya Samajists of the Panjab, a few months before. Consequently we are glad to find that the last Famine Commission have recognised the great importance "of this question and have recommended that the "policy of the Government in regard to orphans, should be formulated in Provincial Codes, helm risk of misconception either its officer's or the public." So far as the principles of this policy are concerned, we believe they have been the same all this time on paper at least. What we are thankful for, is the unambiguous and clear language which the Commissioners have used in making their recommendations. Should the Local Governments formulate their policy in the Provincial Codes in similar style, we feel sure, much of the misapprehension hitherto caused would be removed, and much unnecessary discontent would be stopped. The Hindus will know what they can do to keep children of their community within the pale of their religion. The following recommendations should therefore be hailed with delight by the whole Hindu community, as they are the persons principally affected by these rules, the Mahomedans being sufficiently powerful, united and influential to allow the destitute children of their community to be taken away with impunity by persons and Associations of other denominations. The italics are ours.

Para. 234 of the Report recommends that the following policy be adopted by Government with regard to orphans or destitute children viz. that "the State should be, in times of famine, the temporary guardian of children whom it finds deserted and should not, in our opinion divest itself of the care of them until a reasonable time has elapsed after the close of the famine, during which efforts should be made to discover the natural protectors of the children or, failing these, respectable persons of the same religion who are willing to adopt them."According to this recommendation it is the duty of the State henceforth to discover respectable persons of the same religion who may be willing to adopt children whose natural protectors have either died or cannot be found out.

Failing such respectable persons the deserted children are not to be made over to persons or institutions of different religions until all efforts to find persons and institutions of their own religion willing to take charge of them have failed. This is a most substantial concession for which we are heartily thankful to Sir Antony and his colleagues on the Commission. The next important recommendation is contained in para 235, which proposes to place certain obligations upon private orphanages with a view to enable the District Magistrate to institute the enquiries contemplated by the 1st part of para 234 i.e., the search for natural protectors, and also to enable the parents and relatives of lost children to trace out their children in such orphanages. This recommendation requires the private orphanages to maintain a register containing. The italics are again ours.

Full particulars regarding the children in these orphanages and also further that "a copy of the register should be periodically forwarded to the District Magistrate in order that he may make enquires for the parents or relatives of such children."But the most substantial part of these latter recommendations consists in recognising the right of the ostensible parents and relatives of the inmates of famine orphanages to free access to such institutions in order to reclaim their little ones. The hasty removal of the children to places distant from their homes is proposed to be stopped or checked by the rule "that no unclaimed child be removed from the district in which it is found until a period of three months has elapsed after the close of relief operations in the district, Categorically put the Commissioners first admit :

(1). — That the action of European and native philanthropists in having taken charge of deserted children and in some instances in dispatching them "to private orphanages" and homes in distant parts of the country has given rise to "misunderstanding."

2ndly. — That "it is of great importance that the policy of the Government in regard to orphans should be formulated in Provincial Codes, beyond risk of misconception either by its officers or by the public."

3rdly. — That "it is common experience that besides hose children who are true orphans, others are deserted by their parents or relatives in the stress of famine, and reclaimed when it is over." 4rthly. — That "it is also common experience. The italics are ours. Natives and caste-fellows and sometimes co-religionists are ready to adopt children at the end of a famine."

And then they make the recommendations we have already referred to above. We hope Hindus all over India will profit by these recommendations and exert as they can to relieve and protect the orphans and other deserted children of their community in times of famine Nay, we think, it is only fair that the recommendations contained in para 235, at least, should be given a retrospective effect and persons claiming as relatives and guardians should be allowed free access to all orphanages to find their lost children or the children of their deceased relatives. The Hindus of different provinces should combine and make a joined representation to Government to achieve this end. In the end beyond thanking the Commission for their clear recommendation as far as they go, we have to express our disappointment at the absence of a suggestion that during the pendency of a famine all orphans or deserted children whether found by Government or other private charitable agencies be brought to Government orphanages, and be not allowed to be detained and admitted into private orphanages except after' the requirements of para 234 had been complied with. Lajpat Rai.

COUNTRY DID NOT FORGET

The movement did not abate though Lalaji died. In fact it acquired a new vigor. The Congress Party began the no-tax campaign. Punjab could not easily forget Lalaji's death. To avenge the cowardly Whites' attack on their beloved leader, the people of Punjab rose in fierce revolt. The young revolutionary Bhagat Singh murdered the Police officer Sanders, mainly responsible for the attack on Lalaji, in a dreadful manner. This happened on December 17, exactly one month after Lalaji's death. Next year the British sentenced Bhagat Singh to death.

'THE LION OF PUNJAB'

The lesson which the Lion of Punjab Lala Lajpat Rai taught the country was to be brave. To the Indians in the chains of slavery his message was "Begging or prayer cannot bring freedom. You can win it only through struggle and sacrifice." Because throughout his life he fought fearlessly, he was called the Lion of Punjab. The sacrifice of his life was like a warrior's death in battle.

A Multifaced Diamond

Lala Lajpat Rai the martyr was a store-house of many good qualities. Efficiency, tireless industry and patriotism gave lustre to his personality. He was friendly. For the sake of his country he won a large number of friends both in India and abroad. From the platform he spoke for hourseloquently. His speeches were fiery and galvanizing. People heard him spellbound and his words opened their eyes. He was indeed a lion among men.

He was a brilliant man and he wasdevoted, in body and mind, to the cause of education. The D.A.V. College, the National College, the Tilak School of Politics and others are living monuments to his patriotism. His service in the field of journalism was no less valuable. He founded the Urdu weekly Vande Mataram and the English weekly 'The People'-and both maintained high standards. In the field of commerce too, he will be remembered forever. It was Lalaji who established the Punjab National Bank and the Lakshmi Insurance Company. As a member of the Arya Samaj he worked incessantly. He fought against Untouchability. When Gandhiji started the 'Harijan Sevak Sangh' he worked for it. He was like a father to the orphans. He was responsible for starting numerous orphanages in the country. The Gulab Devi Hospital and the Servants of People Society are living monuments to the memory of that great man.

Lalaji was one of those who sowed the seeds of socialism in India. He was well acquainted with Henry Meyers, Beatrice Webb, Lansbury and others whopromoted the growth of socialism inBritain. He was in the vanguard of labor organization. He founded the 'All-India Trade Union Congress' and was himself its president. He started an organized effort to improve the conditions of the working class. He pleaded that a part of the profits of an industry should be given to the workmen.

The people of India were in chains, and they had to be aroused. They had to be organized. Lalaji was the symbol of the power, which did this. As Mahatma Gan dhi said: "So long as the sun shines in the Indian sky, persons like Lalaji will not die."

Lajpat Rai once said: "If I had the power to influence Indian journals, I would have the following headlines printed in bold letters on the first page:

Milk for the infants

Food for the adults

Education for all,"

2

Lajpat Rai and Indian National Congress

There are others who make name and add to their fames if they are already on the ladder, by uttering plausibly worded platitudes and well-disguised commonplaces in the shape of speeches. Even the last are losing their charm, as platitudes have become too common, and the commonplaces too apparent, to delude any longer people who are possessed of even ordinary intelligence and share a little at least, of common sense I do not know if the Anglo-Indians are much to be blamed, if they judge the prosperity of British India, by the appearance and evidently rich surroundings of the Congress.

The delegates mostly look well-to-do people who can spare enough money for taste, elegance and show. The decorations, receptions, furnishings, etc. are done on a scale which can hardly lend weight to our contention of being perhaps the poorest people on the face of the globe.

These so-called political work done after all this fuss is of such a doubtful and ephemeral character as to raise serious doubts in the minds of even enthusiasts. Whether we are not frittering away our energies in trifles and, besides wasting away our own time and money, keeping the nation in delusion and under work I am not prepared to deny that as a festival alone the annual meeting is not without its value and should not therefore be altogether given up. Let me assure you, my brethren of the congress that by saying these unpleasant things, I mean no offence to anybody.

I am one of you, and all that I have said above applies to me with equal, perhaps greater force than to anybody else. Nor do I mean there are no exceptions. There are honourable and good men amongst us who can be truly called patriots but their number is so small that I will prefer to make no exception. The truth is that till now, we have not realised the full significance of this "partriotism."We have been taking it easy, and never realised in our heart of hearts that patriotism is a cult requiring the most rigid and ascetic course of life from its devoties. It is only one degree lower than the absolute self-denial of a Sanyasi. What I am anxious for is to see, if it is not possible to achieve better and more laudable results and from this annual gathering of the best and most intelligent of the educated Indians. As at present conducted its principal defects are: —

(1) Its unwieldy size which precludes the very idea of serious work whether in shape of deliberations, discussion or action.

(2) The anxiety to speak in the name of all Indians, a good many of whom think otherwise, and repudiate all sympathy with it. This attempt at forced union is mostly at the bottom of the discontent which at present prevails even amongst those who have all along supported it, and who think that till now the congress agitation has been a mere waste of energies, funds find opportunities.

(3) The want of sense of real responsibility amongst its members which results in total inactivity during the course of the year.

(4) The failure to afford the opportunity of comparing notes and exchanging views, by which the unity of the nation or at least of its principal components, maybe really furthered and definite progress in this direction may lead to more exertion towards the same end. This is mainly due to the mismanagement of the short time that is at the disposal of the delegates, owing to the lengthy programme of speeches and resolutions etc.

(5) Failure to take some practical steps to check the growing poverty of the country and to dispel ignorance which is still the crying need of India.

(6) Its unbounded but unreasonably mistaken confidence in its power to enforce the redress of the grievances, to extort political privilege by the passing of Resolutions and the making of speeches, which result in misleading the nation to place unjustifiable faith in the over-efficacy of the Congress agitation, and fails to impress upon them the necessity of a stupendous preparation attended with great sacrifices and mighty efforts before even one step can be gained in the ascent to political progress. The temple of freedom is not easily opened into those who claim admission into it by simply knocking at its gates. Mere aspiration is no guarantee of success. The intending worshipper or claimant for admission must show his mental by sacrifices and trials.

States of a pilgrim, because the goddess of liberty is a jealous of its sanctity that it would admit none but tried of unquestionable sincerity, devotion and faith. I will stop for the present and suggest remedies which in my opinion are calculated to remove the defects and which might be considered by Congressmen, before they meet at Calcutta, and then adopt or reject them with such modifications or alterations as to them seem desirable. Under clause (1) : — I will suggest that the sitting of the general assembly be shortened as much as may be possible to do, at once. In no case should it exceed two days with a maximum sitting of 5 hours every day at the most. The programme might be something as follows: —

- Welcome by the chairman of the reception committee who will in it produce the presidentelect as the nominee of the Indian National Congress committee.
- Speech of the President.
- Omnibus resolution including all matters and subject upon which the Congress has, by the end of the preceding year, pronounced definite views and upon which public opinion in this country is practically settled.
- Resolutions upon new subjects that have cropped up during the course of the year, on which the Indian Congress committee have recommended for inclusion in the Congress programme, and upon which there is a practical unanimity of opening between Indians of all classes creeds, shades of opinion.
- Such other subjects recommended by the Indian Congress committee upon which there is a likelihood of a difference of opinion.

In the general assembly no speaker, whether the proposer or the supporter, should be allowed to exceed the limits of 10 or 15 minutes respectively except the chairman of the Reception Committee, the President or the proposer of the resolution or amendment falling under clasue (e).

This will leave the different committees, sub-committees and other special conferences, already organised or to be organised sufficient time to devote to serious work requiring discussion and deliberation; as, for example, the Indian Congress committee should every session devote at least some hours to the question of starting political organisation in places where there are none, and perfecting those where they already exist 2ndly, the education committee and sadly, the industrial committee. With the work of these two latter we will deal under clause (5). Under clause (2) I will suggest (a) total discontinuance of all such practices as are, if at all, adopted, encouraged or connived at to bring in such people to the congress as are otherwise either not eligible for its membership, or do not possess sufficient interest therein, or are of no use to it, except in increasing the number of delegates from a particular class.

It should be the business and duty of every congressman to jealously maintain the honor, the dignity and the prestige of the congress, and nothing should be allowed or encouraged which has even the least semblance of being dishonourable, undignified, or likely to lower its reputation or to lessen its sense of self-respect. (b) The number of subjects upon which there is any likelihood of a reasonable friction existing, or coming into existence, between members belonging to the different religious nationalities in India, ought to be reduced to a minimum, if there is still any room for the same, in the agenda paper of the general assembly, such subject being reserved for separate treatment by the inclusive organisations of these nationalities.

This will lead to the necessity of a Hindu political or a semi-political congress or conference being organised, and the sooner it is done the better. As at present situated the absence of such an organisation places the Hindu at distinct disadvantage, and takes away from them, the chances of a united action or of a united expression of opinion upon matters, which affect the unity, prosperity the well-being and generally the interest of Hindu all over India.

In order to leave no room for doubt as to the necessity for this step I will be more specific. In my opinion it should be the business of such a Hindu Congress or conference to support and take, as far as possible, such steps which might conduce to their unity and strength as a religious nationality, as for instance, the language question, the question of characters, the advisability of having common Text-books, the teaching of Sanskrit language and literature all over India, the taking of steps which might lead to the protection of Hindu orphans from the hands of the proselytizing agencies of other denominations and if necessary to record a protest against those confidential circulars of the Government, which aim at the favouring of other communities to the loss of the Hindus.

In my humble opinion it is futile to admit at a chimerical and premature union of the various religious nationalities that are to be found in India, the principal of which are Hindus, the Mahomedans and the Christians. The wisest course will be to wait for a physical union and to aim at the same. This is impossible to achieve till these nationalities have had a free hand to strengthen themselves, and to exhaust all means by which they can do so at the cost of other or others.

A physical union presupposes a common danger and a conviction that they cannot overcome it or meet it but by uniting and combining against a common foe. At present this conviction is wanting, and there is still lurking in the mind of at least one community, that they can crush out the other or the others. So long as one community looks the other down and talks of it with contempt, it is ridiculous, nay suicidal, for the latter to try to force a union and make advances which are liable to be misconstrued, as the outcome of fear or of expediency, or of treachery. I quite agree with a talented writer in the Kayaaiha Samachar that the springing up of so many castes or conferences against the Hindus is a menace to the development of the idea of Hindu nationality and might lead to harm. He has, I think, done a distinct service to the cause of Hindu nationality by giving public expressions to an idea, which has been causing a serious anxiety to many a lover of the idea of Hindu nationality or to many a Hindu Nationalist. It is time that the leaders and promoters of these conferences take notes of the warning so judiciously given — not to destroy the fabrics which they have constructed, but to so mould and guide them as to make them instrumental atlas.

Construction and building up of a Hindu Nationality. Theirs should be the attempt to destroy the sub-castes, to bring about a fusion of the different sub-divisions in a caste; and to eventually bring round Hinduism to its four original castes. There will be ample time then to think and talk of the evils of the caste system, and of modification in the latter, to suit the requirements of the times. Then the conferences can be used to spread education amongst the backward classes and to bring them to the level of the times, but their promoters ought to proceed very carefully, lest in their efforts to unite the sub-divisions of a caste they might be creating permanent schisms between the different main castes, and be creating barriers amongst them, impeding the fructification and the realization of Hindu nationality. It is therefore far immature and far before the time, to talk of intermarriages between the different castes of Hindus, as it is futile to think of bringing about a complete political union of Hindus and Mohamedans at once.

The Mohamedans think that the Hindus are physically inferior to them, and wanting in certain qualities — energy, pluck, boldness, fearlessness, stamina of character, capacity to command and ability to make a land — which go to make a good, effective and capable administrator. But, in short, the Mohamedans thinks that they belong to a race of rulers,' and their fellow subjects, the Hindu, having been in slavery so long, cannot claim an equality with them in the scale of nations.

Even the otherwise amiable Sir Syed talked of Hindus with contempt. The result is that every Mohamadan he a pulaha or a Pmya or the Vvke, thinks that he can dominate over the Hindus and claim a superiority over them in the art of governing. The latter, on the other hand, retort that, as a nation they have never displayed 'Cowardliness, always proving equal to the occasion whenever necessity forced them to take up arms and assert their dignity as men, as is abundantly evident from the history of the Rajputs, the Sikhs and the Mahrattas and that the physical inferiority of certain of their sections, even if admitted, is so much counter-balanced by their intellectual and moral superiority over their rivals that in this age of science of Art, they think they are sure to win the race and acquire qualification which alone can confer a political status in these days of learning and knowledge.

This is not the occasion to discuss how far these claims are well-founded, but it is a fact that a large class of educated Mohamedans keep aloof from the Hindus and suspect their organisations and agitations as likely to prejudice them in the race for progress and advancement. They think they have better chances of political prosperity as a separate nationality and in keeping aloof from the majority who are Hindus. There are a good many far-seeing men amongst them who can read the signs of the times and think that this game won't pay but the number, on the other hand, is preponderant, because in the case of the leaders especially and of other newly-educated young Mohamedans generally, personal benefit which follows this line of policy lends great weight to the other arguments and considerations by which their present political attitude aspires to be actuated. All welcome therefore to those who are illiterate.

See the future and join with the Hindus in the struggle for political rights. Let therefore there be a general assembly which can voice the joint aspirations of such Hindus, Mahomedans and Christians by all means, but let not this general assembly stand in the way of Hindu progress and in the name of a higher, though at present impracticable, impulse, lull them to sleep over their interests as such, make them forego the opportunities of furthering their own unity inter se, and neglect the placing of it on a firm, sound and unassailable basis.

Once wisely led, no power in the world can stand in their way, retard their progress and stifle their aspirations. The Hindus have existed as a nation since times to which the memory of man runneth not, in weal or woe they have maintained their individual existence and have from time to time, given to the world lessons in religion and morality, which even to-day when the sun of European civilization is at its zenith, shine in the splendour of their purity and in the grandeur of their truth. Are they then to die as a nation in this twentieth century of the Bikram Era.

True that just now we are in a very sad plight and if judged by the national vices that have crept into our society, and by their national weakness which are too numerous to be mentioned here, the last ray of hope often disappears and turns the most hopeful optimist into a disappointed pessimist. It is only in unity that the safety of the Hindu lies. No wise or prudent Hindu can therefore neglect the opportunities of seeking the safety. Let them once make up their mind to be a united nation and to continue as such. Let them once be inspired by a living their future, and by a conviction that when God has willed the individuality of a nation and given it a mission to perform. He has at the same time given the people constituting that nation means, power, and capacity, by which they can successively resist all those forces which tend to disintegrate or disorganise them, and which trace their existence as a nation.

True that our selfishness and estrangement from national interests is simply indescribable. There have been and there are Hindus who have now and then sold the nation and its interests to the enemy, and aggrandised themselves at the cost of the former, still to a close and thoughtful observer who can feel the pulse of the nation and who has a mind and capacity to read the signs of the time, enough of life and vitality seems yet to be left in Hindustan, to enable the latter to respond to skillful treatment and kind and devoted nursing. Skill and devotion must therefore be put forth for this purpose by the whole Hindu community or at least by the thinking portion of it. It is on these grounds therefore that I suggest the formation of a Hindu congress or conference to meet annually at the place of the congress, and to discuss only such matters and devise such measures as are likely to further the cause of Hindu Unity and otherwise tend to the well-being and prosperity of the Hindus as such. Of course such an assembly should only consist of not very large number of men, say 100 of the best and the most representative of Hindus. One word about the social conference. Indian social conference as at present constituted is no more a Hindu organization than the Congress.

I call the latter also a Hindu Congress. It is as powerless to do anything for the Hindus exclusively as the latter. In the anxiety to give it a national character the Mahomedans and Christians have been allowed to take part in its deliberations, and resolutions have been altered and weakened, nay rendered meaningless, in the attempt to make them acceptable to all. Here again Hindu interest, as such have been sacrificed for a false idea of nationality and in the attempt to achieve it at once. For example, what on earth have the Christians and Mohamadans to do with the Shuddhi movement. The Shuddhi movement, which aims at the purification and readmission of all Hindu apostates is a purely Hindu movement, in which the Hindus alone are interested, the same may be said, of the resolution dealing with orphans. At the last conference both these resolutions had to be modified into vague generalities which deprived the proposition of much of their force and effect, and rendered them incapable of producing any impression either on the public or on the government.

Then the conference is a gathering and an assembly of the advanced Hindus and does not represent the orthodox portion of the community who are still in an overwhelming majority over their English educated brothers. Then again, the conference, as at present constituted, cannot ventilate the grievances of the Hindus and is not in a position to speak for them. Hence the necessity of a general Hindu organisation with its provincial branches all over India. The functions and constitution of the provincial branches will be similar to those of the many Islamic anjumans already existing in the country without criticising the policy of the Government in the abstract, without passing resolutions on abstract political propositions, these Hindu organisations will confine themselves to concrete objects and tangible grievances. As such, the country will not be deprived of the valuable assistance which it can get from the co-operation of those Hindus who are in the employ of government and who in fact constitute the pick and the cream of the nation. I have been rather too long on this part of the subject but the importance of the point necessitated a full expression of my views. Thereupon clause (2) requires no further comments.

Under clause (3) : — I will suggest that only responsible and really working men should be selected as members of the Indian congress committee. Menwhose interest in the movement is confined to annual visits ought not to find a place on this committee. One of the best methods of testing one's earnestness in a particular cause is to see if he is prepared to spend his money for the same. I will therefore repeat the proposal that was made at the last meeting of the congress at Lahore by one of the Punjabi delegates, and which was unceremoniously dismissed at the general meeting and ridiculed in the meeting of the subjects committee by two of our revered leaders that every member of the Indian Congress committee should be required to pay at least 5 Rs. a month towards the funds of the congress. The Provincial committees, moreover, ought to see that only such men are placed on this committee who take a real interest in the Political Reform Movement, and who are prepared to undo some amount of sacrifice, in thc cause of the country's political progress. Members who Call to attend even one meeting in the course of the year ought to be disqualified for re-election.

Clause (4) does not require any further comment. The remedies suggested under clause (1) will remove this complaint.

Under clause (5) : — I will suggest, that the least that should be undertaken at once, is the employment of a paid officer whose business should be to go round and collect information on both these heads. I am glad to find that the Indian congress committee have decided to pass a Resolution whereby it is proposed to ask the Government to undertake an industrial survey of the country. This is a right move, no doubt, bat the mere passing of the resolution does not advance us one inch in the cause which we have at heart. In my opinion we ought to be prepared to give a more substantial proof of our earnestness by voting a certain amount of money to be spent in the coming year, by ourselves on the object in question. One year's experience will give us sufficient ground to judge of the usefulness of the project and will strengthen our demand. I am afraid I have already exceeded the limits of an ordinary article and must stop here for the present.

Lajpat Rai

The following is published in Justice, London, from the pen of an Indian:—

LEGAL aspect.

In considering the legal aspect of the deportations/propose to discuss the question under two heads —

(1) Whether deportation is legal or illegal. In putting this part of the case before your readers I will assume the legality of the Regulation under which the two gentlemen are deported. I may say by the way, however, that the question whether the Regulation is ultravires or not is undoubtedly a very important one and requires to be carefully considered, discussed and thoroughly threshed out. (2) If the deportation is illegal whether there is any tribunal (a) in India or (6) in England, legally authorised to entertain, hear and finally determine an application if one is made on behalf of the sufferers.

As to (1) the second clause of Section 2 of the Regulation in question gives the form of the warrant, and the third clause enacts that the warrant of commitment shall be sufficient authority for the detention of any State prisoner in any fort, gaol, or other place within the "territory subject to the presidency of Fort William."

Then we come to the Punjab Act II of 1872, which extends the application of this Regulation to the Punjab," and if we read the Punjab in the place of the territories subject to the presidency of Fort William," then the persons in the Punjab could be kept in confinement only in some place within the limits of the Punjab.

This is the only possible interpretation of the Reguiation and the Act read together, and consequently the detention of Messrs. Lajpat Rai and Ajit Singh outside the Punjab is clearly illegal.

The Regulation III of 1818 is, be it noted, repealed in part by Act XVI of 1874 amended by Act XII of 1891 and supplemented by Acts XIV of 1850 2.

A drowning man, it is said, catches at a straw, and accordingly, the Government of India will, I am sure, try to rely on the last named Act (III of 1858) in justification of their action. Section 5 runs as follows.

"The Governor-General in Council may order the removal of any State prisoner confined under the provisions of any of the said regulations as amended and extended by this Act from any fortress or gaol or place in which he may be confined within either of the said Presidencies to any other fortress, gaol or place of confinement within the territories under the Government of India. "I submit that neither the Act nor the particular section has any application to the present case for the following reasons:

(1) That the Act is only applicable to cases of persons belonging to a place within the Presidencies of Bengal, Madras, or Bombay, to none of which, either of the two gentlemen belongs, and (2) that the section in question empowers

the Governor-General in Council the removal of a State prisoner who is in the first instance confined in any fort, gaol or place of confinement within the territories under the Government of India. The section hives no power to the Governor-General in Council to confine, in the first instance, a person dealt with under-the said Regulation in any place outside the three Presidencies.

For these reasons and apart from the question of the inherent illegality of the Regulation itself as well as apart from the question of the insufficiency of the grounds in which the powers given by the Regulation are to be exercised, I hold that the detention of two gentlemen is ah initio illegal. Let us now turn our attention to the second question.

(a) As regards courts in India the position is this; the Supreme Court was invested with jurisdiction to issue writs of habeas corpus by charter of the year 1774. The jurisdiction was of a very limited character and was allowed only in cases where a person within the local limits of the ordinary jurisdiction of the Court, or a British European subject without those limits, alleged wrongful confinement.

Under the old Criminal Procedure Code (1872), this writ was issued by the High Courts of Calcutta, Madras and Bombay: Section 82 of that code having empowered them to do so. But such powers now no longer obtain Section 82 is replaced by section 491 (1) of the Code of Criminal Procedure of 1882 which provides that the three High Courts of Calcutta, Madras and Bombay may, whether they think it, issue, not the writ of habeas corpus itself, but directions in the nature of such writ. I may be permitted to set out in full the whole section in view of the fact that some of the English newspapers are very fond of indulging in isolated phrases and commenting on them (at least as regards matters Indian).

Directions in the nature of the Habeas Corpus.

Section 491 (1) : Any of the High Courts of Judicature at Fort William, Madras and Bombay may, whenever it thinks fit, direct powers to issue directions in the nature of habeas corpus.

(a) That a person within the limits of its ordinary original civil jurisdiction be brought up before the court to be dealt with according to law;
(b) That a person illegally or improperly detained in public or private custody be set at liberty;
(c) That a prisoner detained in any gaol situated within such limits be brought before the court to be there examined as a witness in any matter pending, or-to be inquired into in such court;
(d) That a prisoner detained as aforesaid be brought before a court martial or any commissioners acting under the authority of any commission from the Governor-General in Council for trial or to be examined

touching any matter before pending such court martial or commissioners respectively.

(e) That a prisoner within such limits be removed from one custody to another for the purpose of trial: and,

(f) That the body of the defendant be brought in on the sherifs return of cepi-corpus to a writ of attachment;

(2) Each of the said high courts may from time to time make rules to regulate the procedure in cases under this section.

(3) Nothing in this section applies to persons detained under the Bengal State Prisoners Regulation II of 1819, Bombay Regulation XXV, of 1827, or the State Prisoners Act 1850, or State Prisoners Act 1858.

The section is clear. Under its provisions (I) no writ of habeas corpus properly so-called can be issued; (2) even the directions in the nature of habeas corpus are allowed to be issued only in cases of persons within he ordinary original civil jurisdiction of the particular high court, but (3) the most significant part of the section is put at the end and it expressely excepts the Regulation III of 1818 under which the deportation has been ordered: and (4) the section does not apply to the Punjab whence the two gentlemen were taken, nor to places where they are kept in confinement. Thus no courts in India have any authority to hear any application to enlarge these gentlemen.

As regards courts in England the fundamental principle of the English constitution denoted by the various phrases "right of personal security ""liberty of persons" liberty of the subject "which is the essential part of the common law of England and which is defined and declared though in no sense originated by Magna Charta and a number of statutes affirming that enactment, is effectively protected by the common law writ of habeas corpus I will make a passing reference to two of these statutes.

(1) Habeas Corpus Act 1678. It is entitled "An Act for the better securing of liberty of the subject and for the prevention of imprisonment beyond the seas.

(2) Habeas Corpus 1816 which is entitled ' An Act for more effectually securing the liberty of the subject "Under this Act amongst other things, judges are empowered to examine and determine the truth of the facts set forth in the return and in all cases of doubt to bail the prisoner I mention this particularly, as I am, Whilst writing this, put in mind of the most evasive and annoying way in which Mr. Morley has been answering the questions put to him by Sir Henry Congress members of the House regarding his information as to the allied connection of Lala Lajpat Rai with Ajit Singh of the so-called seditious speeches and I wonder if the matter is at all brought before the court empowered to

examine and determine the truth of the facts whether it will not be "injudicious" and "entirely adverse to public interest" for Mr. Morley to open his heart there.

After this Act and in the year 1861, in the matter of John Anderson, a very important decision was given by the Court of Queen's Bench. In that case a writ of habeas corpus was issued to a gaoler in Upper Canada. In the course of the judgment the court said: —

"We are quite sensible that it may be felt to be inconsistent with that higher degree of Colonial independence, both legislative and judicial, which has happily been carried into effect in modern times; at the same time it is observed that in establishing local legislation and local judicial authority the Legislature has not gone so far as expressly to abrogate any jurisdiction which the courts in Westminster Hall might possess with reference to the issuing of a writ of habeas corpus into any part of Her Majesty's dominions. The writ of habeas corpus has been issued even into dominions of the Crown in which there were local judicatures and local legislatures. Hence we feel that nothing short of legislative enactment depriving this court of such a jurisdiction would warrant us in omitting to exercise it when we are called upon to do so for the protection of the personal liberty of the subject."This led to the passing of the Statute 25 and 26 Vict., chap. 20. This Statute has partially restricted the common law jurisdiction vested in Courts of issuing thitj prerogative writ of habeas corpus, which is supposed to issue on the part of the King, and which, therefore, runs into any part of the King's dominions. The title to the statute is "Act respecting the issue of writs of habeas corpus out of England into Her Majesty's possessions abroad "The sections run : —

(1) No writ of habeas corpus shall issue out of England by the authority of any judge or Court of Justice herein into any colony or foreign dominion of the Crown where Her Majesty has a lawfully-established Court or Courts having authority to grant and issue the said writ and to ensure the due execution thereof throughout such colony or dominion.

(2) Provided that nothing in this Act contained shall affect or interfere with any right of appeal to Her Majesty in Council now by law existing.

In construing this statute you will excuse me if I take you back to my observations in the first part of this letter wherein I have made it clear that there is no court in British India authorised to grant and issue the writ of habeas corpus (as it is understood in this country) and to ensure the due execution thereof: that section 161 of the present Criminal Procedure Code allows the issue of the directions in the nature of habeas corpus by the High Courts of Calcutta, Madras, and Bombay: that this limited jurisdiction is again further restricted by the section to cases of persons within the ordinary civil jurisdiction of the respective high courts that even this limited and restricted jurisdiction did not and does not obtain either in the Punjab or in Burma which we are at present concerned and lastly that proviso at the end of the section takes away in one breath what the section gives in another by enacting that persons detained under Regulation III of 1818 have no right to appeal under this section.

In this state of the law I have no doubt that the prerogative writ of habeas corpus in vcue in England still runs in all parts of British India for the reasons given above, with much more force in the Punjab and in Burma.

I may add, in conclusion, that any one has a right to move the proper tribunal in England for the issue of such a writ and venture therefore to express the hope that my countrymen will give the question their most serious attention and careful consideration and organise a campaign to take the necessary steps to regain the liberty of the two gentlemen so ruthlessly taken away by the monstrously illegal and inhuman action on the part of the despotic and irresponsible Government which knows no constitution, recognises no limits to its powers and no apology to offer for anything that it does.

Vande Mataram.

FOUNDATION OF THE INC (1885)

On 20th December (Monday), 1885, 72 people met in the hall of Gokuldas Taj pal Sanskrit College in Bombay for the inaugural session of INC. The emergence of INC marks a significant stage in the process of evolution of India's political awakening and national consciousness. The Congress undoubtedly played a pivotal role in India's political awakening and national consciousness and struggle for liberation from British rule.

Having said this, it is a paradox that INC is founded by an Englishman, A.O Hume who was a retired government servant and who had chosen to stay back in India after the retirement.

It was Hume who toured across the sub-continent talked to prominent political leaders in Bombay, Madras and Calcutta and persuaded them to meet at a national conference that was initially supposed to meet at Poona. He was on a very good term with Lord Ripon, who was the viceroy of India at that time. His views were that the emergence of educated class should be accepted as a political reality and timely steps should be taken to provide legitimate outlet to the grievances of this class and efforts should be made to satisfy its ambition.

Character of the First INC

The Indian National Congress, which was destined to play a dominant role in India's struggle for independence, was formed at a national convention held in Bombay in December 1885, and it was first held under the presidency of W.C. Bannerji.

From the beginning the INC tried to eliminate regional differences. The first congress declared that one of its major objectives would be the "development and consolidation of those sentiments of national unity".

The decision to hold congress every year in different parts of the country and to choose the president from a region other than the one where the session was being held from a region other the one where the session was being held was meant to break regional barriers and misunderstandings.

As noted earlier, the first INC in 1885 was attended by seventy two non-official Indian representatives, and they included the people apparently from various walks of life, or belonging to 'most classes', as claimed by the official report of the Congress. There were lawyers, merchants and bankers, landowners, medical men, journalists, educationists, religious teachers and reformers.

Objectives of the First Indian National Congress 1885:

i) One of the basic objectives of the early nationalists was to promote the feeling of national unity; to weld India into a nation; to help create an Indian people; to meet the imperialist charge that Indians were not a people or nation but a mere grouping of hundreds of diverse races, languages, castes and religions.

ii) The second basic objective was to create a national political platform or programme on which all Indians could agree and which could serve as the basis for all-India political activity.

iii) The third objective was the politicization of the people and the creation of public interest in political questions and the training and organization of public opinion in the country.

iv) Another important aim of the time was the creation of an all-India political leadership. Such a leadership on a country-wide level did not exist in the 1880s. Allied to this was the need to train a common band of political workers or cadre to carry on political work.

Debate over 'safety-valve'

Hume's involvement in the formation of INC gave rise to a lot of controversy regarding the origins of Congress. The safety-valve theory or the conspiracy theory, which was deduced from this simple fact, was for a long time subscribed to by all shades of historians, in the right, left and center. It was even accepted by some of the stalwarts of nationalist movement. In recent researches, however, it has been thoroughly discredited.

The theory (safety-valve) originated from William Wedderburn's biography of Hume published in 1913. Wedderburn, another civil servant, wrote that in 1878, Hume had come across seven volumes of secret reports which showed that there had been seething discontent among the lower classes and a conspiracy to overthrow British rule by force. He became disturbed, met Lord Dufferin and together they decided to establish an organization with educated Indians. This would serve as a safety valve by opening up a line of communication between the rulers and the ruled and would thus prevent a mass revolution. The congress was in this way the creation of British rule.

This safety-valve theory was believed by the earlier nationalist historians; the imperialist historians used it to discredit Congress and the Marxist historians developed a conspiracy theory from this. R.P Dutt, for example, wrote that Congress was born through a conspiracy to forestall a popular uprising in India and the Indian bourgeoisie leaders were a party to it.

In the 1950s, these safety-valve or conspiracies theories were proved to be wrong.

First of all, those seven volumes of secret reports have not been traced in any of the archives either in India or London. Historians argue that given the structure of British information system in the 1870s, it was highly unlikely that so many volumes of secret reports have existed. Except in Wedderburn's biography of Hume by religious gurus, and were not procured from any official sources.

In 1888, Dufferin openly castigate Congress for its dubious motives. He criticized it for representing a "microscopic minority" and this statement if anything else, explodes the safety valves or conspiracy theory.

Historians now more or less agree that the story of seven volumes of secret report was a fiction created by a friendly biographer Wedderburn to portray Hume as British patriot who wanted to save the British Empire from an impending crisis.

So, as Biban Chandra comments, "it is high time that the safety-valve theory was confined to the care of the Mahatma from whom perhaps it originated.

The fact that Hume played a crucial role in the foundation of the Congress, however, remains, although this role might have been grossly exaggerated in the safety valve or conspiracy theories. But even if Hume had not taken any initiative, in India in the 1870s and 1880s, the formation of national organization was clearly in the air.

In its political behavior, quite expectedly, the Indian National Congress in its early career was never a radical organization, as the culture of the open to the government had not yet taken roots. So they were cautious reformers seeking to alleviate certain unpleasant aspects of what Surendranath Banerjee described as the "un-British rule" in India and their method was sending prayers, petitions and memoranda.

W.C. Banerjee, the president of the first Congress, made it clear at the very outset that it was not "a nest of conspirators and disloyalties", they were thoroughly loyal and consistent well-wishers of the British Government. This explains why the founder of the Indian National Congress had to involve A.O Hume in their project.

Gokhale wrote in 1913 that any attempt by the Indians to form an all India organization would immediately attract the unfriendly attention of the authorities. He further wrote that, "If the founder of the Congress had not been a great Englishman, the authorities would have at once found some way or the other to suppress the movement". Thus, to use Bipan Chandra's analogy, "if Hume and other English liberals hoped to use Congress as a safety-valve, the Congress leaders hoped to use Hume as a lightning conductor".

In this way, the Congress movement started in India as a limited elitist politics for limited reforms. But nevertheless, it represented a new and modern trend in Indian political tradition. Despite its limitations, it sought to forge an overarching national unity and raised a very important political demand: the basis of the government should be widened and the people should have their proper and legitimate share in it. It was from her that the mainstream of Indian nationalist politics began to flow.

EARLY PHASE OF THE CONGRESS

The Indian National movement was primarily a movement for freedom from alien domina--nation. The movement has been one comprehensive effort embracing all aspects of the life of the community. The birth of the Indian National Congress, perhaps the oldest and the biggest democratic organisation in the world, did not take place in an atmosphere of a fanfare of trumpets nor did it create a stir by passing flamboyant resolutions.

Hume's Initiative

In 1884, at the annual convention of the Theosophical Society at Adyar in Madras, Mr. Allan Octavian Hume laid bare to his friends his plan to organise the Congress. A committee was formed to make the necessary prepara-tions for a session at Poona to be held in 1885.

The committee consisted of Mr. Hume, Mr. Surendranath Bannerji, Mr. Narendranath Sen, Mr. S. Subramania Iyer, Mr. P. Ananda Charlu, Mr. V. N. Mandalik, Mr. K. T. Telag, Sardar Dayal Singh, Lala Sri Ram.

Mr. Hume, still a government servant, addressed an open letter to the graduates of Calcutta University with a fervent appeal for self help.

He said: "and if even the leaders of thought are all either such poor creatures, or so selfishly wedded to personal concern, that they dare not strike a blow for their country's sake, then justly and rightly they are kept down and trampled on, for they deserve nothing better.

Every nation secures precisely as good a government as it merits. If you the picked men, the most highly educated of the nation cannot, scorning personal ease and selfish objects, make a resolute struggle to secure greater freedom for yourselves and your country, a more impartial administration, a larger share in the management of your own affairs then we, your friends arc wrong and our adversaries right, then Lord Rippon's noble aspirations for your good are fruitless and visionary, then at present at any rate, all hopes of progress are at an end, and India truly neither lacks nor deserves any better government than she enjoys.

"Only if this be so, let us hear no more factious, peevish complaints that you are kept in strings and treated like children, for you will have proved yourself such. Men know how to act. Let there be no more complaints of Englishmen being preferred to you in all important offices, for if you lack that public spirit, that highest form of altruistic devotion that leads men to subordinate private ease to the public weal that patriotism that has made Englishmen what they are-then rightly are these preferred to you, rightly and inevitably have they become your rulers. And rulers and task masters they must continue, let the yoke gall your shoulders never so sorely, until you realise and stand prepared to act upon the eternal truth that self-sacrifice and unselfishness are the only unfailing guide to freedom and happiness."

The First Session

The first session of the Congress was to meet at Poona but owing to an outbreak of cholera the venue was shifted to Bombay and the session began on the 28th December, 1885, with Mr. W. C. Bannerjee, the doyen of the Calcutta Bar in the chair, though originally, it had been decided to request Lord Reay, Governor of Bombay, to be the first President of the Indian National Congress but the idea had to be dropped as the Governor was advised by the Viceroy not to accept the offer. 72 delegates came from different parts of the country and most important among them were Dadabhai Naoroji, Ranade, Pherozeshah Mehta, K. T. Telang, Dinshaw Wacha, etc. The meeting was truly a national gathering consisting of leading men from all parts of India.

The president defined the objective of the Congress as "promotion of personal intimacy and friendship among all the more earnest workers in our country's cause in the parts of the empire and eradication of race, creed or provincial prejudice and fuller development of national unity." In its early sessions, the Congress Organisation, by and large, limited its activities only to debates.

After the Madras Session in 1887, an aggressive propaganda was started among the masses. Hume published a pamphlet entitled "An Old Man's Hope" in which he appealed to the people of England in these words: "Ah men, well-fed and happy, do you at all realise the dull misery of these countless myriads? From their births to their deaths, how many rays of sunshine think you chequer their gloom-shrouded paths? Toil, toil, toil; hunger, hunger, hunger, sickness, suffering, sorrow; these alas, alas, alas are the keynotes of their short and sad existence."

In December 1889, the Congress Session was held at Bombay under the Presidentship of Sir William Wedderburn. It was attended by Charles Bradlaugh, a member of British Parliament. He addressed the Congress in these words; "For whom should I work if not for the people? Born of the people, trusted by the people, I will die for the people, and I know no geographical or race limitation."

Dadabhai Naoroji was re-elected as the President of the Lahore Session of the Congress held in December 1893, His journey from Bombay to Lahore presented the spectacle of a procession, and Citizens at various places on the way presented him addresses. At the Golden Temple at Amritsar, he was given a robe of honour. Addressing the audience at the Session, Dadabhai Naoraji declared: "Let us always remember that we are children of our mother country. Indeed, I have never worked in any other spirit than that I am an Indian and owe duty to my work and all my countrymen. Whether I am a Hindu or a Mohammedan, a Parsi, a Christian, or of any other creed, I am above all an Indian. Our country is India, our nationality is Indian."

The Moderates

The early Congressmen who dominated the affairs of the Indian National Congress from 1885 to 1905 were known as the Moderates. They belonged to a class which was Indian in blood and colour but British in tastes, in opinions, in morals and in intellect. They were supporters of British institutions. They believed that what India needed was a balanced and lucid presentation of her needs before the Englishmen and their Parliament. They had faith in the British sense of justice and fairplay.

The Moderates believed in orderly progress and constitutional agitation. They believed in patience, steadiness, conciliation and union. To quote Surendarnath Banerjee, "The triumphs of liberty are not to be won in a day. Liberty is a jealous goddess, exacting in her worship and claiming from her votaries prolonged and assiduous devotion." In 1887, Badruddin Tyabji observed: "Be moderate in your demands, just in your criticism, correct in your facts and logical in your conclusions."

The Moderates believed in constitutional agitation within the four corners of law. They believed that their main task was to educate the people, to arouse national political consciousness and to create a united public, opinion on political questions. For this purpose they held meetings. They criticised the Government through the press. They drafted and submitted memorials and petitions to the Government, to the officials of the Government of India and also to the British Parliament. They also worked to influence the British Parliament and British public opinion.

The object of the memorials and petitions was to enlighten the British public and political leaders about the conditions prevailing in India. Deputations of leading Indian leaders were sent to Britain in 1889. A British Committee of the Indian National Congress was founded in 1906 and that Committee started a journal called *India*. Dadabhai Naoroji spent a major part of his life and income in Britain doing propaganda among its people and politicians. The object before the Moderates was "wide employment of Indians in higher offices in the public service and the establishment of representative institutions."

The economic and political demands of the Moderates were formulated with a view to unifying the Indian people on the basis of a common political programme. They organised a powerful all-India agitation against the abandonment of tariff-duties on imports and against the imposition of cotton excise duties. This agitation aroused the feelings of the people and helped them to realise the real aims and purposes of British rule in India. They urged the Government to provide cheap credit to the peasantry through agricultural banks and to make avail-able irrigation facilities on a large scale. They asked for improvement in the conditions of work of the plantation labourers, a radical change in the existing pattern of taxation and expenditure which put a heavy burden on the poor while leaving the rich, especially the foreigners, with a very light load. The Moderates complained of India's growing poverty and economic backwardness and put all the blame on the policies of the British Government. They criticised the individual administrative measures and worked hard to reform the administrative system.

The Moderates opposed tooth and nail the restrictions imposed by the Government on the freedom of speech and the press. In 1897, Tilak and many other leaders were arrested and sentenced to long terms of imprisonment for spreading disaffection against the Government through their speeches and writings. The Natu brothers of Poona were deported without trial. The arrest of Tilak marked the beginning of a new phase of the Nationalist movement. The *Amrita Bazar Patrika* wrote: "There is scarcely a home in this vast country where Tilak is not now the subject of melancholy talk and where his imprisonment is not considered as a domestic calamity."

The basic weakness of the Moderates lay in their narrow social base. Their movement did not have a wide appeal. The area of their influence was limited to the urban community. As they did not have the support of the masses, they declared that the time was not ripe for throwing out a challenge to the foreign rulers.

To quote Gokhale, "You do not realise the enormous reserve of power behind the Government. If the Congress were to do anything such as you suggest, the Government would have no difficulty in throttling it in five minutes." However, it must not be presumed that the Moderate leaders fought for their narrow interests. Their pro-grammes and policies championed the cause of all sections of the Indian people and represented nation-wide interests against colonial exploitation. What they wanted was to reform or liberalise the existing system of government through peaceful, gradualist and constitutional means.

The influence of the moderates, however, declined with the rise of the militants who did not believe in gradualism and who criticized the moderates for their great faith in Britain and British political institutions.

Rise of Extremism

The moderates sought to make the provincial e legislatures more representative and to increase the Indian clement in the civil services, but the process was long and thc progress slow. Repelled by the unsympathetic approach of the imperial bureaucracy and enraged by the unpopular policies of Lord Curzon, the Viceroy, and particularly his decision on the partition of Bengal, the youth of India moved towards militant politics and direct action. As a protest against the partition of Bengal (October 1905), the nationalists advocated the boycott of British goods".

In 1907, Bipin Pal made the paradoxical statement, that the "viceroyalty of Lord Curzon... had been one of the most beneficent if not decidedly the most beneficent viceroyalty that India ever had," for Curzon, by pursuing his unpopular policies, had made Indians so discontented that they demanded self-government with greater determination than ever before. Aurobindo similarly declared that he considered the partition of Bengal to be a most beneficial measure because, by arousing intense opposition among the people, that measure had stirred up and strengthened national feeling.

As a result of the growing disillusionment about the activities of the British rulers and as a reaction against Curzon's proposal for the partition of Bengal; there came into existence the extremist party which advocated a policy of boycott, *swadeshi* and national education. In January 1907, Tilak declared: "We are not armed, and there is no necessity of arms either. We have a stronger weapon, a political weapon in boycott." Tilak also said: "When you prefer to accept *swadeshi*. You must boycott *videshi* (foreign) goods. Without boycott, *swadeshi* cannot flourish." Aurobindo, Tilak, and Pal asked the people not to cooperate with the government. The basic theory of Tilak, Aurobindo and Pal, which was later put into operation on a mass scale by Mahatma Gandhi, was that as the existence of the Government depended on the cooperation of the people, the Government would cease to function or to exist the very day the people withdrew their co-operation from it.

With the rise of the militant movement the glamour of England and English institutions began to fade and English influence increasingly came to be replaced by the influence emanating primarily from the indigenous sources as also from the European literature or revolt.

The study of British constitutional history had generated among the moderates a love for and faith in Dominion Status. But such stories as how the Italians had driven the Austrians out of their land gave militant nationalists a new conception and in fact a new ideal of complete independence. Self-government under British paramountcy had been the goal of the moderate school, but the ideal of the extremist or militant school was complete autonomy and elimination of all foreign control.

Bal Gangadhar Tilak (1856-1920) and other extremist leaders, who wanted to adopt a policy of direct act and passive resistance, denounced what they called "the political mendicancy" of the moderates. During the anti partition agitation, in the first decade of the twentieth century, Tilak wrote: "The time has come to demand *Swaraj* or self-Government. No piecemeal reform will do. The system of the present administration is ruinous to the country. It must mend or end." According to him Swaraj was the birthright of every Indian.

"The term *Swaraj*," said Bipin Pal (1858-1932), another exremist leader, was not merely a political but primarily a moral concept. "The corresponding term in our language," he said, "is not non-subjection which would be a literal rendering of the English word independence, but self-subjection which is a positive concept. Self--subjection means.... complete identification of the individual with the universal."

Another Swarajist leader who, like Tilak, spoke of the ideal of *Swaraj*, was Aurobindo Ghose (1872-1950). "We of the new school, "he said, "would not pitch our ideal one inch lower than absolute *Swaraj*-Self-Government as it exists in the United Kingdom." And he added, "We reject the claim of aliens to force upon us a civilisation inferior to our own or keep us out of our inheritance on the untenable ground of a superior fitness."

Lajpat Rai (1865-1928), along with Bal Gangadhar Tilak and Bipin Pal, constituted the *swarajist* triumvirate called "Lal-Bal-Pal". Lajpat, like the other extremists, believed that India must rely on her own strength and should not look to Britain for help.

The *swarajist* said that however much Britain's rule might be improved or liberalised, it could never be as beneficial to Indians as the self-rule. Their attitude was the same as that of the Irish Sinn Fein leader Arthur Griffith, who had said: ".... In those who talk of ending British misgovernment we see the helots. It is not British misgovernment, but British government in Ireland, good or bad, we stand opposed to." The *swarajists* accordingly considered that freedom was their birthright.

The Surat Split

In 1907, there was a split in the Congress and the Moderates parted company with the Extremists. That split was due to many causes. The moderates had controlled the Congress from its very beginning and even now they were in control of it. They had their own ways of thinking and doing which were not acceptable to the younger generation who were impatient with the speed at which the Moderates were moving and leading the nation. Under the circumstances, a confrontation between the two was inevitable and that actually happened in 1907.

The seeds of the split could be traced to the Calculla Session in 1906, where the Moderates had accepted the resolutions on *Swaraj*, national education, boycott and *Swadeshi* on account of the pressure brought on them from all quarters. In their hearts, they had not accepted the new resolutions. Their fear was that the growing pace of the national struggle might lead to lawlessness and that would provide the British with an excuse to deny the reforms on the one hand and to crush all political activity on the other.

They had no self-confidence. They did not believe that sustained and dignified national struggle was possible and desirable. They considered the Extremists irresponsible persons who were likely to put in danger the future of the country. The British Government also tried to win over the Moderates against the Extremists. While the Extremists were roughly handled by the Government, the Moderates were shown all the favours. Lala Lajpat Rai, Sardar Ajit Singh, Tilak and many leaders of Bengal were deported.

The break-up of the Surat Congress was no doubt an unpleasant affair. It marked a direct open breach between the Moderates and the Nationalist panics not only in Maharashtra but throughout India. For the first time in the history of the Congress, there was at Surat an open light between the delegates of the congress and some blood was drawn. But it did not stop at that.

The split led to a cleavage in the sense that the name of the Indian National Congress had to be kept in abeyance for the time and a new entity called the convention was installed in its place. Of course as the name itself implies, the Convention was a stop-gap expedient, intended to function in the place of the Congress only till such time as the national Congress could meet again in its old form.

The old form had this peculiarity that there was not much ceremony observed in the election of the delegates to the Congress. There were no conditions of membership. There was no constitution as such for the Congress, no election of delegates. In fact the membership was open to anyone that might choose to attend the Congress session as a delegate. There was no competition as such in the election of the delegates for the simple reason that there was no numerical allotment fixed for any province. It was an open rally of all that chose to attend.

Tilak and his party were of course ousted from the Convention because they would not sign a prescribed creed of political faith, which practically excluded the ideal of independence, if only an ideal so far.

The Convention and, the Nationalist party met in two separate camps at Surat. It must be noted here that even with this definite split in the Congress each party duly affirmed its love for the Congress which alone was regarded as the true national Assembly for the country and in both the camps the hope was expressed that sooner or later there might again be held a Congress united as before.

Nobody could openly allege the break-up of the Congress as a criminal offence, but the split was taken into consideration by the government as an open challenge to the policy of constitutional agitation. After Tilak's conviction by the High Court, the National party led by him became sullen and almost went underground.

For six years, from 1908 to 1914, the Nationalist Party could not decide as to what it should do about entering the Congress. There was an attempt made to call a meeting of a rival Congress at Nagpur. But while government banned the session, there was also want of unanimity in the party itself about the starting of a rival Congress which might make the split absolutely permanent. The cooler wings in the Party thought that there was no wisdom in setting up a rival to the old Congress as without unity among political parties the show as presented by separate parties was bound to be poor. A group within the Tilak Party was trying to negotiate matters with the leaders of the Moderate party for making the entry of this group and others of its persuasion into the Congress on its own terms, that is to say, without the restriction of a creed and with the old facilities for unfettered election of delegates. But the other view was more insistent and prevailed, namely, that nothing should be done in this matter until Tilak returned from Mandalay.

THE MODERATE PHASE (AD 1885-1905)

During the first twenty years of the Congress, the moderate nationalists or the Moderates, as they were called, dominated the party. Some of the moderate leaders were Surendranath Banerjea, Dinshaw Wacha, Pherozseshah Mehta and Gopal Krishna Gokhale. The Moderates believed in sending petitions and resolutions to the British government asking for:

1. Freedom of speech and expression.
2. Expansion of welfare programmes.
3. Promotion of education.
4. Reduction of land revenue.
5. Recruitment of Indians to high posts in the administration.
6. More powers for the Legislative Councils and more Indian members in these Councils.
7. Holding the Civil Services exams in India as well.
8. Change in the economic priorities of the government so as to benefit Indian industries.
9. Reduction of government expenditure on administration.
10. End of the drain of India's wealth to Britain.

Most of the Moderates came from the English speaking upper classes of society. They believed in constitutional methods for getting their demands accepted. They believed that since their demands were moderate, they would be accepted by the government. They hoped that by peaceful methods of persuasion, they would be able to get their demands accepted.

British Attitude towards the Congress

Initially, British attitude towards the Congress was favourable. Some British officials even attended Congress sessions. However, very soon it changed and the British turned hostile towards it. They began to openly criticize the Congress. They realized that instead of becoming a means of containing the anger of the masses, it had become the focus of Indian nationalism. In order to break the Congress unity, they also started practicing the policy of Divide and Rule. Muslims began to be dissuaded from participating in the activities of the Congress. These tactics of opposition, however, failed the national movement continued to grow powerful.

New Trends in the Congress

The closing years of the nineteenth century AD was a period of great misery for the Indians. Famines struck in large parts of India causing lakhs of deaths. The repressive policies of the government also intensified. And the failure of the Moderates to do anything constructive brought forth new trends within the Congress. A new leadership arose within the ranks of the Congress. Three of these new leaders were Bal Gangadhar Tilak, Bipin Chandra Pal and Lala Lajpat Rai. These leaders felt that the moderate ways of the Congress were inefficient and impractical to achieve anything. They called for strong political action such as strikes and boycotts. Through nationalist publications and popular festivals, they tried to spread political awakening and patriotic feelings among the people. Bal Gangadhar Tilak called for the attainment of Swaraj. He declared-"Swaraj is my birthright and I must have it". The newspapers, Kesari, became the mouthpiece of the new group of leaders. Soon, this newly emergent trend came to dominate the Congress and with it the national movement.

In the first twenty years of its existence, the greatest achievement of the Congress was that it created a platform from where people could speak with one voice. In the beginning, it was an organization of the educated and the privileged members of society. But gradually, the middle classes, the farmers and the workers also became a part of it and the national movement.

LAJPAT RAI: CONGRESS PRESIDENT

Lala Lajpat Rai (1865-1928) was an Indian author and politician who is chiefly remembered as a leader in the Indian fight for freedom from the British Raj. He was popularly known as *Punjab Kesari* (The Caesar of Punjab). He was also the founder of Punjab National Bank and Lakshmi Insurance Company.

Early Life

On 28 January, India in 1865 in a Hindu Family, Lajpat Rai created a career of *reforming Indian policy through politics and writing.* (When studying law in Lahore, he continued to practice Hinduism. He became a large believer in the idea that Hinduism, above nationality, was the pivotal point upon which an Indian lifestyle must be based.) Hinduism, he believed, led to practices of peace to humanity, and the idea that when nationalist ideas were added to this peaceful belief system, a non-secular nation could be formed. His involvement with Hindu Mahasabhaite leaders gathered criticism from the Bharat Sabha as the Mahasabhas were anti-secularism, which did not conform with the system laid out by the Indian National Congress. This focus on Hindu practices in the subcontinent would ultimately lead him to the continuation of peaceful movements to create successful demonstrations for Indian independence.

Political Life

As the need for partition and independence took an important turn for the possible, Lala Lajpat Rai's involvement became imperative to the Indian Independence Movement. His actions in anti-imperialist movements led to numerous arrests. He became an important member of the Arya Samaj. This political group was full of British-educated Indians who believed that Hinduism had a specific and direct impact on what it meant to be an Indian. The group also took the ideas of a merged western and eastern world and promoted the view that the subcontinent had benefited from its coagulation. The involvement of the Arya Samaj in constitutional reform supported the freedom movements which took hold of the Indian population. Lala Lajpat Rai led political rallies which taught how the history of the subcontinent had always been heading to the philosophical idea that it would become an independent nation.

(Lajpat Rai presided over the first session of the All India Trade Union Congress in 1920. In 1923, he became a member of the Imperial Legislative Assembly. He also went to Geneva to attend the eighth International Labour Conference in 1926 as a representative of Indian labour. He had an opportunity to watch the labour movement in the USA and England where he was required to prolong his stay for political reasons.)

In addition to espousing his philosophical principles, Lajpat Rai engaged heavily in direct action and protest against British rule. (He led the Punjab protests against the Amritsar Massacre (1919), the Non-Cooperation Movement (1919-1922), and the "Simon go back" demonstrations against the Simon Commission (1928)). He was repeatedly arrested. He disagreed, however, with Mohandas Gandhi's suspension of the movement due to the Chauri Chaura incident. (He formed the *Congress Independence Party*, which was particularly pro-Hindu in voice and policy).

He was not only a good orator but also a prolific and versatile writer. His journal *Arya Gazette* concentrated mainly on subjects related to the Arya Samaj. *Bande Mataram* and *People*, contained his inspiring speeches to end oppression by the foreign rulers. He founded the Servants of the People Society, which worked for the freedom movement as well as for social reform in the country. He also wrote an autobiography in English titled *The Story of My Life*.

Demonstration and Death

The Government of India Act 1919 had introduced the system of dyarchy to govern the provinces of British India. However, the Indian public clamoured for revision of the difficult dyarchy form of government, and the Government of India Act 1919 itself stated that a commission would be appointed after 10 years to investigate the progress of the governance scheme and suggest new steps for reform. In the late 1920s, the Conservative government then in power in Britain feared imminent electoral defeat at the hands of the Labour Party, and also feared the effects of the consequent transference of control of India to such an "inexperienced" body. Hence, it appointed seven MPs (including Chairman Simon) to constitute the commission that had been promised in 1919 that would look into the state of Indian constitutional affairs. The people of the Indian subcontinent were outraged and insulted, as the Simon Commission, which was to determine the future of India, did not include a single Indian member in it. The Indian National Congress, at its December 1927 meeting in Chennai, resolved to boycott the Commission and challenge Lord Birkenhead, the Secretary of State for India, to draft a constitution that would be acceptable to the Indian populace. A faction of the Muslim League, led by Muhammad Ali Jinnah, also decided to boycott the Commission.

An All-India Committee for Cooperation with the Simon Commission was established by the Council of India and by selection by the Viceroy The Lord Irwin. The members of the committee were: Sir C. Sankaran Nair (Chairman), Sir Arthur Froom, Rajah Nawab Ali Khan, Sardar Shivdev Singh Uberoi, Nawab Sir Zulfiqar Ali Khan, Sir Hari Singh Gour, Sir Abdullah Al-Mamun Suhrawardy, Kikabhai Premchand and Rao Bahadur M. C. Rajah.

In Burma (Myanmar), which was included in the terms of reference of the Simon Commission, there was strong suspicion either that Burma's unpopular union with India would continue, or that the constitution recommended for Burma by the Simon Commission would be less generous than that chosen for India; these suspicions resulted in tension and violence in Burma leading to the rebellion of Saya San.

Protest and Death of Lala Lajpat Rai

Almost immediately with its arrival in Bombay on February 3, 1928, the Simon Commission was confronted by throngs of protestors. The entire country observed a *hartal* (strike), and many people turned out to greet the Commission with black flags. Similar protests occurred in every major Indian city that the seven British MPs visited. However, one protest against the Simon Commission would gain infamy above all the others.

On October 30, 1928, the Simon Commission arrived in Lahore where, as with the rest of the country, its arrival was met with massive amounts of protestors. The Lahore protest was led by Indian nationalist Lala Lajpat Rai, who had moved a resolution against the Commission in the Legislative Assembly of Punjab in February 1928. In order to make way for the Commission, the local police force began beating protestors with their *lathis* (sticks). The police were particularly brutal towards Lala Lajpat Rai, who later that day declared, "The blows which fell on me today are the last nails in the coffin of British imperialism." On November 17, Lajpat Rai died of his injuries on his head.

3

Lion of Punjab

After all the controversial writings which have appeared in the Indian Press about Lala Lajpat Rai's deportation it would be idle to dwell here on the merits and demerits of a measure whose only redeeming feature is that it is an Act of State. It is as idle now to expatiate on the retrograde and impolitic act of government as it is to dwell on the social and domestic virtues and also the political foresight of him whom Indians at all events believe in their heart of hearts to be a martyr. Ever since

Mr. Morley condescended to recognise the belligerency existing between Educated India and Bureaucratic India by calling the former "enemies"in open Parliament, it is as foolish on the part of the people to pray for favours — even the favour of releasing Lajpat Rai, as it is on the part of the Goverment to expect more loyalty and less sedition from the people. For Belligerents never waste their breath in exchanging prayers and admonitions, but look to their own resources, "If you adopt a manly policy be prepared for the logical consequence "said the Lala to the Benares Congress delegates. Bureaucracy at least is arming itself with all the formidable weapons at its command to suppress a people's legitimate aspirations and, under the impression that all India is one great Kurukshetra, is bringing forth one by one its battalions of Acts and Ordinances to bind, gag and suppress all freedom of speech in the land — Yes, Bureaucracy is more earnest than the people in recognising the belligerency in India! What though guns and swords play no part in this great one sided war? In their place are hurled Edicts, Circulars Ordinances and Acts— all in the perhaps sincere belief that the whole of India is seditious and on the verge of a civil war!

Bureaucracy is arming itself meanwhile what is the Nation doing ? The Nation at present appears like a house divided against itself. Its house is not in order — it is not prepared for the struggle. Some would fain give up the struggle for political rights in despair. They argue that a house divided against itself cannot stand.

Yes, it may not stand — still It must march on! Let Lajpat Rai's noble-Orders come to the rescue of thosewho are destitute of faith in the Nation's cause : —

"Struggle, hurd struggle is the lair of progress. Yes, struggle we visit both inter se as well as against others. There must he a struggle between truth and untruth, between vice and virtue, between honesty and dishonesty between expediency and righteousness, between indolence and energy, between enterprise and a spirit of lethargy and between timeserving selfishness and noble interest evilness. Without this struggle no nation can ever aspirer to be great and influential. This struggle we have just entered upon."

Yes, we have just entered upon this struggle both inter se as well as against outside forces. The so called dissensions of the Congress on the one hand prove it; Mr. Morleys famous epithet proves it on the other. We have enemies in the camp as well as in Downing Street. Shall we yield?"is the cry of many and many a wearied weakly soul, that expected Liberty to grow like a common Jack Fruit by the way side, that expected freedom to drop from above like a ripe mango all ready for the eating ! Shall we yield and close this agitation of ours for more rights and more privileges and be content with the morsels thrown now and then from a lord's dining table as at a favourite dog?

No! "A people once awakened, and awakened rightly, cannot be put down."says the Lala! It is impossible even for an all-powerful Bureaucracy to put down an awakened nation, let it hurl its edicts ever so assiduously. The more such edicts, the more unpopular the Bureaucracy — the stronger becomes the Nation's cause. But the people need a warning not to commit political harry-carry in their premature despair. To such as are weak of heart and dull of political faith, a perusal of Lala Lajpat Rai's ' Study of Hindu Nationalism "might be recommended as a wholesome tonic."Let us not be impatient of what in my humble opinion seems to be a healthy sign of (political) growth. Let us not strangle it by drawing its undesirable (yet unavoidable) concomitants in high colours or by attaching undue importance to the same.

Because there are some violent men, some bad tempered, some dishonest men, some traitors and some time-servers, it is no reason to record a wholesale condemnation of the same or to be disappointed with (or feel despair for) them."Like the deadly poison that arose at the Churning of the Ocean for making Heavenly Nectar, undesirable concomitants will always turn up when least expected. And in many instances they are unavoidable. But has not our religion taught us that even that Deadliest Poison may be rendered harmless to Iswara's children by His Heavenly Grace! The Lalas writings therefore call on the readers have more faith in the political regeneration of the country. For "how can a Nation destitute of faith produce Martyrs ?

He might well have said: —
Hold ye fast, the storm is coming!
Hold ye fast, brother to brother: —
The storm may continue — the wind may rage.
But hold ye fait and brave the xreather.

It requires all the nerve and all the strength of the Nation to brave and break the repressive fetters that are now being forged for the People's benefit by the Bureaucracy, and a proper study of the Lala's writings is sure to inspire the reader with the sanguine enthusiasm and robust faith in the Nation's glorious destiny with which every page of those writings is replete.

It has well and truly been said that Lala Lajpat Rai is the leader of the New Movement — the movement which recognises the limitations to the British Supremacy in India and emphasises the part which the Nation Las still to play in the history of the world. The New Party's articles of faith need not be here explained — they are fully expounded in the speeches and writings of Babu Bepin Chandra Pal and Lala Lajpat Rai. The new party prefers to pursue a manly policy, and in the language of Lala Lajpat Rai, it is "prepared to follow the logical consequences of tLat policy."It craves no favours from Bureaucracy; it in fact recognises the state of belligerency darkly hinted at by Mr. Morley. Only Babu Bepin Chandra Pal called it a game of Chess instead of a game of War. And in that game, he said, "We do not know what shall be our next move until we know the move of our opponent. "So the New Party and Mr. Morley seem to understand each other well enough! The political atmosphere has thus been cleared and the fog of political dissimulation no longer clouds the scene of operations. Each side knows what it is about. The Kew Party wants the complete manhood of the Indians to assert itself in spite of every obstacle: the Bureaucracy wants to retain its hold as long as possible upon the country. The opposite parties have met face to face. The resources of Bureaucracy are matched against a people's determined will. There ought not to be any doubt as to the result of the contest. The bureaucracy will have to yield to the people what the latter have long been striving after, viz. — Popular Government.

And what form of Government will it be? We hear this query many a time put in the Indian Press; and in many ways Las it been answered. The last Congress declared for Swaraj — and Swaraj will be either self-government under British Control or it will be absolute independence, according as the British are sympathetic or otherwise towards the manly aspirations of Indians. The well wishers of the British Raj indeed pray that it may be under the sympathetic guidance of Britain and they say it will be Britain's fault if she forces this foster child of hers to completely break away from her. One thing, however, is clear — the struggle for Political Progress must go on — whether with or without British sympathy, time alone can decide. In fact, it cannot afford to wait for British sympathy. A wise father retains the affection of his grown-up children — but what shall be said of him who stands in the way of his grown-up son setting up Louse for himself and feels peevish whenever a better ariatigetnent in the house itself is suggested ?

The struggle is just begun. The arrest of Lala Lajpat Rai was the beginning of the struggle. The Bureaucracy with Mr. Morley at its head acknowledges it. The New Party with Mr. Lajpat Rai at its head recognises it. Of the two opponents, Bui'eaucracy and the People, the former is an organised entity with the traditions and heritage of over a century, the latter is a new growth, yet somewhat nebulous, its numbers yet uncertain, its resources yet untried, its heroes still in the making. The Bureaucracy is in its age, the Nation is still in its youth, in its budding adolescence. All the good that Britain has till now done not only for India but for all humanity, the victories she has won, the arts and sciences she has developed, the education she has spread, the equality of man she has preached, the Christianity she has advocated — these and numberless other acts of benevolence and grace that characterised the giantess of Britain in her early days of conquest in India — all these stand as bulwarks in support of a jealous and timeworn Bureaucracy. There are many among Indians who gladly and sincerely forgive the present day haughty Englishmen all their sins on remembering the good deeds and qualities of their old-time predecessors. But with all their virtues and with all the benefits hitherto afforded to Indians by Engishmen — the fact still remains that Indians hanker after something more than a mother's milk more in fact than even bread and butter. The tender care bestowed upon the infant by its father may have been angelic; but "there is a whisper rising in this country that loyalty is not a phrase, faith not a delusion, and popular liberty something more diffusive and substantial than the profane exercise of the sacred rights of sovereignty by political classes; that we live in an age when to be young and to be indifferent are no longer synonymous and that we must prepare for the coming hour."

It is asked if the New Party desires immediate separation. This question has been repeatedly asked and been as repeatedly answered in the Press. The new party contemplates no such thing — it only keeps the goal clear in view — it may take decades and even centuries to reach the goal; but the goal is there and it is held aloft for public view in a serene atmosphere of open truth, unclouded by simulation, trickery or any paltering with conscience. For an Indian to deny that he has that goal in view is for a youth to deny that he will ever reach manhood. If all Indian parties were as clear in their statement of their ideals as this new party is, our political progress would be achieved much quicker. Does the new party then desire an immediate revolution as has only too often been alleged by the Anglo-Indian Press?

From what we have read and heard of the writings and speeches of the leaders of the New Party we can emphatically say, No and why?

'Sybil or the two Nations"by Disraeli.

"Recalling all the evil passions that a revolution arouses, all the ties it dissolves, all the blood it commands to flow, all the healthful industry it arrests, all the madmen that it arms, all the victims that it dupes — it is doubtful whether any man really honest, pure, and humane, would ever hazard it, luikss he was assured that the victory was certain — ay, and the object for which he fights not to be wrested from his hands amidst the uproar of the elements that the battle has released."

Xo, the New Party contemplates no such thing as an immediate revolution! This should be clear to even a cursory reader of the writings and speeches of Lala Lajpat Rai. The Lala is conscious of the defects and weaknesses of the Indian Nationality, and like a sagacious politician his writings are mainly aimed at remedying those defects and removing those weaknesses. But be refuses to be overwhelmed by the difficulties in the way and asks his compatriots not to mind the thorns but to Lave the eye fixed on the divine rose of political freedom. His writings strengthen weak minds, while they encourage the timid and censure the indolently inclined. In these days of political activity — when the very air is surcharged with politics, nobody who follows the march of events with any pretentions to careful study can afford to miss a perusal of the speeches and writings of the first great martyr in the sphere of India's Politics.

Who is a great man? asks Lord Beaconsfield, and answers the question himself. It is he who affects the mind of his generation/Judged by this test Lala Lajpat Rai is undoubtedly a great man. Whether one agrees with his views or not, no one who reads these pages will doubt the earnestness and sincerity of purpose with which he has worked for the National Cause, understanding by the term the development and enrichment of the people along all lines of activity, moral, social, intellectual, educational, spiritual, political and economical; nor will anybody think him capable of engaging in enterprises which cannot bear examination in broad daylight. Every one of the virtues which Mazzini attributes to Garibaldi — a whole life devoted to one object — his country; consecrated by deeds of honour first abroad and then at home; Valour and constancy more than admirable; Simplicity of life arid manners which recalls the man of antiquity; all the more mournful trials and losses manfully endured: Glory and Poverty ! Every particular relating to such a man is precious — finds a counterpart in the life of the great leader of the Punjab.

Lala Lajpat Rai was born in 1865 of humble but respectable parents in the small town Jagaran in the district of Ludhiana. He comes of an old Agarvara Baniya family. Lajpat never wearied of acknowledging his indebtedness to his mother. The Baniya cate is famous throughout India for its thrift — thrift practised as assiduously by the women who spend as the men who earn. In such a community Lajpat Rai's mother was remarkable for her skill in household management. None could excel her in the art of making a little go a long way. There was one uniform level of comfort maintained in the family whatever be the amount of income. The son testifies ' that when he was earning thousands his family was not more truly prosperous than when the family income was less than fifty — thanks to his mother's management. In the mother of Lajpat RatJ was realised the noble Hindu ideal of a grihaim.

His father Munshi Madha Krishen Lala, who is fortunately living, has been a teacher of Persian and Urdu in a Government School. He is an excellent Urdu writer and the author of numerous pamphlets and hooks. Straightforward and honest, he is a great lover of knowledge. Among his works is a political pamphlet which attracted attention at the time of publication, written in reply to the famous monograph of the late Sir Syed Ahmed Khan in which the latter enunciated the policy which the Aligarh party is still pursuing.

When again Sir Syed Ahmed Khan wrote an article against the principles and composition of the Indian National Congress, Lala Radha KrisLen, surprised at the changed attitude of the leader of the Mussalman community, addressed an open letter to him which appeared in the Urdu paper ' Kohinoor'. Lala Lajpat Rai translated these letters into English and published them in 1888 when the Congress met at Allahabad under the Presidency of Mr. George Yule.

The veteran's pen is far from idle to-day. Munshi Radha Krishen's mofcto is plain living and high thinking. He would not on principle allow himself to be dependent on any of his sons and so he carries on a small business at Jagaran — his native town — which brings in enough to meet his modest requirements. Within the last few years he has suffered S9veral grievous bereavements including the death of the second of his four sons — a promising graduate of the Punjab University — and of his noble wife. Now that Lala Lajpat Rai has been snatched away — not by death I — from his side, what a storm of mingled feelings must be raging in the breast of the venerable old gentleman: with the natural pang of sudden and forced separation from his first born, there must be mixed up a feeling of exultant pride at his beloved son having justified the training in public spirit and self-sacrifice which he had received from his father. The burden upon his heart must have no doubt been to a great extent lightened by the consciousness of sympathy demonstrated from end to end of this vast continent with the sufferings of Lala Lajpat Rai and his family. But those who wish to know that heroic stuff the old gentleman is made of and how bravely he has stood the shock of his son's deportation, cannot do better than read, mark and ponder over the following epistle which he thought fit to address to the public press just three weeks after the mournful event: —

"Scarcely 50 years ago the Hindus of the Punjab were a grossly ignorant and superstitious body. The religion consisted of silly fables and they could not face the attacks of Christianity and Islam. Conversions to these two religions were therefore somewhat common. Then arose Swami Dayanand, who nationalised Hinduism sweeping away the inventions of priests and charlatans, and striking at the root of image worship The reconstructed Hindu mind of this Punjab now stood forth boldly to attack those before whom it had cowered so long. Can versions and deflection to other religions came to an end; and carrying the war into the enemy& country, the Arya Samajists began to take back into thefolds of their neoflinduism people who had gone over to Christianity, or to Islam. Controversy raged furiously and very often courts of law had to be appealed to Christians and Moslems who had been in the habit of a having it all their own way when fighting Hinduism began to feel a new pressure and, being worsted in controversy, gave out that the Aryas were a spiteful and contentiously. Christian Missionaries to whom each successive famine had been a veritable time of harvest, found their vocation gone; for, the Hindus led by Aryas began to look after their own orphans instead of handing them over to Christian propagandists. It was not seldom that English judges were appealed to, to decide who. should be given the guardianship of Hindu widows and orphans and had to make the Christian Missionary hand over his future convert to his enemies. It became a common thing for a Missionary preaching in the bazaars, to suddenly depart at the approach of an Arya.

"It was thus that the Arya Samaj became unpopular with certain very influential classes. As ill-luck would have it, the Editor of the Punjabee was an Arya Samajist. But it is difficult to find out why some orthodox Hindus in the Punjab have been rejoicing at Lajpats deportation. They should know that the efforts of the Samaj, and of men like Lajpat Eai, have conferred great benefits on orthodox Hindus. Their children and destitute widows have been saved for Hindu Society. The thousands of souls rescued by Lajpat Rai, from famine and conversion were not the offspring of Arya Samajists,but belonged to orthodox Hindus. The chief sin of my son Lajpat consisted in this, that he stood forth a champion of his people and I rejoice that I had a son like him."

How many a father in similar circumstances would feel and think as the Munshi Radha Krishen has done! If ever India is to become a self-respecting member in the commonwealth of nations it can only be through such self-respecting fathers and self-respecting sons. Despite his advanced years Krishen Lala's step is as elastic, his frame is as erect and his brow as serene as in the happiest days of his youth.

Lajpat Rai had a brilliant career as a student. He distinguished himself at every stage, his weak health and narrow circumstances notwithstanding. His intellect was as strong as it was quick: he was regarded by his fellow students as an intellectual prodigy. He studied in the Government College at Lahore for two years being in receipt of a University scholarship. Having passed the first certificate examination of Law of the Punjab University he started practice in 1883, when he was hardly 18 years of age.

Two years later he passed the final examination standing second in a list of thirty candidates. This bare record of his student career does not however bring out clearly the influences amidst which he grew to be the man he is. In the evolution of character hereditary tendencies mark only the starting point of a man's career, the direction of which is however very considerably determined by the influence of environment. Endowed with a rich legacy of moral and intellectual attributes peculiar to the genius of the eastern Aryan, the good Lala had the benefit of an education in which the practical rationalism of Western science combined with the religious purity and moral elevation of Eastern literature put on him the hall-mark of true culture. He was naturally attracted towards some of the noblest spirits of his age of whom the most notable were Lala Hansraj, the late Guru Datta Vidyarthi and Chethanand. All these men, differently gifted as they were and differently circumstanced too, were moved by one common impulse — viz. a keen desire to work for the regeneration and elevation of the Motherland which to them was no vague patriotic abstraction but was concretised in the land, of the five rivers.

In their close association with one another were born those ideals of patriotism, of self-sacrifice, of untiring work and of unconquerable faith which have sustained Lala Lajpat Rai in later years of strain and stress and have also inspired the formation during the last two decades of enthusiatic bands of ardent young men who in their turn, each in his own way and in his own sphere, have been leading most of the progressive movements of north western India. Not a single movement started in recent times for the furtherance of educational, social religious or political reform but has had the benefit of Lajpat Rai's counsel or participation, and has received the impulse of his vivifying genius. While sympathising with and aiding every movement which made for progress, Lala Lajpat Rai early in his life identified himself with the Arya Samaj in which he found at first ample scope for the exercise of his patriotism, philanthrophy and religious zeal.

The visit of Swami Dayanand in 1877 marked a turning point in the social and religious development of the Punjab. The Brahmo Samaj, while it emancipated the souls of men from the thraldom of superstition and blind alligeance to custom, was too eclectic for men who wanted a definite and tangible standard to rally round, and wandered too far afield in the region of belief and practice to satisfy the patriotic craving for a national heritage. Swami Dyanand, though assisted in his lour by the more liberal Brahmos especially of the Adi Samaj, noticed this tendency of the Brahmo movement and sought to supply a corrective by insisting on the authority of the Vedas as the revealed Word of God and proclaiming the social and religious ordinances of the Rishis as all sufficient for the social, moral and spiritual needs of the Hindu people.

This was just the sort of teaching for which the young Punjab was dimly yearning. By pointing to the pristine purity and simplicity of the Vedas, Swami Dyanand condemned on one hand the corruption and decay which had crept into popular Hinduism, and on the other satisfied the cravings of the National spirit which in those early days sought to realise itself in the field of social and religious reform.

A gospel like the illustrious Swamis was a trumpet call for men to array themselves in opposite camps. Men had to declare themselves either foes or friends. No middle way was possible.

The orthodox were pronounced in their opposition, while the Brahmos sought to take the life out of this rival reform movement by starting a number of associations in connection with their own Samaj which sought to supply the deficiency which the Swami pointed out. But it was too late. Swami Dayanand felt the need of an organization which would on one hand ensure healthy progress and on the other be a bulwark against denationalization. He conceived the formation of a grand National Vedic Church in which Patriotism and Reform went hand in hand and supplied the corrective one to the other. The opposition to Swami Dayanand's work was as determined as the zeal of his followers was fervent

The struggle between his followers whose number was rising by leaps and bounds and the eclectic and ultraconservative Hindus was at its keenest between 1880 and 1885 when Lala Lajpat Rai was studying at Lahore. Lala Lajpat Rai and his friends were not the men in those stirring days to look on unconcerned as if they had no part to play in the fray. They determined to throw in their lot with the Dayanand party which was sorely in need of young men to defend its cause against the redoubtable champions of orthodoxy. Guru Dutt, Hansraj and Lajpat Rai were constituted Apostles of the new evangelIt was true they were students. But they did the work of grown up men, — preaching, debating and spreading the cause throughout the length and breadth of the Punjab. Their organizing capacity was truly marvellous. Hansraj being the eldest of the three counselled, Guru Datt inspired, and Lajpiat Rai carried out the plan of missionary operations. In internal constructive work too, the three young men took a leading part. If the Arya Samaj of to-day may be said to be the creation, next toSwami Dayanand, of any particular men — those men were the three who fought its battle in their student days and nourished it with their earnings and their energy in adult age.

Having qualified as a leader Lala Lajpat Rai elected to settle down to practice at Hissar in the Punjab. As in. his early days, so now in his manhood good fortune followed him in the matter of genial associates and happy comrades. Among his new acquisitions were the noble hearted Pandit Lajpat Rai who has only recently given away all his life's earnings for philanthropic and educational undertakings; and Lala Churamani, the founder of a famous Industrial School for waifs and strays, the father of Jaswant Rai, the proprietor of the Punjabee, Lajpat Rai practised down to 1892 at Hissar when he became the leader of the local bar. He also acted for three years as honorary secretary of the Hissar Municipal Board.

It may be mentioned in passing that.professional avocations did not take up the whole time and energy of Lala Lajpat Rai and his Hissar friends, the greater portion of their time being nobly and unselfishly spent in discussing questions concerning the welfare not only of their province but of India as a whole. Lajpat Rai's abilities and gift of speech earned for him an extensive practice, but his unambitious, unassuming and self-abnegating spirit, his plain simple mode of living combined with his profound and varied erudition in western and eastern literatures enabled him to attract a circle of friends and admirers to whom the Deportation has come as a personal calamity. In i892 he transferred his practice to the wider field of Lahore, the nerve centre of the Punjab, whose Chief Court is practically the High Court of the Punjab.

Fortune's smile attended his advocacy, but since 1902 he has slackened his professional activity partly we believe on account of successive attacks of illness but mainly in order to devote himself more fully to the cause of his country. He has taken it upon himself to utilize his income from professional pursuits for the benefit of the Indian public.

In education, secular and religious, Lala Lajpat Rai has long taken a very active interest. He took part in. the foundation of the Dayanand AngloVedic College at Lahore, a First Grade college with an endowment of some five lacs which he was largely instrumental in collecting; it is, according to the Government Inspector's report in 1905, "the most numerously attended college in the province". He is a vice-president of the institution, and oft' and on for about a dozen years he has acted as its honorary secretary. He has taken an active part in teaching, having several times acted as honorary lecturer in History. He has made large donations to its funds. He is secretary also to the Anglo-Sanskrit College at Jalunder and a member of the managing committees of a number of Arya Samaj schools in the province."

It was chiefly his interest in education that took him to America in 1905, where he visited many educational institutions and took careful notes for future guidance. We may also mention that he gave important evidence before Lord Curzon's University Commission in 1902. After his return from the political mission on which he went to England as a colleague of the Honble Mr. G. K. Gokhale, he organised a political society and collected funds for educating the patriotic sons of the Punjab in politics and economics with a view to send them out as political missionaries on the model, we believe, of the Servants of India Society' of Poona.

His attention was not confined to matters educational. In other departments of social service as well, the Lala's activity has been marked. His noble heart bled for the needy, the friendless, the houseless, the suffering and the starved. He organized relief works and orphanages, the outcome of his disinterested love for humanity in general and his community in particular. For several years he has been General Secretary of the Arya Samaj Orphanage at Ferozepur, by far the largest Hindu orphanage in Northern India, having several hundreds of orphans in its books. He is a member of the managing committee of the waifs' orphanage at Meerut, also a well endowed and flourishing institution. In 1897, and again in 1899 — 1900, he organised a Hindu Orphan Relief movement which succoured over 2,000 orphans, and he acted on both occasions as its General Secretary. The Government availed themselves of his experience in 1901, when he was invited to give evidence before the Famine Commission.

His evidence was especially valuable as he had personally inspected the areas largely affected by famine. In April i9o5, on the occasion of the great earth-quake in the Kangra District, he organised a relief committee on behalf of the Lahore Arya Samaj; and as Secretary of that-committee he visited areas particularly afflicted, collected funds and himself supervised the administration of relief. The orphanages and relief works which Lala Lajpat Rai has organised and supervised with scrupulous care and pious devotion are standing monuments which bespeak the high and noble character of the Lala who on this respect followed faithfully the ideals of humanity and charity which are enshrined in the scriptures of India. A veritable Darmaraj of the Punjab, no earthly motive or ambition could deter him from the noble work of love and sacrifice into which he completely threw himself, heart and soul, despite tremendous difficulties in the way. The Karnan of his age, he has been the sunshine of many a gloomy and despondent heart. His philanthropic undertakings — living embodiments of his Thyaga and Paropakava — testify to his high capacity as financier and organizer.

Lala Lajpat Rai is also a man of extensive business connections. He is a Director of the Pan jab National Bank, the first and the largest Indian Bank in

Lahore. He is interested in several cotton mills and cotton presses in the Punjab, being in several cases on the Board of Directors.

Lala Lajpat Rai claims attention as a man of letters. As a journalist, he has for several years edited a vernacular magazine and a vernacular weekly journal, both conducted in the interests of religious and social reform and educational progress; He has published in Urdu biographical monographs on Mazzini, Garibaldi, Sivaji, Swami Dayanand and Sri Krishna — books which have been widely read and greatly appreciated in the province. He has been in constant touch with several newspapers conducted in English, contributing to them frequently on the leading questions of the day. He has also written in English a life of Pandit Gurudatta Vidyarthi, m.a., the Indian reformer.

He has compiled a concise historical account of Hindu civilisation down to the commencement of the Musalman period. He has published various pamphlets and booklets of an occasional character.

Lala Lajpat Rai has always felt drawn towards politics: which indeed was a subject on which Hansraj and he could not look eye to eye. The elder patriot held that the work of the Arya Samaj Avas work enough for one life nay, for hundreds of lives. The younger and more forward leader's view, like Justice Kanade's was that the work of national regeneration was a larger and more comprehensive object than could be accomplished by any single agency however catholic it may be, and that it needed to be pursue along many lines of activity, moral,, social, intellectual and political. He felt it hrs duty therefore, to promote, political activity first in his own province and through that in the whole country. It was in 1888 A. D. that Lala Lajpat Rai joined the Indian National Congress movement when it met at Allahabad under the Presidency of Mr. Georgs Yule. Ever since his connection with this "un-official but

National Parliament,"to quote the words of Mr. Lal Mohan Ghose, his political activity has expressed itself in various shapes and forms, and in the political field, as in other fields, he has done all that, a man could do with pen, tongue and purse.

In 1905, the Indian National Congress Committee having recognised in him an austere, sincere and selfless devotion to his country and her cause, selected him as one of its delegates to place before the British public the political greivances of the Indian people. The Indian Association of the Punjab voted Rs. 8,000 for the expenses of his tour in Knjjland : but he who had himself disbursed money for philanthropic and patriotic objects would have none of the money but gave it back to the support and benefit of students, and met his expenses out of his own pocket. The two Indian national delegates worked together for some time in England: but the Panjabee leader determined to visit America and study the working of institutions in the far western country —

that latest born child of Modern Democracy. On his return he resumed Lis woi-k in England with Mr. G. K. Gokhale; and in the political campaign carried on in several parts of England the Indian representatives brought home to the Mind of the Britisher the evils of unsympathtic bureaucratic government under which India was labouring, and pleaded in eloquent language, adducing facts and figures in support of their contention, the cause of the half-starving and half-dying people of India. This political campaign, it may be confidently said, was a success, were it for nothing else but the message which as Lajpat Rai put it' the people of England wanted to send to you through me viz, the message that in our utterance, in our agitation, and in our fight and struggle for liberty, we ought to be more manly than have been hithertofore."

After his return from England he has been busy devising and organising ways and means for the political advancement and industrial emancipation of his country. In the deliberations of the Indian National Congress which assembled in 1 905 at the holy city of Benares under the presidency of Mr. G. K. Gokhale, he took a IcaeuJing part, and supported a resolution on the "repressive pleasures in Bengal". His wit and humour, his thorough grasp of the situation, his warm appreciation of and eloquent tribute to the Bengali manliness, his sturdy patriotism, and above all, his unquestionable loyalty to the British Raj and his anxiety to befriend every popular measure of the Government, these are discernible in that short stirring speech (reproduced on page 149 of this book) which he delivered in the sacred hall of the National Congress.

The greatest fact in Lala Lajpat Rai's career and the one which has made his name a household word in every part of India is his Deportation. How this event has come to pass — though happily at the time of writing, the news of his release has caused joy in the heart of every Indian, be he Moderate or Nationalist — be he Mahomedan or Hindu — orthodox or Aryasamajist — how that unique event has come to take place, will not be fully and accurately known until official records supplemented by non-official testimony are in the hands of the public. But Lala Lajpat Rai, though perhaps surprised by the warrant of Deportation, was not quite unprepared for what has taken place. Coming events east their shadows before."Lala Lajpat Rai, true mariner that he is, read the signs of the coming storm and the letter {vide page 220) which he handed over to the editor of the Vunjuhee a few hours before his arrest, remains the most remarkable example of political prescience which has ever emanated from the pen of any Indian politician.

India was passing through stormy weather. The notorious Partition of Renewal was the precursor of a new political phenomenon in India — the birth of the nascent Nationalism. This infant political Town, the Anogo-Indian bureaucrats could not and would not tolerate. Of the ways and means they devised to strange the national movement one was to strike a blow at the influence of popular leaders. Lajpat Rai was the first to thunder against Sir Bampfylde Fuller who insulted the elite of Bensjal Society, including Babu Surendranath Banerji, on the occasion of the Barisal conference.

He protested against the insinuations of Lord Minto in speaking of Honest Swcuhshiam. In his own province executive high-handedness reigned rampant, the Government of Sir D. Ibbetson had one rule for the Punjabee and another for the Civil and Military Gezette, Unpopular measures, like the Colonization Act which has since been wisely disallowed by the Viceroy, had stirred popular feeling which vented itself in public meetings. Of these meetings the Lala, according to Mr. John Morley himself, attended only two meetings, not on his own initiative but at the express request of the people. When the Lala who was sent for by the people to explain the object of the unpopular measures of the Government, was on his way to the meeting at Rawalpindi he was intercepted by Mr. Agwew — magistrate who was persecuting: the leaders of the Rawalpindi Bar for their alleged championship of the cause of the people— and by the Superintendent of Police, and was advised not to deliver any lecture on pain of forcible dispersal of the meeting, and the loyal Lala La j pat Rai accordingly informed the assembled people of the intentions of the magistrate and cause them to disperse peacefully. But the genius of Bureaucracy which little knows the feelings and thoughts of respectable citizens of India would not stop where it had during all these years stood, repressing the growth of full national life. The policy. pursued by officers of Government is forcibly exposed in the Hiniustan 'Review : —

"You first drive a people into frenzy, to the point of desperation, by passing a number of highly unpopular and oppressive measures, without consulting them and without paying the slighest heed to their most reasonable objections urged in temperate language, if they keep their counsel to themselves and do not take the trouble to represent their opinions, you misconstrue their silence in to acquiescence in your doing. If they make known their views in respectable and mild language you pass by their representations in contumptuous silence. If they speak loudly and strongly, and seek to make themselves felt, you clap them into jail and go the length of banishing them from the land of their birth, without hearing, without trial, without consideration. Let this violent act of yours raise further loud-tongued protest, you set aside the legislature of the country and pass an executive ordinance wiihdrawing the indefeasible right of British citizens to meet in public for the ventilation of grievances."

When public affairs come to such a sad pass in this country, persons of unselfish motives, of noble intellect and of unswerving loyalty to the highest interests of their mother-land, will come forward and espouse the cause of the people even at risk to their own Jives, and they will not surrender their conscience and patriotism to the dictatorial mandate of panic-stricken Bureaucrats, alien in race, complexion and habits, in thoughts and feelings, in ideas and ideals, in interests and ambitions. The frown of the authorities cannot in itself make an action bad or ignoble. The law is glorified when thieves and robbers, decoits and murderers, and persons of moral and spiritual depravity are visited with condign punishment. But when the flower of a nation are chosen for arbitrary punishment, the law degenerates into a savage weapon. Lala Lajpat Uai is undoubtedly among the choicest spirits of the age and of the race. Like Captain Dreyfus, he is an innocent victim of the rulers of the land.

"A man so open-hearted and straightforward, so genial and disposed to be fiiendly to one and all without distinction of class or creed; whose services were at the public command no matter from what quarter it came : of unsullied private character and spotless public career, his life was an open book that any one might pass and read; who loved light and worked in the light; to whom nothing was so abhorrent as the powers of darkness — of tyranny and treachery, of persecution and perfidy, of bad faith and low associations; who shunned dark corners of dubious patriotism and always kept himself before the public gaze and in the sunlight of public criticism — howcould, every one felt puzzled, such a man of open movements and open actions bring upon himself a blow aimed in the dark that in its terrible swiftness will not even allow him to lay bare his heart and show to all concerned Low clean, how spotless, how devoid of mischievous thought and intent in any shape whatsoever it was' (Punjabee).

We wonder how a Government which had indented on the splendid, versatile services of the Lala on the occasion of the University and the Famine Commissions, can, in' the name of consistency, policy or even expediency justify its conduct and character in inhumanly depriving one of the most intelligent and serviceable supporters of the British Raj of the elementary rights of liberty and selfvindication by banishing him from his native land on the beautifully vague pretext of state reasons' under the sanction of a military, despotic Regulation which it does not blush to call a "law. "His letter addressed to the Punjabee a few hours before his secret arrest and dark deportation seems providential; but his appeal and warning to his Bengal friends assembled in the Benares Congress is prophetic, "If you have adopted this manly and vigorous policy, be prepared for the logical consequence (cheers). Don't conceal your heads, don't behave like cowards. Once having adopted that manly policy, stick to it till the last."

The orie reads like an unconscious autobiography, but the other fully lays bare the straight forwardness of a mind standing four square to all the winds that might blow. Questions without number were put in the British Parliament to the biographer of Gladstone and Burke, but these have been treated with scant courtesy. Under great pressure, Mr. Morley first tried diplomatic methods of persuasion to inspire confidence in the persistent members of Parliament who are interested in Indian progress, and these proved futile. It was only after his conference with Sir D. Ibbetson, "one of the ablest and most experienced Lieutenant-Governors,"that, he gave out the grounds on which he sanctioned this extreme and quite uncalled-for action. The Indian Parliamentary Committee met and denounced this high-handed measure and also passed a resolution that the Regulation of 1818 and other similar measures must be repealed : but why would Mr. Morley listen to their proposals, seeing that the Regulation comes so handy to an infuriated and frightened officialdom ?

There is not a single Indian or unbiassed foreign journal that has not condemned this Military Act and the executive action of the Government of India. The most prominent politician, the Honble Mr. G. K. Gokhale, has challenged the alleged conspiracy on the part of the Lala. Legally the action of Government Las been questioned; and this aspect of the matter is ably handled in a letter which we reproduce at the end of the book from the pen of an Indian and originally published in the Justice, the organ of Social Democracy in England. The Lala may have entertained very strong political views, but he is the last man to hatch a conspiracy in darkne.ss and secrecy. In the deportation of the Lala — an idealist, enthusiast, litcyntciiy, practical philanthropist, hijld politician, accomplished lawyer, cool-headed financier, cautious investor, earnest religious preacher and devout Arya Samajist, politics in India has entered upon a new phase and will, ere long, develop into a force which it will be impossible for any human power, armed though it he with the most drastic laws and a formidable array of soldiers and a magazine of shots and bullets, to change; and on the right evolution of the collective and mutually inter-dependent forces brought into play, the salvation of India depends.

It is a happy sign of the times that this fact is recognized even in the highest quarters. For what said Lord Mill to a few weeks ago in his place at the head of the Vice regal Legislative Council? "I am well aware of the growing strength of political hopes and ambitions in this country and I welcome them as the natural result of the education British administrators have done so much to introduce and encourage. I have said so over and over again and I deny the accusation of want of regard for the growing influence; of the educated classes of India. Far from wishing to check the growth of political thoughts, I have hoped that, with proper guidance, Indian capacity and Indian patriotism might earn for its people greater share in the Government of their country, They have proposals before them now which I trust will greatly contribute towards that end. The Government of India would be blind, indeed, to shut its eyes to the awakening wave which is sweeping over the Eastern world, overwhelming its old traditions and bearing on its front a cloud of new ideas. We cannot check its flow, we can but endeavour to direct it into such channels as may benefit the generations that are to come. We may repress sedition — we will repress it with a strong hand — but the restlessness of new-born and advancing thoughts we cannot repress. We must be prepared to meet it with help and guidance. We must seek for its causes."

One wonders whether Lord Minto has realised all that his words signify in the shape of a conciliatory policy and a policy of encouraging, without stifling, the aspirations of the people after a self-respecting national existence. If Lord Mi n to and his adjutants in the Government of India had only sought the help of men like LalaLajpat Rai in seeking for the causes of the unrest in the Punjab and in the whole country, they would have found in them friends and not "our enemies,"such as they have imagined him and other popular Rawalpindi lawyers to be.

At any rate, it is a matter for rejoicing that the Government of India have at last thought lit to restore the spotless and illustrious Lala to his proper sphere. The Government of India, more than the happy Lala, deserve congratulation on an act of justice for which. there should have been no occasion.

Long: Live Lala Lajpat Rai.

Come onward, come ! Ye sons of Ind !
The motherland your aid implores.
With dauntless hearts and ardent zeal,
Enlist ye in your country's cause.
Let one resolve your actions guide,
One spirit move your heart and soul :
Your feelings, efforts, hopes and aims,
Let them all tend to the self-same goal.
Go, roam abroad in distant lands.
And ever newer wisdom gain;
Awake, arise with ardour fresh,
And chant a nobler — manlier strain.
Let not applause be your sole aim.
Nor let abuse your soul subdue.
Devote your life to what is good.
And what is great, and what is true.
Let all our party-stfifes and feuds,
Be scattered to the winds and skies !
Let Hindu clasp his Moslem friend
For, all are one in Mother's eyes."

OPEN LETTERS TO THE HON'BLE SIR SYED AHMED KHAN BAHADUR, K. C. S. I.

No. I.

Sir, — Would you excuse me if I encroach upon your valuable time for a short while? Before I address you on my matlah, I think it advisable to state for your information that I have been a constant reader and admirer of your writings. From childhood, I was taught to respect the opinions and the teachings of the white-bearded Syed of Aligarh. Your Social Reformer was constantly read to me by my fond father, who looked upon you as no less than a prophet of the nineteenth century. Your writings in the Aligarh Institute Gazette and your speeches in Council and other public meetings, were constantly studied by me and preserved as a sacred trust by my revered parent. It was thus that I came to know that you once approved of the contents of John Stuart Mill's book on "Liberty,"and it was thus that I came to know (if my memory does not deceive me) that the present Chief Justice of Hyderabad, a staunch opponent of the National Movement, once translated Jeremy Bentham's book on Utility "for the readers of your Social Reformer. Is it strange then that I have been astonished to read what you now speak and write about the "National Congress "? Any person, in my circumstances, would shout on it: Times have changed and with them convictions! Flattery and official cajoleries have blinded the eyes of the most far-seeing; cowardice has depressed the souls of the foremost of seekers after truth, and high sounding titles and the favours of worldly governors have extinguished the fire of truth burning in many a noble heart. Is it not a sad spectacle to see men whose days are numbered, whose feet are almost in the grave, trying to root out all the trees planted with their own hands.

Under these circumstances, Syed Sahib, it is, surely, not strange if I ask what has been the cause of this lamentable change in you. Old age and exhaustion of faculties may, perhaps, have some share in causing you to forget what you once wrote and spoke. Has your memory lost its retentiveness, or is it the blindness of dotage which has permitted you to stray into your present unhappy position?

If the former, I from amongst your old admirers will take upon myself the duty of reminding you of what, in moments of wisdom, was recorded and published by your pen and tongue, and this duty, I promise, I will fulfill with the utmost pleasure and with feelings of the highest satisfaction.

I will begin with your book on the "Causes of the Indian Revolt," which was written in 1858, though only translated and published in English in the year 1873. It may be worthwhile to note here that the translators of this were no others than Sir Auckland Colvin, the present Lieutenant-Governor of the

NorthWestern Provinces, and Lieutenant-Colonel Graham, the writer biography. In this book, after having tried to prove that the mutiny of 1857 was no "religious war," nor the result of a preconcerted conspiracy, you say that "most men, I believe, agree in thinking that it is highly conducive to the welfare and prosperity of Government — indeed, that it is essential to its stability — that the people should have a voice in its Councils. It is from the voice of the people that Government can learn whether its projects are likely to be well received. The voices of the people can alone check errors in the bud and warn us of dangers before they burst upon and destroy us."

To make the matter more clear you go on saying that "this voice, however, can never be heard, and this security never acquired, unless the people are allowed a share in the consultations of Government. The security of a Government, it will be remembered, is founded on its knowledge of the character of the Governed as was on its careful observance of their rights and privileges."These are noble words, nobly spoken; words of sterling honesty and independence of spirit. Can they bear any other meaning than that which attaches to that resolution of the National Congress which prays for the introduction of a representative element into the constitution of our Legislative Councils? Pray, tell me how can the people have a voice in the Councils of a Government if not by representation?

How can the people of a country have their voice constantly heard if not through their representatives? But, to leave no doubts on the subject, I will go on giving quotations in proof of my assertion, that you have yourself in former times strongly advocated the introduction element into the Legislative Councils of India After lying much stress upon the necessity of a Government respecting the opinions of the people it governs you say: "The evils which resulted to India from the non-admission of natives into the Legislative Councils of India were various. It (i.e., the Government) could never hear, as it ought to have heard, the voice of the people on the laws and regulations which it passed/ Again you say: "But the greatest mischief lay in this, that the people misunderstood the views and the intentions of the Government. They misapprehended every act.' After this you proceed to say that "if Hindustanis had been in the Legislative Councils, they would have explained everything to their countrymen, and thus-these evils which have happened to us would have been averted. In your opinion, as expressed there, this non-representation of the voice of the governed in the Legislative Council of the realm was "the one great cause "and the "origin of all smaller causes of dissatisfaction."Nay, further, not to leave any doubts in the matter, and to prove that in your book you even go to the length of saying that your countrymen should be selected to form an assembly like the English Parliament (which demand at the time you advanced it, was certainly more premature than it now is, though the National Congress, with all the advantages that the country has had in the way of education and enlightenment since that miserable year of 1858, only advocates the partial introduction of a representative element in the Legislative Councils), I shall give some more extracts from the same work.

There you say : "I do not wish to enter here into the question as to how this ignorant and uneducated natives of Hindustan could be allowed a share in the deliberations of the Legislative Council, or as to how they should be selected to form an assembly like the English Parliament. These are knotty points. All I wish to prove here is that such a step is not only advisable but ABSOLUTELY NECESSARY, and that the disturbances are due to the neglect of such a measure'.

Could clearer words be used than what have been quoted above? Is there any doubt as to their meaning? Because, if so, I shall be obliged to quote the exact Hindustani words Hissed by you to express the ideas propounded in the above lines. But no, I do not suppose you can feel any doubt on that point, because the English rendering was undertaken by no others than Sir Auckland Colvin and Lieutenant-Colonel Graham, the former of whom, at least, is now being proclaimed (whether rightly or wrongly, God knows) as an opponent of the National Congress.

Sir Syed, does it not sound strange that the writer of the words above quoted should put himself forward as the leader of the Anti-Congress movement? Is it not one more proof of India's misfortune that the writer of the above words should impute bad motives to the supporters of the National Congress, mainly because they advocate the introduction of some sort of representation in the Legislative Councils of India? Is not your charge of sedition against the promoters of the Congress, in the face of these, a mere mockery, a contradiction in terms?

Thirty years ago, you advocated the institution of a Parliament, and yet you chide us saying that we want an Indian Parliament, notwithstanding that protest that for the present, and for a long time to come, we do not claim any such thing ? Mark the difference.

India is no longer what it was 30 years ago. In the course of this period it has made a marked advance towards a higher civilization The natives of India are no longer, with very few exceptions, ignorant or uneducated.

The rays of education are penetrating and shedding their wholesome light inside most Indian homes; hundreds of thousands of Indians are as well educated as any average English gentleman, and we see scores of our countrymen every year crossing the "black waters to witness with their own eyes the proceedings of the great British Parliament and personally familiarize themselves with the political institutions of the English nation. Can you in face of these facts still call us ' seditious"?

According to your writings, we are the most loyal subjects of the Government, and if, notwithstanding what you have written, you still deserve to be called "the ablest of our loyal Mahomedan gentlemen,' why, we deserve to be styled "the ablest of the most loyal subjects of the English Government.'

To give a still more clear idea of what you thought about the fitness of India for this sort of Government, I give one more extract to the point, and then I will havedone with your old writings for the present. After giving: many arguments in proof of your position that the law which allowed the sales of land for arrears of Government revenue was also a cause of the outbreak of disturbances in 1858. you say: "A landed estate in Hindustan is very like a kingdom. It has always been the practice to elect one man us the head over all. By him matters requiring discussion are brought forward ' (mind, not decided), and every shareholder, in proportion to his' holding, has the power of speaking out his mind on the point."You are wrong when you say "in proportion to his holding.'

However, let it remain as it is. You proceed and say: "The cultivators and the choudhries of the villages attend on such an occasion and say whatever they have to say. You have here, in fact, in great perfection a miniature kingdom parliament."How is it that now you have changed your mind and have come to opine that these kingdoms, as you called them, should have no voice in the making of laws which materially affect the person, the property and the reputation of the people ?

Some persons insinuate that these writings which I have quoted came from an honest, uncorrupted mind, at a time when the writer had no prospect of being raised to the Legislative Council by mere favour No, Sir Syed, no I I, on my own part, do not want to make such an insinuation against the fearless writer of those noble words which have been quoted above.

Then the problem to be solved remains the same, viz., why this change, why this inconsistency ? I pause for a reply, with a promise of more in my next, and in the meanwhile be to be allowed to subscribe myself.

Sir, — It is more than two weeks now since my first letter was published, and I think, I have waited long enough for the reply which, it seems, you have no mind to send However, in fulfillment of my promise, I am bound to go on giving quotation after quotation, bringing home to you your own former political teachings, and I hope I shall be able clearly to prove that you once believed in all the principles upon which the different Resolutions of the National Congress are based. This will leave you no alternative but either an open and unreserved confession of your apostasy or an unreserved retreat from politics. Do not think, Sir Syed, that I shall rest satisfied with the publication of these letters in India. No, they will be duly published and distributed in free England, side by side with the pamphlets of your own pet Association of yesterday.

In the book, already so often referred to, i.e., "The Causes of the Indian Revolt," you say: "Government were but slightly acquainted with the unhappy state of the people. How could it well be otherwise ?

There was no real communication between the Government and the governed, no living together or near one another, as has always been the custom of Mahomedans in countries which they subjected to their rule.

Government and its of officials have never adopted the course without which no real knowledge of the people cm be gained."Further on you say that "this cannot be expected from the English, as they almost all look forward to retirement in their native land, and seldom settle for good amongst the natives of India."

Now, I take the liberty of asking has there been any improvement of late in this direction? Have the majority, or even one per cent, of the retired English officers, permanently settled in India?

On the contrary, we find that they are birds-of-passage just as much now as, or perhaps more than, they were when the above sentences were written. Then, have the Englishmen and the natives taken to living together or near one another? Do you ever see Englishmen living in the Mahallas of your towns, however large the towns or however respectable the Mahallas may be ? None of the Englishmen have ever been seen doing that. In fact, their mode of living is so peculiar that they cannot. Or, do you think that the point has been gained by a few Anglicised natives like yourself having taken to living in Bungalows? If that 18 what you argue, I assure you, you are sadly mistaken.

Your living in Europeanized houses cannot be said to be a gain to native society. It is rather, if I may be allowed to say so, a very severe and deplorable loss. In the sentence quoted above, you admit that living together or near one another enhances our sympathies and gives us more occasions of seeing, mixing with, and obtaining a more intimate knowledge of each other. It is thus clear that Europeans can only really know us if they see us in our native homes, in our small thatched huts full of misery and sickness.

How poor and miserable India is, they can feel only if they live amongst or near the houses of our agriculturists, and there see with there own eyes respectable native rooms into which an English beggar would scorn to step Why is this? Is it because we Indians do not know how to live?

Now, if you say that, go to those Indian residences which are occupied by our few rich or even well-to-do countrymen, and there you will find that our mode of living is quite on a par with that of Europeans. Does any one then ask how it is that I say that respectable natives live, everywhere, in buildings which can only properly be called hovels? The answer is, because they are miserably poor and cannot afford to build comfortable houses.

Taxation is so high that they never feel themselves secure of their respectability. In fact, it is always in danger. The poor fellows are daily and nightly engaged in making the two ends meet What I mean to say is that the fact of you or a few other natives having taken to live in Bungalows and imitating the English customs of eating and drinking and dressing cannot do any good either to India or to England.

In fact, this will never help the English to realize the unhappy state of the people. Then the question is, how can the Government know the wants and wishes of its subject? They cannot know them through official reports, because these reports are almost all prepared by parsons who seldom see the real state of the people whom the reports concern.

You' yourself said: "But even these officials themselves were ignorant of the real thoughts and opinions of the people, because they had no means of getting at them "(vide your Biography by Colonel Graham, p. 49.) Then can the Government get this knowledge through the petitions of their subjects? I say, as you said — no.

You said that these petitions "were," and I say they are, "seldom if ever attended to and sometimes never heard "(vide the same page of your Biography.) I add to this that even if they are ever attended to, enquiry into the allegations made in them is often entrusted to the same officials whose conduct forms the subject of complaint. Their reports are taken to be gospel truth and the petitions are thrown out.

Then, can the Government know the real opinion of the people through the Native press? No, because the Government officials have always been hostile to it and have ever asserted that these papers represent nobody but themselves. Public meetings even are not effectual, because these are invariably declared to be the work of professional agitators, stump-orators and wire-pullers.

The question then is, that admitting as you do, that it is essential for the purpose of good administration that the people should have a voice in the consultations of the Government, should that voice reach the Council Chambers, and how should the people be consulted before laws are passed?

You once said that laws affecting the subject should be made after consultation with the representatives of the people "— ba salah wa mashwarah riyaya ke naibon ke —Social Reformer of the 15th Shawwal, 1290, Hijri, equivalent to the 6th December, 1873, p. 163), and there cannot be any other answer to this question.

Further on you said : "I am very sorry that this is not being done in India, and in not doing so Government is in error to a certain degree but in a larger measure of the subjects, but I am confident that after a certain period — (baad chand roz) — sufficient education will remove both."{Vide the same Journal, same page.) It 18 fifteen years now, Sir, since the above lines were written, and it is, surely, time to ask, or, at least, to consider, whether that period, or "chand roz," to speak in your own words, has not expired yet. I am ready to concede, though it may be for argument's sake only, that "the period has not expired, but are we not making steady (progress towards the desired end?

Your objections, unfortunately, are not based upon considerations of time, but are put forward as matters of principle. Then admitting, as you do, that this voice can only reach the Council Chamber through the representatives of the people, the only question to be solved is — who should be those representatives, or, in other words, how should they acquire that position?

Can men, like Rajah Shiva Prashad and yourself, be properly considered as representatives of the people, and can the method of selection, by which you were sent to the Council Chamber, be accepted as of any value? I think no reasonable man would contend that it would have been possible, if Rajah Shiva Prashad had been an elected representative of the people of India, for him to have libeled the whole Indian nation, as he did, in his notorious speech-on the Ilbert Bill.

Could Rajah Peary Mohan Mukerjee and other native members have consented to the raising of the Salt tax if they had thought that their seats depended on the voices of the people, whose throais were, to speak, to be cut by that obnoxious and inhumane measure?

Then the correct solution is this and no Other, that the people must be represented by delegates, elected by themselves; and subject of course to the restrictions to be imposed by the Government Co-sharers in the business of governing or legislating, these representatives must be such as to be totally independent of official favour or disfavour. If the selection of members for the Legislative Councils is to be entrusted to officials, I say it is a downright farce, and there can be no representation.

The majority of the quotations given above comer from a book which was written about 30 years ago, and you may find an excuse by saying that the state of the people has since then undergone a mighty change, and that, in consequence of this, the remedies then suggested are no longer suitable. My dear Sir, this reply cannot stand a moment's examination.

I am going to show that in 1881, which is only seven years ago, you held the same views and felt rather proud of them.. When it was proposed to raise the old Punjab University College to the status of a University, you were one of the foremost opponents of the proposal. You, your admirers and followers, should not have forgotten that you wrote certain articles under the heading of 'Our Vernacular,' and got them published and circulated in a pamphlet form.

These articles were published in almost all the leading vernacular papers of Northern India, and the educated community of the Punjab, who were strongly opposed to the establishment of a University on the lines suggested by Dr.

Leitner, obtained effective support from these writings of "the ablest of the loyal Mahomedan gentlemen. National progress and National Government are both sisters born of the same mother. When a nation loses its independence, its progress only depends upon its learning the language and sciences of Conquerors and thus taking a part in the Government of the country. Flattery whatever may be said, and as a matter of policy whatever may be stated, the fact is that in reality the relations of Hindustanis to their rulers are no better than those of slaves to their master.

The italics are mine. I have tried to give a faithful translation of your Urdu sentence. If I have erred, I hope to be excused, and that my mistake may be pointed out. However, to satisfy the scruples of sceptical readers, I prefer to give the last portion of the sentence in Roman characters and leave them to judge for themselves whether the rendering is correct or not.

The original words are: "Khushamad ki baten jo chahe kah le, aur political tariqe men jo kuchh beyan karna ho, keya javve, magar Hindostanion ka hal apni fatahmand qaum ke sath gulami ki halat se kuchh ziyada nahin hai."In the same article, further on, you said that the University College was being raised to the status of a University with the object of throwing obstacles in the way of our National advancement, and that the result of the clamour after Oriental studies could be nothing but that of keeping ourselves in the state of serfdom."<Iska natija yehi hai ki gulami ki halat men rakhne ke liye).

Sir Syed, would you still call us "seditious"? Remember that we are the product of that education which you so strongly recommended and which you have never been known to condemn. Our English education, the study of eminent European minds and European sciences — alas! that you cannot feel this — has expanded our souls, and we can no longer be selfish "Sat Bachina" prodigies of your Oriental language.

Sir, your fall seems to remind me of the fall of Adam. Just as Satan is said to be the cause of the fall of that progenitor of our race, this seeking after wordly honours seems to be the real explanation of your decline. It is nothing to you, because your term in this world must at no very distant period expire; but to us, who are yet, we hope, to live long and to fight out the bloodless battle of liberty, it is destined to remain a permanent disgrace.

The line of argument against us would be that the races which produce such inconsistent philosophers are not fit to receive the boon of Local Self-Government. Sir Syed, if you have changed your political opinions, the sooner you announce it the better it will be, both for yourself and for us. It is simply childish to persist in your claim to consistency in the face of the above quotations. Better announce this change and explain why and how this took place. Again pausing for a reply, with a promise of more in my next, I beg to subscribe myself.

Sir, — Well may we apply the opening sentence of Dickens Tale of Two Cities to the present times in India. Well may we say that it is "the best of times "as well as "the worst of times". Best as the country is on the point of having a nation, worst as a particular section of the community wants to check the progress of the country and unfortunately is headed, or at least is said to be headed, by a man who has been a frequent advocate of representative Government in India. It is "the age of wisdom" as the country has risen from its deep lethargy and made up its mind to assist the Government by wise counsels.

It is "the age of foolishness' as a particular party has the audacity to believe that their opposition will cause the national movement to die in its infancy. It is "the epoch of belief" because the different sectional interests have begun to believe in each other's sincerity: it is "the epoch of incredulity "because you, Sir, are said to be now-a-days against the introduction of a representative element into the Legislative Councils of India. It is the "spring of hope "when we see eminent English statesmen advocating the rights of the dumb millions of India. It is the "winter of despair" when we see her own sons deserting the cause of awakened India.

Sir Syed, I must remind you that it is the same India for the welfare of whose sons you established "The Siddors's Union Club "at Aligarh.

Do you remember? Sir, that in that Club the alumni of the Mahomedan College were trained in the art of discussing public matters in public councils? I ask you, Sir, why that Club? Why did you formulate those rules of discussion which predict the establishment of representative institutions in the country? Oh, if we had only known that it was to end in this!! I feel that I have gone astray and must look to those extracts from your writings and sayings so dear to me, which foretold the establishment of representative Councils in India.

Will you please turn to page 49 of your Biography by Lieutenant-Colonel Graham where you are described as saying: "The people were isolated, they had no champion to stand up for their rights and to see justice done them, and they were constrained to weep in silence." Can you in the face of these words still say that the people never needed such champions, and that the Government has been doing and will go on doing without demand what it has thought and what it will think necessary for the welfare of the people ? That it never needed the voice of such champions for the redress of grievances and the attainment of rights?

Having pointed out what the Government ought to have done to make itself popular (quotations as to which have been given in letters Nos. I and II) you said in the end of the same book, "The Causes of Indian Revolt," that "it was necessary for the Government to win the friendship and the good feeling of its subjects."Further on you said: "As yet, truth compels me to state, Government has not cultivated the friendship of its people as was its duty to do the father loves his child before the child loves him. If a man of low degree try to win the esteem of one in high position he is liable to be styled.

It was, therefore, for Government to try and win the friendship of its subjects, not for the subjects to try and win that of the Government. If Government say that what I say is untrue — that they have tried to cultivate friendship and have only been repaid with enmity — I can only say that if it had gone the right way to work, its subjects would most undoubtedly have been its friends and supporters instead of, as in many instances, rising up in arms against it.

Now, friendship is a feeling which springs from the heart and which cannot be kindled by admonitions.' Government has hitherto kept itself as isolated from the people of India as if it had been the fire and they the dry grass — as if it thought that, were the two brought in contact the latter would be burnt up."

I have given this large quotation to recall to your mind some of the reasons upon which you formed the opinions which I have already quoted in my letters Nos. I and II. These reasons may also go to prove that the prayers of the National Congress as to the concession of volunteering to be allowed to the native subjects of Her Majesty are nothing but reasonable and consistent with the noble principles involved in the above lines. Now I have done with your book on "The Causes of Indian Revolt," so far as it concerned that resolution of the National Congress which prays for the introduction of a representative element in the Legislative Councils of India. Most of these extracts, except one or two here and there, were abstract, and perhaps you may, with your usual calmness, have the boldness to say that there is nothing in these quotations which goes to prove that you ever meant to say that these representatives to the Council of India should be elected by the subjects.

Very good, I will search out quotations which will leave nothing doubtful. You may not have forgotten that two months after the opening of your Scientific Society you delivered "a vigorous speech "at the laying of the foundation stone of the New Gazhipore, now the Victoria College. In the course of that address you said: "Bear in mind, gentlemen, that Her Most Gracious Majesty Queen Victoria has had proclaimed in this country that her servants and subjects, European and native, are to be considered as being on an equal footing; and this assurance gentlemen, is not a mere matter of form hut a reality: The italics are mine. Now, Sir Syed Ahmed, will you still laugh at us because we believe this — this very proclamation — to be our Magna Carta?

Further on in the course, of the same address you said: "The appointment of natives to the Supreme Council was a memorable incident in the History of India. The day is not far distant I trust, and when it does come you will remember my words when that Council will be composed of representatives from

EVERY Division or District, and that thus the laws which will pass will be laws enacted by the feelings of the entire country."

"You will see that this cannot come to pass unless we strive to educate ourselves thoroughly. I once had a conversation with one in high authority on this very subject, and he said that Government would be only too glad if a scheme, such as I have sketched above, were practicable, but he felt doubtful; if it were stated that there were qualified men in every District, Government would gladly avail itself of their knowledge and give them seats in Council. I knew this only too well and felt ashamed that such was the case.

What I have above stated is only to inculcate on your minds the great fact that Her Most Gracious Majesty wishes all her subjects to be treated alike; and let their religion, tribe, or colour be what it may, the only way to avail ourselves of the many roads to fame and usefulness is to cultivate our intellects and to conform ourselves to the age."Sir Syed, have the happiness to know that the day, which you in 1864 said was not far distant is coming nearer, and nearer, and that you need no longer feel so much ashamed of your countrymen for not conforming to the age.

Your prophecy is not fulfilled yet, but we are certain that sometime or other it is sure to be fulfilled, and then you will have the satisfaction of feeling that you did not prophesy in vain. Sir Syed, do you wish to withdraw this prophecy of yours, and if so why? Please explain — I and others like me are waiting in suspense.

Only say that this prophecy was one of the hallucinations of a head which had been turned by the sudden inrush of Western ideas and we will be satisfied. Only say that with the return of sobriety and the calmness of old age you have come to know your own errors, and we will no more trouble you with these prophecies. Sir Syed, would you please point out what else could be the meaning of the above sentence except that, that India would some (in 1864, not far distant) day be governed by Councils composed of members elected by the people themselves ? If not this, how can the laws be said to be "enacted by the feelings of the entire country.'

Two months before you spoke the words quoted above, you, on the 9th January, 1864, started a Translation Society now known as the Scientific Society of Aligarh; and in the course of a speech then delivered pointing out the ignorance of your countrymen you said: From their ignorance of the events of the past, and also of the events of the present — from their not being acquainted with the manner and means by which infant nations have grown into powerful and flourishing ones, and by which the present most advanced ones have beaten their competitors in the race for position among the magnates of the world — they are unable to take lessons and profit by their experience."Sir, we took your advice, and your countrymen have learnt the means and the manner by which they can advance the growth of their "infant nation "to the position of a "powerful "and a "flourishing" one.

How is it that this growth which you so much desired in 1864 is an eyesore to you now?

How is it that now at this period you cannot feel any pleasure in seeing a combination of all the different races and sects towards the accomplishment of the great end for which you have been until recently struggling so hard?

How is it that you are going to prove that you did not deserve the distinctions so deservedly, as we thought, bestowed upon you?

By your present attitude, by your present utterances, you mean to prove that all that you once said, all that you once did, for which you were rightly honoured both by the Government and for which you were said to be deserving of being awarded a conspicuous place on the list of benefactors of India, was, after all, but utter nonsense — because that is the phrase you now apply to the repetition of those same principles which you once so strenuously advocated by the supporters of the National Congress.

On the 10th of May, 1886, you addressed a large and influential meeting of the European and native residents of Aligarh on the necessity of Indian affairs being more prominently brought before Parliament and of forming an association for this purpose (at least so says your biographer on pp. 88 and 89). In the course of this speech you compared the British rule with that of the "former emperors and Rajas" of India. You said "it "(i.e., the rule of the latter) "was based upon nothing but tyranny and oppression; the law of might was that of right; the voice of the people was not listened to; the strong and the turbulent, oppressed the feeble and the poor, and usurped all their privileges with impunity for their own selfish ends. It is only therefore by such usurpers and turbulent spirits that a despotism, such as flourished in Hindustan for many long centuries, is at all to be desired."Know, sir, that the National Congress wants nothing but that the voice of the people be listened to, and that the "strong and the turbulent" may not oppress "the feeble and the poor.'

The National Congress wants to achieve these ends by peaceful means and in fact by prayers; while it can only be the usurpers and the turbulent who desire to threaten, as you now do, the use of arms. It can only be the self-assumed ' strong ' who can threaten the poor "with the use of the arms, by ' the followers of the prophet. Further on you regretted the indifference, with which the affairs of India were treated in the Parliament, and laid the blame of it to a great extent upon the shoulders of your own countrymen. You said: India, with that slowness to avail herself of that which would benefit her so characteristic of Eastern nations, has hitherto looked on Parliament with a dreamy apathetic eye, content to have her affairs, in the shape of her Budget, brought before it in an annual and generally inaudible speech by Her Majesty's Secretary of State for India."

You entreated your countrymen to discontinue this apathy, and you asked them to exert themselves towards securing the proper representation of their interests in the governing body of the British Nation. You appealed to the "entire native community ", "to co-operate "with the London Association established for the purpose. To your countrymen you continued to say: You will have only yourselves to reproach when in after years you see the European section of the community enjoying their well-earned concessions whilst your wants remain still unmet."Sir Syed, the country then responded to your call, though imperfectly, and it is now that the country has felt the value of your words and begun to throw away the deep indifference which you so forcibly lamented. Pray will you tell me whether, prior to the movement of National Congress, there was no agitation for the redress of the grievances of Indians in India? If so what was all this which you were doing?

Why did you establish and support all these associations?

"Why did you call upon the entire country to with these Associations if the Government had of its own accord been doing all that was needed for the welfare of India? In your criticism upon the Lucknow speech of the Honble Pandit Ajudhia Nath of Allahabad you meant to ask (if I did not err in understanding and reproducing it from memory) the Congress-wallahs if any of their agitations had been existing when the Government granted all the boons which we enjoy. I have quoted largely from your own writings to show that such an agitation did exist, and that you yourself were one of the most prominent agitators. You even went the length of saying that no fear need be entertained of your (i.e. of those who meant to take part in such associations) being called discontented by the Government. To quote your own words you said: "I am afraid that a feeling of fear — fear that the Government or the district: authorities would esteem you factious and discontented, were you to inaugurate a measure like this — deters you from coming forward for your country's good.

Believe me that this moral cowardice is wrong — the apprehension unfounded, and that there is not an Englishman of a liberal turn of mind in India who would regard with feelings other than those of pleasure and hope, such a healthy sign of increased civilization on the part of its inhabitants. The natives have at present little or no voice in the management of the affairs of their country, and should any measure of Government prove obnoxious to them, they brood over it, appearing outwardly satisfied and happy while discontent is ranking in their mind."Further on you said that the natives were in the habit of in weighing against such measures in their homes, but to the Europeans they represented that they were satisfied with the justice and wisdom of these very measures.

You loudly proclaimed that such a state of affairs is inimical to the welfare of the country. Far better would it be for India were her people openly and honestly to express their opinions as to the justice or otherwise of the acts of Government."Would you pray tell me, Sir, why they are sedition mongers; is it because we speak "honestly "as to the justice or otherwise of the acts of the Government is it because we have overcome the moral cawardice with which you charged us ? Are we seditious because we do not want to keep "discontent rankling" within our hearts?

Are we disloyal because we, according to your own teachings, have come forward to speak up for our country's good? If we deserve all these epithets on account of all these I must say, Sir, that you are the father of all this. You taught us to do exactly what we have begun doing now. You not only taught but encouraged us by your own example. Why do you now deprecate "this healthy sign of civilization "as you once called it on the part of Indians? If we, the followers of your old principles, have exceeded the proper dimension which, I humbly maintain, we have not, it is surely not advisable to root out these instincts from within us, but rather to point out the place and the occasion where we have exceeded.

How have you come to oppose the principles themselves, the principles so lovingly promulgated by you? Say that the principles are not to be discarded but the men abusing these principles are to be despised. We will then know how to love the men. We loved you because you held these principles, because we thought you loved your country above everything, because we considered you to be one of the fathers of the present India, and if we have erred we must say we think that you should have pointed out our error in time. Truly has a poet said : "Khwab tha jo kuchh ki dekha tha afsana tha jo kuchh ke suna tha,

' i.e., "what I saw was but a dream, what I heard an idle tale."Ah I human delusions are then destined to delude the human eye for ever I Again with a pause, with a promise of more in my next, I am yours, &c., 22nd Nov., 1858. The Son of an old follower of Yours.

No. IV.

Sir, — The fourth meeting of the Indian National Congress is soon to be held at Allahabad, and so I think

I must hasten to give some more of the most important quotations in this letter of mine. The less important ones I leave for some future occasion.

When this letter reaches you, you will be, possibly, smiling over the ex-Viceroy's speech delivered at the

St Andrew's Dinner, Calcutta. If you will only take the trouble of reading that speech with your eyes open, you will find that your uproar against the introduction of some representative element in the Legislative Council of India is not liked even by those whom you have undertaken to flatter, and whose National traditions you try to belie.

Sir Syed, for God's sake, reconsider your position and do not disappoint us just when the morning of hope has begun to draw over us and our motherland.

Now to proceed with your old writings and sayings; please turn to pages 207 and 208 of your Social Reformer for 1298 Hijri, equivalent to the year 1881 A. D. There, while giving an account of your voyage to London, you said that on the way you happened to see Mr. D. Fitzpatrick, the former Deputy Commissioner of Delhi, with whom you talked about "the goodness or badness of the Punjab administration."Therein you profess to have said that the Government of the Punjab was a Despotic one, though a thousand times [better than that of the Sikhs. Further on you say "the people of the Punjab may be happy and perhaps may like it because they have been just taken out of fire and made to sit in the sun. But we cannot like it.

The goodness or badness of the Punjab Government, i.e., of the Government of the nonRegulation Provinces, should be asked of the inhabitants of the Delhi, Panipat Rohtak, Hissar and Sirsa Districts, which once used to belong to Regulation Provinces and have now been subjected to a non-Regulation (or heqanum) Punjab Administration As far as I know people think that of many other punishments, which had been awarded to the inhabitants of Delhi and its adjacent districts in the Mutiny, this was also one that they were made over to the Government of the Punjab and thus made the subjects of non-Rulation Provinces."These lines were written when the NorthWestern Provinces did not enjoy the blessing of having a Provincial Legislature of its own, and so the only superiority in the administration of the N.W. P. over that of the Punjab then, was the existence of a High Court instead of the Chief Court in the Punjab, and the constitution of a Board of Revenue instead of a Financial Commissionership here.

The word Despotic is your own, and is used in your Urdu style, and thus you cannot say that the word has been unwittingly thrust upon you by the translator. Even at the risk of unidiomatic English I have tried to give a literal translation of your Urdu sentences. If you think that this translation is incorrect, I trust you will not, for the sake of your own reputation, fail to publish a true translation of the sentences quoted. Now, will you please explain on what principles you designated the Government of the Punjab as Despotic, and how you distinguished it in that respect from the Government of India or that of N.W. P.?

I can venture to say that the Government of the Punjab was never more Despotic than the Governments of other sister Provinces. No doubt the merit of each Government to a considerable degree depends upon the personal character of its head. The Governments of Montgomery, Aitchison and even that of Sir James Lyall cannot be said to be more Despotic than that of any of the Governors of other Provinces. Can you, Sir, in the face of this broad accusation of yours, still designate us as reckless accusers of Government and its policy? Further on in the same article you go on saying: "In fact the present time is not one in which people may like a Despotic Government, nor are those virtues (which in ancient times used to be mixed with a thousand vices) of a Despotic Government, and by which the influence of the former were an antidote for the latter, to be found in these days. Now-a-days it is not possible for those virtues to exist in any Despotic

Government, and the people who think that in India a Despotic Government, such as it used to be in by-gone times, would be more appropriate and useful than the constitutional form of Government, are greatly mistaken. They are just like one who judges a garden by its state in the autumn without caring to think what it will be in the spring. "The word Despotic throughout this quotation is your own.

At another place, on page 132 of the same journal for the same year, under the heading of the Eastern

Arts and Sciences, you exhort us not to devote ourselves to them but to the study of Western ones. You ask us even "to forget our mothertongue "(an impossibility in itself) because you said our National advancement only "depended upon the spread of Western Sciences. "You said: "Let us by all means remain loyal to the Government, let us always regard it to be our patron and well-wisher, and let us at the same time try to extricate ourselves from that servile and savage state in which we are."

Nobly and truly did you say that this, and this only, should be the object of a generous-hearted Government who rules over a nation for the good of the latter, or, say, for the good of the human race. In the course of the same article on the same page of your "Tahzib-ul-Ikhlaq ' you say "no nation can ever advance in parallel lines all point to another. Nations always advance in the shape of a triangle, whose one corner projects in advance of the others. To think that we may not be divided in different sects is to pray that we may not be enlightened by the light of Western ideas "1 n contrast to this, please reconsider your Meerut speech, in which in fact you wanted to express that the whole nation must remain in the background because you think that the Mahomedan community has not sufficiently advanced to fully reap the benefits to be enjoyed by the granting of the boons prayed for by the National Congress. (I do not admit that the Mahomedan community is not sufficiently advanced.)

On page 136 of the same Journal you say: "I sincerely believe and wish to assure the Government that the same discontented educated critics "(meaning those educated gentlemen who severely criticize the Government measures and who are blamed for it) "yield to none in their appreciation of the British rule; hence it is not just to effect the ruin of our education on account of any apprehension of such criticism."These are the words which you addressed to those politicians who advocate the closing of Government Colleges and Schools, and who are of opinion that education in Western ideas and sciences has made the Indians disloyal.

You would, I suppose, like to re-read those words also by which you encourage your own educated countrymen to fight out the battle of their national advancement bravely and without fear. You say; "Without doubt, there are many difficulties in the way of our doing so "(i.e., promulgating those blessings of education, instruction and enlightenment which we acquire in those civilised countries to which we go or completing our education).

"On one side we are to contend against the prejudices and ignorance of our own countrymen, and on the other side we are to bear the opposition of those narrow-minded men of the conquering race to whom our social and political advancement is an eyesore, and who dislike us because we have adopted English life, English politics and the manners of an English gentlemen; and change of dress even infuriates them to such a degree that they look at us with angry eyes as a pious man looks at a great criminal. But we should keep the good of our nation at heart and should bear all the difficulties and troubles which beset our way with the greatest possible forbearance and perserve ranee. I do not wish to conceal that Time, the Great Reformer, will let all these things, and no opposition or discontent will be able to keep them back. But still there is no doubt that this narrow-mindedness is kindling the feelings of discontent, and is surely calculated to cause all sympathy and love between the governors and the governed to be banished.'

Sir Syed, have the happiness to learn that your countrymen took you to be a true prophet — that they are going to stick to every word which you wrote — are not to be daunted or baffled by any opposition, — no, not even by yours. How is it that you preached to us to persevere and yourself could not do this? ("Digran ra nafihat wa khud ra fazihat. ") We have persevered, but the old man has fallen; what a pitiable spectacle of human weakness.

Next I will give a native volunteers with which one of the Resolutions of the National Congress deals. On page 332 of your Biography, says your Biographer, that in March, 1883, when Mr. A. O. Hume (the beloved General Secretary of the National Congress) advocate the cause of native volunteers in India, and stated that in the mutiny he had a brigade of infantry, cavalry and artillery in the Etawah yeomanry levy — all Volunteers — he (i.e., Lieutenant-Colonel Graham) addressed a letter to the Editor of the Pioneer in which he tried to rebut many of the arguments advanced by Mr. Hume, which letter he says brought you (Sir Syed Ahmed) down upon him in a letter which you wrote to him. He gives an extract from that letter on page 334, which runs thus: I have perused your reply to Mr. Hume's letter advocating the volunteering of the Natives of India.

In not allowing the natives to become Volunteers, the Government mean to say that they do not trust the Natives of India. Its consequences should be judged from the saying: IP you want U3 to trust you, you should also trust us.' There yet exists a wide gulf between European and the Natives of India, and unless it be filled up nothing can secure and improve the prosperity of the country, "The italics are mine. This you wrote in the middle of 1883, and now in 1887 and 1888, you say Indians do not want anything. On the same page Lieutenant-Colonel Graham writes as follows : "What I would advocate would be the selection by the local authorities in all large stations in India of a certain number of picked Native Volunteers — men of good family and well-known for their loyalty — to be placed under the command of the Officer commanding the European Volunteers. I would let them select their own company officers, and once started I would also permit them to select their own recruits as vacancies occurred."

I say "give us this much and we will be satisfied for a long time to come."

A few important extracts more and I will have done with your old writings and sayings for the present.

Contrast the meanings attached to the words "Nation and National by you in your Meerut speech with those promulgated by yourself at Gurdaspur on the 27th of January, 1884. At Gurdaspur you said that "we (i.e., the Hindus and Mahomedans) should try to become one heart and soul and act in unison; if united we can support each other. If not, the effect of one against the other would tend to the destruction and downfall of both (Cheers.)

In old historical books and traditions you will have read and heard, and we see it even now, that all the people inhabiting one country are designated by the term one nation. The different tribes of Afghanistan are termed as one nation, and so are the miscellaneous hordes peopling Iran, distinguished by the term Europeans, though abounding in variety of thoughts and religions, are still known as members of one nation, though people of other countries also do come and settle with them, but being mixed together they are called members of one and the same nation. So that from the oldest times the word Nation is applied to the inhabitants of one country though they differ in some peculiar characteristic of their own. Hindu and Mahomedan brethren, do you people any country other than Hindustan? Do you not inhabit the same land? Are you not burned and buried on the same soil? Do you not tread the same ground and live upon the same soil?

Remember that the words Hindu and Mahomedan are only meant for religious distinction — otherwise all persons, whether Hindu or Mahomedan, even the Christians who reside in this country are all in this particular respect belonging to one and the same nation. (Cheers)

Then all these different sects can only be described as one nation; they must each and all unite for the good of the country which is common to all.

Again in your Lahore speech, which was delivered in reply to the address of the Indian Association of Lahore, you, on the 3rd of February, 1884, said as follows "Even granting that the majority of those composing this Association are Hindus, still I say that this light has been diffused by the same whom I call by the epithet of Bengalees. I assure you that Bengalees are the only people in our country whom we can properly be proud of, and it is only due to them that knowledge, liberty and patriotism have progressed in our country. I can truly say that really they are the head and crown of all the different communities of Hindustan. I myself was fully cognizant of all those difficulties which obstructed my way, but notwithstanding these I heartily wished to serve my country and my nation faithfully. In the word Nation I include both Hindus and Mahomedans because that is the only meaning which I can attach to it (i.e., NATION or quamy Here in the end the word nation is originally used by yourself (see the account of your trip to the Punjab by Maulive Iqbal AH, p. 167, line 18th). The capitals are mine. To resume : "With me it is not so much worth considering ivhat is their religious faith, because we do not see anything of it. What we do see is that we inhabit the same land, are subject to the rule of the same Governers, the fountains of benefits for all are the same, and the pangs of famine also we suffer equally. These are the different grounds upon which I call both those races which inhabit India by one word, to Hindu, meaning to say that they are the inhabitants of Hindustan. While in the Legislative Council I was always anxious for the prosperity of this nation." The italics are mine. This letter of mine has already exceeded its proper dimensions, and therefore I think I must not give more extracts, and must leave the rest to be commented upon by abler hands than mine.

Anybody reading these extracts will be once for all convinced of the former loftiness and present lowness of your position. Foreigners reading these extracts will not believe that your now famous Meerut and Lucknow speeches were in reality delivered by the same Sir Syed Ahmed Khan who was once proud (whether rightly or wrongly God knows) of his broadmindedness. This much seems certain: either you were not the author of those ideas reproduced in the above quotations, your recent utterances were inspired by some mind or other than your own. Poor Sir Syed, you must feel sorry for all.

Can it be that your once massive, manly intellect to the feeble, schoolgirl-like sop this inconsistency, though you may not have the boldness to say so. Sir, I assure you that you should not despair; a small sacrifice at the alter of your country, a renewed profession of the faith that was once in you will suffice to regain for you the confidence of your countrymen. If you are not prepared to do so, I must think myself justified in impeaching you in the name of consistency, in the name of honesty and fair play, in the name of the great Mahomed whose descendant and follower you profess to be, in the name of Madhi Ali, your old devoted friend who once felt proud of showing to the world that the original Mahomedan rule was based upon democratic principles (see your Social Reformer for 129D Hijri, p. 136, lines 8 to 23); and lastly in the name of the pupils of your own Mahomedan Anglo-Oriental College, Aligarh, whom you trained in the principles which you now affect to detest. It is a year since you actually engaged yourself in creating and keeping up an opposition to the National Congress, but up to this time your countrymen have not been clearly enlightened as to what It is that you object to in the proceedings of the National Congress. You say we are not fit for a Republic and so do we say. You say we are not yet fit for a parliament and so do we say.

If you say that the introduction of some representative element even into the Government would be injurious to our community, we ask why and how, and employee? That Merlin-like, the great heart that once beat true for India is now pulse less, and that you lie bound, inextricably, by the treacherous spells of a modern Vivian, even more despicable than his female prototype? Pray when did you receive that revelation, because up to 1884 you yourself acknowledged the necessity of these Legislative Councils being reconstituted upon some representative basis. Then, again, when were you inspired with the idea that the Hindu and the Mahomedan interests are sure to clash at least in this respect?

Because up to 1884 you belived in the doctrine of Hindus rand Mahomedans having one and the same political interests and being members of one and the same nation. To your friends Maulvles Mahdi Ali and Madhi Hussain, whose tergiversation is not less amazing than your own, I have only a few words to say. To the former that he had better now suppress his Lecture published in the Social Reformer for 1290 Hijri on pp. 136 and those preceding and following it. To the latter hat he should now publicly recant the views set forth in his article under the heading of "Liberty "published in jour Social Reformer for 1298 Hijri, 1881, from pp. 231 to 341. Until they do this I will ask them to abstain, if they desire any human being to credit them with common honesty, from abusing us and denouncing our principles, and to my other countrymen as well as to our rulers 1 have only to say further— "I know a maiden fair to see.

Take care.
She can both false and friendly be.
Beware ! Beware !
Trust her not,
She is fooling thee.
She has two eyes so soft and brown,
Take care.
She gives a side-glance and looks down,
Beware I Beware I
Trust her not,
She is fooling thee I
And she has hair of a golden hue,
Take care !
And what she says it if not true,
Beware I Beware I
Trust her not,
She is fooling thee.
She has a bosom as white as snow.
Take care !
She knows how much it is best to show
Beware I Beware I
Trust her not.
She is fooling thee."

With a promise to begin afresh in the year 1889,
I beg to subscribe myself, Sir,
Yours, &c., &c.,
December, 1888. The Son of an Old Follower of
Yours.

OUR STRUGGLE FOR FREEDOM

No patriotic Indian can return to his country after a trip to England, including a visit, however short, to other countries in Europe, without being forcibly struck by the intense desire for political liberty and freedom that fills the European atmosphere and that distinguishes the West from the East. He finds that in Europe people are always agitated about their political rights and are extremely jealous of interference with or sup pression of popular rights and privileges.

Life in Eng land or in Europe is a great struggle — constant, unend Jng struggle for right and liberty. Freedom from limitations and restrictions, removal of trammels, be they of any nature, perfect bondage of everykind, is the ever increasing and ever recurring cry of modern Europe. Democratic spirit is the key-note of Western Civilization in all its branches and departments, but in politics it rules almost supreme.

The Government of the people, by the people and for the people is the ideal all over whether in Domocratic England, Monarchical Germany, Autocratic Russia or Republican France. The Press, the pulpit and the plat form are all ringing with the cries of "away with the tyrants and autocrats who stand in the way of the demo cracy and who desire to check or stop the wheel of pro gress onwards or who have the audacity of trifling with the wishes of the people."One should be here in Europe to realize the truth of the above remarks on occasions when anything is done or attempted to be done by the various Governments in power, which is opposed to the democratic spirit of the times or by which a popular de mand is thrown out or anything else is done which is opposed to the wishes of the people or which does not tend to further their interests.

In July last the rejec tion of the London Tramways Bill by the House of Lords afforded such an occasion. The City of London, as our readers know, is situated on the banks of the Thames. The river divides the city into two main divi sions one on each side of the river, the tramways end on each side and are not allowed to run across the bridges. This results in great inconvenience to the people as they have to leave the tramway at one end of the river, cross the bridge on foot and then take other end. The London County Council, therefore, pro posed to take their trmways across the bridges and thus add to the comfort and the convenience of that great mass of people who cannot afford to engage cabs and hansoms. The Bill passed the House of Commons and was rejected in the House of Lords on the ground that its acceptance involved the destruction of the spectacu lar effect of the bridges and would make them look ugly. The days and nights that followed the rejection of this bill presented a spectacle in London which re quired to be seen in order to be fully realized and which is past all description. People were mad with rage and frenzy and on all sides and from all quarters you heard the cry "down with the Lords," down with these heri ditary robbers and thieves."

In clubs, in theatres, in political meetings, on the tramcars, on the buses, in trains, everywhere in fact, the audacity of the House of Lords was the one absorbing topic of discussion and comment, and the proposal for abolishing the House of Lords was being freely and seriously discussed. It found loud expression in the columns of the democratic press, was re-echoed in society papers and was exhibited on the stage. Angry resolutions were passed at the meet ings of the London County Council and at other public meetings whether convened for that special purpose or not. For a few days the atmosphere was surcharged with revolutionary ideas. The semi-official liberal and radical press joined in the cry of the House of Lords. Press could not but disapprove of the action of the Lords and was either discreetly silent or printed in different paragraphs. No serious attempt was made to defend the action of the Lords by anybody.

In short, the whole city seemed to be in a state of ferment and the public mind was intensely agitated. Even the Dailii News, the organ of the Whigs, demanded an abolition of the House of Lords. The country re sounded with the cries of "end it or mend it."Almost im mediately following this, came the defeat of the Govern ment on Irish supplies and the statement of the Premier that he intended neither to resign nor to dissolve the Parliament. On this question, of course, the country was divided and the Whigs and the Tories sided with their respective parties. But even the Tory papers acknow ledged that a crisis had come and in a suppressed tone the Times also admitted that a great constitutional issue Ihadbeen raised.

One of the Radical extremists wrote : —

"It is no less than Revolution I The King is dead. Mr. Balfour has established an autocracy to supplant the monarchy. As defiant of the nation as the Tsar and his bureaucracy, he laughs at public opinions and-governs by paper constitutions. He has only to pro pose a measure prolonging the life of the Government indefinitely and the cowardly criminals at his back aided by the land thieves in the hereditary chamber will pass it. Defeated in the House of Commons, he ignores a hostile vote and continues the petence and corruption.

Let us rejoice, then, that we have been reminded before the election and not after it, of the Permanent Tory Opposi tion which will confront us after the battle is won. Now that we have the issue raised again, in sheer wantonness by the old and new nobility. Let us not suffer it to be dropped. We will come into power in 1906, not only with a mandate upon the fiscal question and education and the publicans and Chinese slavery and labour legislation, but upon that monstrous survival of the bad old times which we call the House of Lords.

At about the same time occurred another incident which showed the ascendancy of the deinocratic spirit in this country. The Government announced what was practically a dropping of the Unemployed Bill and said there was no chance of the Bill being passed into law this session. This announcement met withr a chorus of disapproval from the public, and at once a number of monster demonstrations of the unemployed were organised.

Thousands of the unemployed assembled in different places and protested. In some cases thousands marched to London to prove to tne Government the intensity of feeling on the subject.

At a meeting of the unemployed at Manchester a regular march to London was proposed. In discussing: the proposed measure one of the speakers said : "They had no hesitation in declaring that such a march would be a menace to the towns they passed through, but if the Government wanted to prevent it, th must ive the legislation asked for."Another speaker said that if in the opinion of the authorities, "Human life was not worth any consideration, they, the unemployed, would say that they were not prepared to consider property (Hear,. Hear). They would take immediate steps to see to it that they had that which was necessary for their suste nance and they would not be particular where they got it."The demonstrations of the unemployed men were supplemented by similar demonstrations of the un employed women, and the wives of the unemployed in London who eventually sent a deputation to the House of Commons to meet the Premier. The result was that all parties had to give in and the "Unemployed Bill ' was taken up and passed into law.

Then there is another question that has been agi tating a section of the British public for several years past, viz., the Education Act. This Act forces Non-Con formists to pay rates which they consider iniquitous. The Bill was passed in the teeth of a great and vigorous opposition and the Non-Conformists have not yet been reconciled to it. \ great number of them every year refuse to pay taxes voluntarily and the same is realized by the seizure and distress of their property. This has been going on for the last three years and still continues. The methods of agitation followed by the Irish national ists are too significant and well known to need special mention. In the House of Commons they obstinately obstruct business and at times make the transaction of it almost impossible. Their policy in this respect is open and avowed. In the country itself they throw as many difficulties in the way of the Government.

Their success in these methods is well known and, as a result thereof, they have extorted many valuable concessions from unwilling and hostile Parliaments. In 'Other parts of Europe they go a step further and in the demand for political liberty have recourse to Anarchist tnethods, which at times culminate in murders, assassi nations and crime.

This is wicked no doubt, but it shows how intense is the desire for political liberty and at what risk and under what conditions people are striving to get it, in their own way and according to their own means. Now, on seeing and studying all this, one cannot help contrasting the same with political conditions that prevail in India.

Not that he necessarily wishes that all of these methods may be adopted by his countrymen but because he keenly feels by contrast the apathy, the indifference, the want of ear nestness, the absence of a spirit of sacrifice for the cause and for the principle, the collossal timidity and the con •sequent failure of those who carry on political agitation in India. There are neither leaders nor followers who fully realize what political freedom is and what stupend ous efforts and sacrifices are required of them in order to get to even the fringe of the same. One is apt to feel that a set of wordly-wise (or perhaps unwise), greedy and cowardly people as we are, we do not deserve a better treatment at the hands of our rulers than what they accord to us. Why? What sacrifices do we under go to deserve what wc want?

Anything more than the trouble oi attending the annual session of the Congress and enjoying a holiday? They write articles and deliver speeches do even more than that, they subscribe small sums of money for the political propaganda. But what propor tion does that bear to their incomes or to their expendi ture on luxuries and holidays, &c., you should not ask. Because in answer to that question even the greatest and the loudest of Indian Patriots will have to hide his head in shame. But why be so hard on them ? Have they not big families, sons, grandsons, daughters, wives, mothers, and last but not the least, their great selves to provide for ?

Why, have they not to leave estates, build palaces and otherwise provide for the dim uncertain future ? Yes, they have to do all that, and we have no quarrel with them for doing so. Only we object to their assuming that they are patriots./In our humble opinion no one is entitled to call himself a patriot who holds any thing (excepting his religion, of course,) dearer than his country. But this is a very high and almost unapproach able ideal, you will say. Very well, let us in any case try to do something better and more tangible than we have been doing heretofore. Let us, at the close of each fear, feel certain of some progress. Let us take stock and say if we are, to be sure, making substaintial pro gress.

Looked at from this point of view even, I am afraid we cannot hold out a cheerful and promising record. Our past record shows that in truth, the strug gle for freedom has not even yet commenced, we have done absolutely nothing to inaugurate it. The country is as yet wanting in those conditions which must precede the dawn of an era of real, earnest struggle.

Where are the politiciations whose sole thought by day or by evening, should be, how to initiate and carry on the struggle for freedom ? Where are the political Sanyasis whose sole work in life should be the preaching of the gospel of freedom, who should, even at the point of the bayonet, say with Galelio, "there they are, I see them moving? Where are the Vaishyas of the movement who will only earn and make money for the struggle and who will finance it; who will live poorly and modestly and save every pie for the sacred cause in order not to let it suffer for want of the sinews of war ? And last but not least where are the peopJe who will quietly, ungrudgingly, without complaint or rwirmur, suffer for the cause and in their persons prove theNtruth of the saying that "the blood of the martyrs is theVseed of the church ' ? In short, where are the people w'ftio will raise agitation for political rights and liberty to thettlig"ity church and live and die for the same.

Let us look round and find ouif if there are men in the country who are fit to properly initiate and inaugurate the struggle for freedom. Bengal is renowned for its writers and speakers. Let some of it best sons con secrate their lives to the cause. Their business in life should be to write books, tracts, pd imphlets, articles and notes, also to give speeches all country expounding what liberty is, how it wiii won by other people and how it can be won by us. Payment for their labours but what is susustenance. Let them build no houses, estates and live simple frugal lives. If possible, librates, Maharashtra has justly earned statesmanship and powers of organisation. Let best sons consecrate their lives to the work of organising political movements in India.

Our revered friend, Mr Bal Gangadhar Tilak, is one of the fittest persons to undertake the work, if the Government which has been persecuting him so long, is inclined to let him alone, which is not likely, he having roused its worst suspicions. Well, in that case, the best thing for him is to bid good bye to his motherland, be a voluntary exile and take his residence somewhere abroad. He should devote himself to the task of influencing English and foreign public opinion in favour of political reforms in India. The other leader who is fitted to do this work is Mr. Gokhale. I may be pardoned for hazarding an opinion to the effect that the Supreme or any other Legislative Council Chamber is not the place for him. He has shown the way to others, he has proved to the world sufficiently that even poor Indians can hold their own against clever autocratic bureaucrats of the class of Lord Curzon, and that is enough. Let the non-official members of the Bombay Legislative Council find another representative champion for the Supreme Council and leave Mr. Go khale alone, to be the whole-time Secretary of the Con gress, to organise a central office, to go about, and guide the Provincial Congress Committees. The other provinces, also, should, if possible, prevail upon one or two capable persons in each centre to renounce their profes sions and take to the work of carrying on political agita tion and spreading political propaganda.

If there are any provinces which cannot fix upon their own leaders, let them follow the lead cf the better situated and more lucky ones and assist in bringing abavit. one compact political organisation determined to carry on the struggle for political right.

As to actual work, we think, the time has come for more vigorous measures and for a substantial change in the methods of our agitation.

Bengal has just shown the way in agitating against the Partition of Bengal. What Bengal has done should be done by every province in ventilating its grievances. Besides occasional provincial demonstrations like those recently held in Bengal, we ought to improve upon the general annual demonstration at the Congress session by arranging to bring about a greater and a bigger meeting every year attended by less than a hundred thousand persons from all parts of India. The educational and the political value of such gatherings cannot be overestimated. Let the next session of the Congress at Benares set the example. Actual deliberative work should be done by a smaller conference attended by not more than a hundred of the best men of the country.

Two whole days may be reserved for this work and one day, the opening day, for popular demonstration, at which speeches may be delivered to the assembled masses from different platforms by different men in their own vernaculars. The executive and administrative work of guid ing the movement all round the year should be done by a still smaller standing Committee of 20 to 30 men. This committee ought to meet at least twice or three times a year, and if Sir Pherozeshah Mehta cannot spare time to attend its sittings at some central place, let us unanimously agree to fix Bombay as the headquarters and meet only there. Or if that be not acceptable to our Bengal friends who are equally indispensable, let Bombay and Calcutta have the honour of being the meeting place every alternate year.

For the sake of unanimity and for the sake of our motherland let us all agree to this even though it may be inconvenient and expensive to Madrassees and Punjabis to do so. Then the next thing which the whole country ought to do simultaneously with the above is the adopting of and giving effect to the

Bengal resolutions re the boy cotting of English goods. This in my opinion is the most effective way of bringing the Government to its senses and will be most telling on England.

Even if we cannot do without foreign goods let us import them from Japan and China first and from Germany, France or the United States next. Let us try to gain the sympathy and goodwill of the Indian retail-sellers, and there cannot be the least doubt that we can carry on an effective political propaganda. There is another thing which I would do, viz,, to spread a knowledge of English laws and Regulations broadcast.

Let the people realize the full significance of the laws under which they live and demand the full pound of fles'i given to them by the same. If all these measures carried out for a number of years fail to make an impression upon the Government, though I am sure they will, then there will be time to think of more effective methods of constitutional agitation to bring about the desiiel reforms in the government of the country.

I have my own ideas about carrying on the Indian political campaign in England which I reserve for another occasion. \ Lajpat Rau

INDIA AND ENCLISH PARTY POLITICS

I am of opinion that those who talk of identifying the Congress with the Liberal Party in England, pre sume too much. Firstly, they assume without justifica tion and perhaps against all experience that the Libera! Party, as a party, are prepared to open their arms to them. My experience tells me just the otherwise It is true that the response to the circular letter of the Chairman of the British Committee of the Indian National Congress, asking for platforms for the Indian Delegates came mostly from the Liberal and Radical Associations of England, including Trade Unions, Labour and Socialist circles. It is equally true that what little %hearing we received in England was given to. us by the Liberals, but then we cannot shut our eyes to the fact that the Liberal leaders and the Liberal executives kept themselves as much aloof as the Conservatives. These latter are in substantial agreement with the Conserva tives in keeping Indian affairs out of party politics.

At the discussion of the last Budget in June there was only one influential Liberal (Sir Charles Dilke) who spoke in favour of Mr. Herbert Robert's motion for a Parliamen tary enquiry. The other leading Liberals went in a body against it. You have only to be a few days in England to come to the conclusion that the Liberal exe cutive is as indifferent to the Indian affairs as the Conservatives and that as a party the Liberals are not prepared to receive your advances. For the time being some of them may utilise you for party purposes in those matters in which they differ from their rivals, the Tories, but beyond that they will not go. As such, it is futile to discuss the wisdom or the no nwisdom of iden tifying the Congress with the Liberals as a party.

The question is, at present, outside the range of practical politics. Though it were possible to do so, I would rather have the Indian affairs fought and discussed on party lines. So far I am quite in agreement with Sir Pherozeshah Mehta. Any one even slightly acquainted with political life in England will tell you that, as a rule, English politicians are not prepared to devote any time and attention to any matter which does not further party interests. Matters outside party politics receive hardly any consideration. Nobody cares for the same. People do not feel sufficiently interested to spare any time or at tention formatters which do not seem to concern them in any way.

The Press cannot afford to spare space for them or it does not pay them. The man in the street is absorbed in his own affairs. The ordinary citizen or voter argues that a matter upon which both parties agree and hold the same views must be well looked after and needed no care on his part. To be just and fair to English Liberals, I must say that those who could be approached were found to be very sympathetic and for the time being at least appeared to have been touched by the tale of woe narrated before them. Some of them passed resolutions of sympathy and so on, but beyond that I don't believe they will take any further trouble of pressing it either on their representatives in the House of Com mons or on their party leaders as such. So far the great est sympathy has been expressed by the Labour and Democratic and Socialist circles.

The working men in England are now awake and they are as much with the present system of class Government as we are, They are pushing forward their own candidates and they hope to return a solid body of Labour members in the next General Election. The Democratic and Socialist sections are in favour of Home Rule for India and so, of course, are the Irish. These are the people upon whose active sympathy Indians can safely rely and who might help Indians if they are sufficiently strong to make themselves heard. But they are poor; and poverty in England is, perhaps, a greater curse and calamity than anywhere else in the world.

They generally denounce the Liberals as well as the conservatives, though their members in Parliament seem to have a certain sort of alliance with the Liberals. They are perfecting ttieir organisations and are advancing steadily. The Socialists and the Democrats are allied with them. I was much impressed with their sincerity of purpose and genuineness of sympathy, and I am of opinion that it is this class only with which at present an alliance is possible, if any. It is no doubt true, that in high circles this class is not looked upon with favour and very reasonably too. They aim at their overthrow and claim a share of the power of which the former have been enjoying an exclusive monopoly so far.

The fact that of all countries in the European world, England is the most Conservative and very slow to adopt new ideas makes it probable that the Labour and Democratic influence will take a long time to develop and to attain the power which they aim at. But all the same it is hopeless to expect anything at the hands of India. When in power they may setup Viceroy but that they cannot and will not follow a systematic, persistent policy of advance in applying Democratic principles of Government to India, is as certain as that Sun will set this evening and rise to morrow morning.

There are some good Liberals who sincerely desire to rule India on sound Liberal principles, but at present.they are in a hopeless minority, their voices do not count for much and there is little chance of their gaining any prominence or coming to the front Benches, in the.near future.

Under the circumstances, the only advice I can offer my countrymen is as follows:—

(1) That they should mainly look to themselves and their own exertions for political progress. The English voter, whether Liberal or Conservative, is a sympathetic creature no doubt, but then he is absorbed in his own troubles and affairs and to care for us has neither the time nor the inclination to attend to anything which does not directly concern him or which is likely to affect his pocket injuriously.

(2) That if there is any class in England which deserves our confidence and upon whose votes we can place any reliance at all it is the Labour party, including the democrats and the Socialists and the Irish of course

REPRESSIVE MEASURES IN BENGAL.

RESOLUTION XIII, OF THE 21 ST INDIAN NATIONAL CONGRESS HELD AT BENARES 1905.

I give it my heartiest support on two grounds. You have been hearing of the misfortunes of our brethren of Bengal. I am rather inclined to congratulate them on the splendid opportunity (cheers) to which an all-wise Providence, in His dispensation, has afforded to them by heralding the dawn of a new political era for this country (cheers). I think the honour was reserved for Bengal, as Bengal was the first to benefit by the fruits of English education. Bengal up to this time — excuse me for saying thattKe Bengal lion, by some cause, had degenerated into a jackal, and I think Lord Curzon has done us a great service by provoking the lion in his own den (cheers) and rousing him to a sense of conscientiousness of his being a lion. I think no greater service could have been done to India, to the cause of India or to Bengal, by any other statesman.

There are times, gentlemen, when I am inclined to pray that from time to time God might be pleased to send Viceroys like Lord Curzon to this country, in order to awaken the people of this coun try to a sense of their responsibility in this matter. Gentlemen, I believe, and I believe earnestly, that the political struggle has only commenced, it was only in the fitness of things that, when Congress attained its majority, the attaining of that majority should have been preceded by a manly and vigorous protest on the part of the people of this country. It is only in the fitness of things that the movement's coming to age of majority should have been preceded by a vigorous and manly declaration of its approaching manhood.

I think in the circumrstances like ours, in conditions like ours, we are perfectly justified in taking the attitude that our brethren of Bengal have taken. What else was left for you? It has been explained that all possible things that could be done in the name of constitutional agitation have been exhausted. What was the example given to you by your fellow-subjects in the other parts of the Empire? Englishmen have been our teachers in all branches of human knowledge. Englishmen have given us constitutional rights. Was it not perfectly right to take a page from the book of the Englishmen on the methods of constitu tional agitation and adopt those methods which will be appreciated by themselves ? Now let us see what Englishmen in England do. I do not say that our condi tions allow of our exactly copying or imitating them, but surely we have a right to adopt that spirit, understand that spirit and follow it. Let me tell you what are the methods adopted by Englishmen in England when they have a grievance to be listened to by Government. The method which is perfectly: legitimate, perfectly constitutional and perfectly justifiiable, is the method of passive resistance (cheers).

I though I am not at the present moment quoting any social democrat or labourman, I must admire them; I have great respect for them. I must tell you that the message which the people of England wanted to send to you through me was the jnessage that in our utterance, in our agitations and in our fight and struggle for liberty, we ought to be more manly than we have been heretofore (cheers). An Englishman hates or dislikes nothing like beggary. I think a begger deserves to be hated. I want to do the duty to show Englishman that we have risen to the sense of consciousness, that we are no longer beggars and that we are subjects of an Empire when people are struggling to achieve that position which is their right by right of natural law (cheers). Gentlemen, in every stage people were arbiters of their destiny, but we are not so at the present moment.

We are perfectly justified in trying to become arbiters of our own destiny and in trying to obtain freedom. I think the people of Bengal ought to be congratulated on being leaders of that march in the van of progress (cheers). I rather envy them. I am rather jealous of them; at the same time I am proud of them. They have begun the battle, they have begun the fight and they have begun it in right manly style.

They have effaced all those taunts, they have effaced all those insinuations against them of being timid and cowardly; they have exhibited a manliness, they have exhibited a spirit in this battle which has to be commended to other Provin ces of India. If the other Provinces of India will just follow their example, I say the day is not far from distant sights. But if you simply go there as a beggar without the consciousness of your power, of your right to demand your rights, you go there simply to be rejected (cheers).

If, therefore, you want to be heard, and you want to be heard with respect, you must approach with determination, with evidences of determination, with signs that yom are determined to achieve your rights at any cost. You do that, the goddess of liberty is very nears. The goddess of liberty is the most sacred goddess in the world, and before you can approach her, you should show by your life, life of self-denial, that you are fit to enter her temple (cheers).

What have we been doing to be fit to approach that temple? I am afraid that our record is extremely poor and extremely humiliating: it is extremely bad to look at. But there are signs of the rising sun. And if the people of India will just learn that lesson from the people of Bengal, I think the strug gle is not hopeless. We are just awakening to a sense of our duty and a sense of responsibility to the mother land. It may be that with th consciousness of that strength we may tread the right way, the right path in the struggle for freedom. I have only to say one word about that part o: the resolution which deals with repres sive measures. I think the repressive policy of this 'Government is very encouraging. A Government com manding 280,003 or 50,000 soldiers stooping to strike us hy striking at our boys (cries of shame)!

I say what have these wise statesmen of Government conrie to? Are they not displaying disgraceful weakness, a weakness of which the people are conscious? It would be difficult for them to remain where they are. What wouki people conclude that thi"mighty Government, with so many guns and canons, wih so many armies and with such :array of statesmen, have begun to series of shame)? We advise them to eschew these weak methods, disgraceful methods, and re-assert their manliness by pursuing paths of righteousness, if we were to adopt the methods of revolutionists if we were to adopt to some secret methods which the Government of Lord Curzon has adopted in pushing forth the Partition Scheme, if we were to adopt the same methods that the Government of India and beauracratic rulers are adopting in dividing people against people, in setting the Hindu against the Mahomedan (shame), the Hindu against the

Sikhs, it will be a dangerous game. I say that the Government is giving weapons which are sharp but which are disgraceful and which show signs of weakness.

I, therefore, say that it is a dange rous game which the Government is playing. It might in jure them at any moment. Therefore, as friends of Government, as friends of order, we warn Government against treading this path of danger and diHiculty. Let Government remember, and let you, gentlemen, also re member, that people once awakened and awakened right ly, cannot be put down (cheers).

It is impossible for the Government of India, after a century of British rule, after a century of liberal education, after havinc; put the books of Burke, Bain and Mason in our hands, to put us down like d(s and slaves. That is impossible. The Bengalis have just now shown. They are only now showing that the task is impossible even for a mighty government like the British Government. Therefore, wisdom requires statesmanship requires, that people should be governed on right lines, on liberal principles, on those democratic principles which are just now stirring the whole worlds

The wave of democracy is out. I defy any Government in the world where there is any just civilization to keep the people out of their rights for any length of time. The history of Europe is before you. What is the fate of the autocratic methods ? We pray our Government not to adopt those methods. As my friend the Chairman has been telling English audience, the British Government is foolish in following Russian methods. We are great admirers of British rule. As people who are benefited by that rule, we call upon Government not to trample underfoot the best traditions of British rule, but to re-trace those steps and not leave the people of this country mider the impression that their Government 18 going to adopt nothing better than Russian methods If these methods continue, gentlemen, what will be the difference between the Russian Government and the British Government?

There will be nothing left for the people of this country to be loyal to the British Govern ment if these things are taken away — if the rights of meetings, if the rights of petitions and if the rights of constitutional agitation are taken away from us. Let my Governors tell me what shall be left to us to be loyal to them ? Why shall we be loyal to them ? I therefore, say that it is in their own interests that they ought to retrace their steps and follow the noble example which has been set by some of their noblest statesmen, and remedy the state of things that exist One word more and I have done. I see the time is going fast (cries of "go on). No, I am not going to break the rule. I think I have already exceeded the limits.

adopted this manly and vigorous policy, be prepared for the logical consequence (cheers). Don't conceal your heads. Don't behave like cowards.

Once having adopted that manly policy, stick to it till the last. Glorify your selves as I have told you. Is it not a matter of shanie for us that this National Congress in the last twenty-one years should not have produced at least a number of political Sanyasis that could sacrifice their lives for the political regeneration of the country ?

Now that the Congress has come to a stage when it could become a father, a parent, I earnestly appeal to you to let it have its legitimate offsprings, a band of earnest missionaries to work out the political regeneration of the country (cheers).

There is no use of our talking aloud, there is not much use of our showing signs of discontent and disaffection, unless we are true to ourselves, true to our noble country, true to the mother-land, true to the cause of political regeneration and political agitation. If you show, in a few years, to our rulers that we are steadfast in our determination, that we are steadfast in our devotion to our cause, I assure you that there is no power in the v.orld that can prevent us from going for ward (loud and continued cheers).

4

Educational Views of Rai

It has now more than abundantly been established that the efficiency of a nation depends upon the amount and nature of brain power which it can put forth ifl The conclusions and comments noted above are based on thtf figures of 1901-1902. We know that since then someting more tmi been done by the Government of India towards extending the scope and the affairs of life.. In an address delivered some two years back, Sir John Lockyer, the illustrious President of the British Association, traced conclusively and con vincingly the intimate relation that exists between the provision made by a nation for the higher education of itft people and the position taken by that nation in the ceaseless competition between the great countries of the world.

Relying upon facts and figure, he compared the educational facilities and the intellectual output of Great Britain and Ireland wth those of its rivals, Germany and United States, and came to the conclusion that the latter were much in advance of the former. Nay, he went a step further and held out young Japan as an example to be followed with profit in the matter of intel'ectual efforts. Those who are in touch with the cur-ent litera ture of the West, must have been struck by the extreme importance which all the civilized nations of the world have, by experience, begun to attach to education as the foundation of all national greatness both In point of wealth as well as of intellect.

If, then, in the struggle for life, education and educational efforts are matters of supreme importance to advanced, independent and If governing nations like the English, the German and the American, it only stands to reason that they are of still greater importance to a country like India where igno sphere of education in this country. An examination of what has been done in these jears and whether that justifies the Policy and attitude of tBe Government towards private enterprise in education may better form t& subject of a separate article wherein we may compare the results Mlieved by the Government of American and European states ia the matter of Education. Ranee and superstition reign supreme, where penury and poverty are the order of the day, where want and starvation are generally prominent, where independence of thought and action is almost unknown, and where the destinies of the nation are completely in the hands, and at the mercy, of a handful of foreigners who, in spite of all the generosity and benevolence of intentions that they can put forth in the Government of this country, are loth to admit the sons of the soil to any decent share in the management of the affairs of their own land.

In a country where the economic circumstances brought about by an alien rule force the people to look to other countries for even the necessaries of life, where the unlimited resources provided by a bountiful Providence are closed to the sons of the soil and are only accessible to clever, energetic, and enterprising foreigners, where the wealth of the country is being daily drained out of the country, and where a fairly intelligent population are, for want of education and opportunities, being reduced to the position of drawers of water and hewers of wood, education, I say, is a question of life and death. Our future principally depends upon the amount and the sort of education we shall receive.

Having once put the educational machinary into motion, our rulers have of late been showing signs of great dissatisfaction with the results. The history of English education in this country shows that originally the framers of Government Educational policy were actuated partly by selfish and partly as high motives. To the words.

MEANING AND IMPORTANCE OF EDUCATION

Meaning

To know the meaning of education we discuss about it's etymological, narrow and broader meaning of education.

- Etymological meaning of education:-The term education is derived from Latin word educere, educare, and educatum which means 'to learn', 'to know', and to 'lead out'. That is education means to lead out internal hidden talent of a child or person.
- Narrow meaning of education:-The education provided under the premises of schools, colleges and universities is the narrow concept of education. The narrow meaning of education limited under the premises of educational institutions. It doesn't include the education outside of four walls of institution. Narrow meaning of education emphasize on bookish knowledge.
- Broader meaning of education:-Opposite of narrow meaning of education is broader meaning of education. That is the education provided under the educational institution's premises is only education is wrong. According to it's concept education is universal, we can gain

education from anywhere, anytime. There is no bound of place and time. Education is the long life process. It starts from cradle and ends to the grave.

The Importance of Education

Education is very important for an individual's success in life. Education provides pupils teaching skills that prepare them physically, mentally and socially for the world of work in later life. Education is generally seen as the foundation of society which brings economic wealth, social prosperity and political stability.

Higher education helps in maintaining a healthy society which prepares health care professionals, educated health care consumers and maintaining healthy population. Education is major aspect of development of any modern society since if there is a deficit of educated people then society will stops its further progress. Government should pay serious attention to education and support it economically and morally all over the country.

Education is the best investment for the people because well educated people have more opportunities to get a job which gives them satisfaction.

Educated individuals enjoy respect among their colleagues and they can effectively contribute to the development of their country and society by inventing new devices and discoveries. Today's ever growing numbers of people mostly are not satisfied with their basic education and try to get secondary or tertiary education in order to meet the demands of contemporary society. Some of them enter higher educational institutions and some search additional information on the internet. Good People sacrifices their time and money and sometimes even their health to raise educational level because they realize that education is their passport to the future and for tomorrow.

Main purpose of education is to educate individuals within society, to prepare and qualify them for work in economy as well as to integrate people into society and teach them values and morals of society. Role of education is means of socializing individuals and to keep society smoothing and remain stable. Education in society prepares youngsters for adulthood so that they may form the next generation of leaders. It will yield strong families and strong communities. Indeed, parents taking an active role in their child education produce a willingness in children to learn. Education and society provides a forum where teachers and scholars all over the world are able to evaluate problems in education and society from a balanced and comparative social and economic perspective. Education is an important aspect of the work of society and it will raise the countryside issues and promote knowledge and understanding of rural communities. One of the education essential tasks is to enable people to understand themselves. Students must be equipped with knowledge and skills which are needed to participate effectively as member of society and contribute towards the development of shared values and common identity. Education has a vital role to play in assisting students to understand their cultural identity. Education acts as the distribution mechanism of the cultural values such as it more layered the society and participate in society that carries the culture.

Education and society provides a forum where teachers and scholars all over the world are able to evaluate problems in education and society from a balanced and comparative social and economic perspective. Education is an important aspect of the work of society and it will raise the countryside issues and promote knowledge and understanding of rural communities. One of the education essential tasks is to enable people to understand themselves. Students must be equipped with knowledge and skills which are needed to participate effectively as member of society and contribute towards the development of shared values and common identity.

Education has a vital role to play in assisting students to understand their cultural identity. Education acts as the distribution mechanism of the cultural values such as it more layered the society and participate in society that carries the culture. In our culture today, there is a great emphasis on higher education. In a society, more educated you are, better off you are. Every society has specialized individuals that require extended education to fulfill certain main positions.

These persons are normally known as professors, priests, doctors, mechanics or artists. Education has been a higher part of every culture on earth and education is a systemic project. Whole society should care for and support the education patriotism, cause and socialism among the young people. Everyone must do work hard to cultivate moral conduct. Education mainly begins at home; one does not acquire knowledge from a teacher, one can learn and get knowledge from a parent or a family member. In almost all societies, receiving education and attending school is very necessary is one wants to achieve success. Education is the key to move in the world, seek better jobs and ultimately succeed in life. Schools play a vital role in preparing our children and young people for effective participation and responsible citizenship in society. The development of education and educational opportunities is built on creativity tempered by knowledge and wisdom gain through the experience of learning.

Investment in human capital, life long learning and quality education help in the development of society. Teachers are the most important factors for an innovative society because teachers' knowledge and skills not only enhance the quality and efficiency of education, but also improve the prerequisites of research and innovation. Many members of our society are not provided with a safe and secure environment in which children can develop, child abuse, violence against women and interpersonal violence cause a cancer on our society. Society play a key role in the realization of life long learning. The improvement of social education facilities such as libraries and the learning opportunities are implemented by the local governments. Students today are exposed to loads of technology and information at everywhere.

PRIMARY EDUCATION

Coming down to the Primary School we find the state of things still gloomier. The total expenditure on Primary Education is Rs. 1,05,45,000 to which the Pub Hc funds (Revenues, Local and Municipal) all contribute only Rs. 60,50,090 while from fees are realised Rs. 31,15, 211. The Provincial and Imperial Revenues contri buted only 13i lacs (see page 178 of report.) As compared with the magnificent figure of 13J lacs of Rupees spent by British Government on Primary Education in India, the Parliament of Great Britain and Ireland voted £ 1,24,1 7, 368 for elementary education in those islands in 1901 alone. The extent and enormity of the evil have been recognised by the Government of India in their resolution of 1904, Paras 14, 15, and 16.

How, then, do matters stand in respect of the exten sion among the masses of primary education ? The population of British India is over two hundred and forty millions. It is commonly reckoned that fifteen per cent of the population are of school-going age According to this standard there are more than 18 millions of boys who ought now to be at school, but of these only a little more than J are actually receiving primary education. If the statistics are arranged by Provinces, that out of a hundred boys of an age to go to school, the number attending primary schools of some kind, ranges from between eight and nine in the Punjab and the United Provinces, to twenty-two and twenty-three in Bombay and Bengal.

In the census of 1901 it was found that only one in ten of the male population, and only seven in a thousand of the female population were literate. These figures exhibit the vast dimensions of the problem, and show how much remains to do done before the propor tion of the population receiving elementary instruction can approach the standard recognised as indispensable in tnore advanced countries. While the need for educatloa grows with the growth of population the progress towords supplying it is not so rapid as it was in former years. In 1870-71 there were 16,473 schools with 607,320 scholars; ifl 1881-82 there were 82,916 with 2,061,541 scholars. But in 1891-92 these had only increased to 97,109 schools with 2,837,607 scholars, and the figures of

1901-02 (98,538 schools with 3,268,726 scholars), suggest that the initial force of expansion is somewhat on the decline, indeed the last year of the century showed a slight decrease as com pared with the previous year.

On a general view of the question the Government of India cannot avoid the conclusion that the primary education has hitherto had insufficient attention and an inadequate share of the public funds. They consider that it possesses a strong claim upon the sympathy both of the supreme Government and of the Local Governments, and should be made a leading charge upon provincial revenues; and that in those Provinces where it is in a backward condition, its encouragement should be a primary obligation.

It may be remarked that these obligations were also admitted in 1882-83, but little was done to fulfill them, as will be clear from a perusal of the following facts and figures which we cull from vol. II of the Government of India's reports on the progress of Education between

7.98 to 1901-02.

No. of Primary Schools for Boys.

1886. 91-92, 96-97. 1901-02.

84,673 91,881 97,881 92,226

-which means an actual decrease of 5,655 in the last 5 jrears. The Punjab showed this decrease to the extent of 42, i.e. in 1901-02 there were 42 Primary Schools less in the Punjab and N. W. Frontier Provinces combined. In 96-97 there was one school for a group of 58 towns and villages. In 1901-02 there was one for a group of 62. In the Central Provinces there is one Primary school for 234 towns and villages, in the United Pro vinces of Agra and Oudh one for 156 and in the Punjab one for 145. In the Central Provinces the mean average distance in miles between each boy's Primary school is 82 miles and in the Punjab 7'1. This does not mean that schools are equally distributed over the whole area. The fact is that in some districts there is no school for many tens of miles.

During the last 5 years, while the number of Schools fell by 5,655, the average strength per school rose only by 2 (i.e. from 31 to 33 per school). The following figures will show the progress made by primary education in the number of scholars receivir education. In 96-97,. 30 lacs and 28 thousand boys received instruction in Primary Schools for boys but in 1901-02 the number fell to 30 lacs and 9 thousand (a fallof 17,000). In the Primary Schools attached to secondary schools the numbers in 96-97 were 31 lacs and 83 thousand and in 1901-02 the numbers were 31 lacks and 84 thousand Le.r an increase of 1,000. Total loss 16,000. In the Punjab and N. W. F Province (combined) the numbers in the former schools were 10 lacs and 8 thousand in 96-97 and the same in 1901 and 1902, but in the latter class of schools it rose slightly, i.e., by 4,000.

In the Census Returns of 1901-02 only 13 million males in British India have been entered and write out of a total male population of 11.7 millions which means that 104 millions cannot read and write at all. In 1901-02 only 174 out of a 1,000 boys of school going ag« were receiving instruction, i.e.. 826 went with out any education at all. But in the Punjab 914 out of a 1,000 went without any instruction at all. Thus in the matter of Primary education, the Punjab — that nursery of the Indian soldier — the land of the brave and the loyal Sikh — is the most backward of all the Provinces even Assam, Burma and Central Provinces showing much better figures (i.e., 197, 167, 137 per thousand res pectively) against 86 of the Punjab.

Now to judge of the quality of education imparted in hese schools we have only to examine the figures relat ing to the average cost of a school and the average annual cost per pupil, the former being lesdthan 10 Rs. a month and the latter being 37 (per year). The following figures show that there has been practically no improve ment in this direction within the last 10 years. Average annual cost of a boy's Primary School : —

91-92 96-97 1901-02.

94 101 114

or say the improvement can be valued at less than one Rupee per month.

Coming nearer home we find that in the Punjab the progress has been in the other direction. In 91-92 the annual cost of a boy's Primary School in the Punjab was Rs. 222, in 96-97 it fell to Rs. 195 and in 1901-02 it could only slightly rise to Rs. 202. The net result is that as compared with 91-92 there is a falling off of 20 per year. The increase in the average cost of educating a boy may be judged from the following figures.

91-92. 96-97. 1901-02.

General average cost... 32 32 37

Punjab 4'4 44 49

Now let us examine the so-called "unparalleled liberality' of the British Government in paying the teachers employed in the schools. I do not know how to characterise the conduct of a Government who expect teachers who get the royal salary of Rs. 2 to 5 a month to spread and strengthen the sentiment of loyalty amongst their pupils. In these days even an ordinary illiterate day-labourer gets 6 annas per diem. The prosperity of this country under British rule may better be judged by these scales of pay which we have given above. Any furthur comments are not needed

Compare with this the following figures giving the annual cost per child in the Primary Siage in Great Bricain and Ireland.

Board School. Private School,.

England £3.0-9J. i, e., Rs. 45-9. £2.6s.4d., ?. e. and Wales. R. 34-12

Scotland. £2 17-4 i.e, Rs. 43. £2-15s-6d-i.e. Rs. 37

Ireland. £2-10-11 i.e, Rs. 38.

The average pay of a teacher of Primary School i Great Britain and Ireland is £129 sterling per annum, 2. e. RS. 1,935 or say more than Rs. 150 per month. So long as the cost of General Administration re mains what it is, and no reduction is effected by the larger employment of native agency for the high-paid and costly European agency, and so long as the military is maintained on that ruinous scale as at present, there is little prospect of increased expenditure being incurred on education from Provincial and Imperial Revenues, Every sensible man will agree with the Government that the wider extension of education in India is chiefly a matter of increased expenditure; and any material im provein en t oF its quality is largely dependent upon the same condition. A Government which could heretofore afford to spend only a crore and lacs upon the education of more than 24 crores of its people in its charge is not in a position to assume that supreme position in matters educational which it has, by its recent policy, decreed to itself. While the Government in India cannot afford to give more than 1 crore and 4 lacs for the education of more than 24 crores of its people, compared with about 19 crores spent by the Parliament of Great Britain for the same object, the former aims at officialising, super vising and controlling every educational agency in the land. In the name of sound education they decry those institutions which, if not up to date in the supply of appliances and apparatus, if not quite up to the mark in the efficiency and competency of their teachers, if not located in beautiful buildings, if not possessed of grand and inspiring surroundings, are at Isast helping the cause of education and literacy in the land.

A Government which pays teachers at the munificent rate of from 5 to 10 or 20 Rupees a month in Government and District and Municipal Board Primary Schools, and at the lowest rate of 4 and 5 Rupees a month to teachers in the Secondary Schools is surely not in a position to vote the Private Schools out of existence even if the managers of the latter cannot treat their teachers better than or 80 well as the Government does. In a country where the number of male literates per 1,000 of the male population ranges from 54 to 378 with an average of 102 for the whole of India; where the number of boys in the Primary stage per 1,000 of male population of school See page 71 Vol. II. of the report going age ranges from 63 in the N. W. F. P. and 68 in the Punjab to 232 in Bengal with an average of 174 for the whole of British India; where the Government can only spare 13 lacs of Rupees upon elementary educa tion for a population of more than 24 crores; in a country where in some parts of it, only one out of 278 is in the s«condary stage of an English School and one in 1,032 in the same stage of a vernacular school; in a country where on the average only one out of 1,079 of a population of school-going ae is in an Arts College, the Government can hardly be justified in assuming that aggressive and dictatorial attitude towards private enter prise in education which it has lately done.

Even in advanced countries where a very large part of Government Revenues is spent upon education; where education is considered as a national asset; wherethe num ber of literates in the population is over 93 per cent; where education is compulsory; even in such countries the Government is not so hard or does not require high and rigid and almost impossible standard of efficiency from private Schools and Colleges as the Government has lately been laying down for the same class of institutions here in India.

We wonder why the Government of Lord Curzon should have forgotten that the systems of educa tion now prevalent in England, United States and Germany, which he has taken as his models, are the growths of more than a century at least if not 10 centuries; that all those countries are self-governing countries, where the interest of the rulers and the ruled are identical and where the former only exist for the benefit and the protection of the latter. To apply the systems, standards and principles in force in these countries to India is more absurd than even the putting of the cart before the horse. But even in England the voluntary and denominational schools were the pioneers of education and till lately enjoyed — nay, to a great ex tent even now enjoy — the freedom which the Government of India by their recent policy refuse to the private Schools, and Colleges of this country.

it is not strange, then, that the people of India should [y be suspicious of the intentions and the motives of the Government, and that the recent policy of the Government in matters of education should have raised a storm of indignation in the land. We say, why should the Government prescribe a tuition fee for the private school and the private college in this land where dense ignorance prevails, where more than 90 per cent, of the population is illiterate, and where the Government of the country cannot spend more than 1 annas per head on education?

Again, we ask why should the Government, if it is honest and actuated by the best and the highest motives, in a country like this, throw obstacles in the way of private enterprise in education; why should it try to prevent the same from competing with the Government institutions; why should it frame such rules and regulations as to take away all liberty of action and freedom of initiative from them and compel them to submit to dictation and supervision from Government and its officers ? If under the circumstances the Government is misunderstood and its motives and intentions misconstrued, it has only to thank itself for these misunderstandings and misinterpretations. Under the new regulations the Government has al most made it impossible for a new private educational institution to come into existence and to thrive.

No private school or college can, under the present rules are to make an humble beginning. Large funds, high class buildings, official good will and a very high state of efficiency in all respects, are the conditions precedent even for a start. Under the present rules, institutions like the great Metropolitan one of Calcutta, the Fergusson College of Poona, the D. A. V. College at Lahore, would not have come into existence. Similar attempts are as a matter of fact, impossible under the new policy. The conclusion, which the people then are irresistably led to, under the above circumstances, is that the Government of this country is neither willing to spend its own Revenues on education, nor will it tolerate the doing of it by people for themselves unless the latter are prepared to place their funds and efforts under the control of the former.

RIGHT OF CHILDREN TO FREE AND COMPULSORY EDUCATION ACT

The Right of Children to Free and Compulsory Education Act or Right to Education Act (RTE), is an Indian legislationenacted by the Parliament of India on 4 August 2009, which describes the modalities of the importance of free and compulsory education for children between 6 and 14 in India under Article 21a of the Indian Constitution. India became one of 135 countries to make education a fundamental right of every child when the act came into force on 1 April 2010.

History

Present Act has its history in the drafting of the Indian constitution at the time of Independence but is more specifically to the Constitutional Amendment that included the Article 21A in the Indian constitution making Education a fundamental Right. This amendment, however, specified the need for a legislation to describe the mode of implementation of the same which necessitated the drafting of a separate Education Bill.

A rough draft of the bill was composed in year 2005. It received much opposition due to its mandatory provision to provide 25% reservation for disadvantaged children in private schools. The sub-committee of the Central Advisory Board of Education which prepared the draft Bill held this provision as a significant prerequisite for creating a democratic and egalitarian society. Indian Law commission had initially proposed 50% reservation for disadvantaged students in private schools.

Passage

The bill was approved by the cabinet on 2 July 2009. Rajya Sabha passed the bill on 20 July 2009 and the Lok Sabha on 4 August 2009. It received Presidential assent and was notified as law on 26 August 2009 as The Children's

Right to Free and Compulsory Education Act. The law came into effect in the whole of India except the state of Jammu and Kashmir from 1 April 2010, the first time in the history of India a law was brought into force by a speech by the Prime Minister. In his speech,Manmohan Singh, Prime Minister of India stated that, "We are committed to ensuring that all children, irrespective of gender and social category, have access to education. An education that enables them to acquire the skills, knowledge, values and attitudes necessary to become responsible and active citizens of India."

Highlights

The Act makes education a fundamental right of every child between the ages of 6 and 14 and specifies minimum norms in elementary schools. It requires all private schools to reserve 25% of seats to children (to be reimbursed by the state as part of the public-private partnership plan). Kids are admitted in to private schools based on caste based reservations. It also prohibits all unrecognised schools from practice, and makes provisions for no donation or capitation fees and no interview of the child or parent for admission. The Act also provides that no child shall be held back, expelled, or required to pass a board examination until the completion of elementary education. There is also a provision for special training of school drop-outs to bring them up to par with students of the same age.

The RTE act requires surveys that will monitor all neighbourhoods, identify children requiring education, and set up facilities for providing it. The World Bank education specialist for India, Sam Carlson, has observed:

The RTE Act is the first legislation in the world that puts the responsibility of ensuring enrolment, attendance and completion on the Government. It is the parents' responsibility to send the children to schools in the US and other countries.

The Right to Education of persons with disabilities until 18 years of age is laid down under a separate legislation-the Persons with Disabilities Act. A number of other provisions regarding improvement of school infrastructure, teacher-student ratio and faculty are made in the Act.

Implementation and Funding

Education in the Indian constitution is a concurrent issue and both centre and states can legislate on the issue. The Act lays down specific responsibilities for the centre, state and local bodies for its implementation. The states have been clamouring that they lack financial capacity to deliver education of appropriate standard in all the schools needed for universal education. Thus it was clear that the central government (which collects most of the revenue) will be required to subsidise the states.

A committee set up to study the funds requirement and funding initially estimated that Rs 171,000 crores or 1.71 trillion (US$38.2 billion) across five years was required to implement the Act, and in April 2010 the central government agreed to sharing the funding for implementing the law in the ratio of 65 to 35 between the centre and the states, and a ratio of 90 to 10 for the north-eastern states. However, in mid 2010, this figure was upgraded to Rs. 231,000 crores, and the center agreed to raise its share to 68%. There is some confusion on this, with other media reports stating that the centre's share of the implementation expenses would now be 70%. At that rate, most states may not need to increase their education budgets substantially.

A critical development in 2011 has been the decision taken in principle to extend the right to education till Class X (age 16) and into the preschool age range. The CABE committee is in the process of looking into the implications of making these changes.

Advisory Council on Implementation

The Ministry of HRD set up a high-level, 14-member National Advisory Council (NAC) for implementation of the Act. The members include

- Kiran Karnik, former president of NASSCOM
- Krishna Kumar, former director of the NCERT
- Mrinal Miri, former vice-chancellor of North-East Hill University
- Yogendra Yadav – social scientist. India
- Sajit Krishnan kutty Secretary of The Educators Assisting Children's Hopes (TEACH)India.
- Annie Namala, an activist and head of Centre for Social Equity and Inclusion
- Aboobacker Ahmad, vice-president of Muslim Education Society, Kerala.

Status of Implementation

A report on the status of implementation of the Act was released by the Ministry of Human Resource Development on the one year anniversary of the Act. The report admits that 8.1 million children in the age group six-14 remain out of school and there's a shortage of 508,000 teachers country-wide. A shadow report by the RTE Forum representing the leading education networks in the country, however, challenging the findings pointing out that several key legal commitments are falling behind the schedule. The Supreme Court of India has also intervened to demand implementation of the Act in the Northeast. It has also provided the legal basis for ensuring pay parity between teachers in government and government aided schools

Haryana Government has assigned the duties and responsibilities to Block Elementary Education Officers–cum–Block Resource Coordinators (BEEOs-cum-BRCs) for effective implementation and continuous monitoring of implementation of Right to Education Act in the State.

Precedents

It has been pointed out that the RTE act is not new. Universal adult franchise in the act was opposed since most of the population was illiterate. Article 45 in the Constitution of India was set up as an act:

The State shall endeavour to provide, within a period of ten years from the commencement of this Constitution, for free and compulsory education for all children until they complete the age of fourteen years.

As that deadline was about to be passed many decades ago, the education minister at the time, M C Chagla, memorably said:

Our Constitution fathers did not intend that we just set up hovels, put students there, give untrained teachers, give them bad textbooks, no playgrounds, and say, we have complied with Article 45 and primary education is expanding... They meant that real education should be given to our children between the ages of 6 and 14 – M.C. Chagla, 1964

In the 1990s, the World Bank funded a number of measures to set up schools within easy reach of rural communities. This effort was consolidated in the Sarva Shiksha Abhiyan model in the 1990s. RTE takes the process further, and makes the enrolment of children in schools a state prerogative.

Criticism

The act has been criticised for being hastily-drafted, not consulting many groups active in education, not considering the quality of education, infringing on the rights of private and religious minority schools to administer their system, and for excluding children under six years of age. Many of the ideas are seen as continuing the policies ofSarva Shiksha Abhiyan of the last decade, and the World Bank funded District Primary Education Programme DPEP of the '90s, both of which, while having set up a number of schools in rural areas, have been criticised for being ineffective and corruption-ridden.

Quality of Education

The quality of education provided by the government system remains in question. While it remains the largest provider of elementary education in the country forming 80% of all recognised schools, it suffers from shortages of teachers, infrastructural gaps and several habitations continue to lack schools altogether. There are also frequent allegations of government schools being riddled with absenteeism and mismanagement and appointments are based on political convenience. Despite the allure of free lunch-food in the government schools, many parents send their children to private schools. Average schoolteacher salaries in private rural schools in some States (about Rs. 4,000 per month) are considerably lower than that in government schools. As a result, proponents of low cost private schools, critiqued government schools as being poor value for money.

Children attending the private schools are seen to be at an advantage, thus discriminating against the weakest sections, who are forced to go to government schools. Furthermore, the system has been criticised as catering to the rural elites who are able to afford school fees in a country where large number of families live in absolute poverty. The act has been criticised as discriminatory for not addressing these issues. Well-known educationist Anil Sadagopal said of the hurriedly-drafted act:

It is a fraud on our children. It gives neither free education nor compulsory education. In fact, it only legitimises the present multi-layered, inferior quality school education system where discrimination shall continue to prevail.

Entrepreneur Gurcharan Das noted that 54% of urban children attend private schools, and this rate is growing at 3% per year. "Even the poor children are abandoning the government schools. They are leaving because the teachers are not showing up." However, other researchers have countered the argument by citing that the evidence for higher standards of quality in private schools often disappears when other factors (like family income, parental literacy-all correlated to the parental ability to pay) are controlled for.

Public-private Partnership

To address these quality issues, the Act has provisions for compensating private schools for admission of children under the 25% quota which has been compared to school vouchers, whereby parents may "send" their children in any school, private or public. This measure, along with the increase in PPP (Public Private Partnership) has been viewed by some organisations such as the All-India Forum for Right to Education (AIF-RTE), as the state abdicating its "constitutional obligation towards providing elementary education".

Infringement on Private Schools

RTE Act In September 2012, the Supreme Court subsequently declined a review petion of the Act.

Barrier for Orphans

The Act provides for admission of children without any certification. However, several states have continued pre-existing procedures insisting that children produce income and caste certificates, BPL cards and birth certificates.

Orphan children are often unable to produce such documents, even though they are willing to do so. As a result, schools are not admitting them, as they require the documents as a condition to admission.

Admissions

Children are admitted in to private schools based on caste based reservations.

INDIA RESOLUTION OF 1904

They regarded it as a sacred duty to confer upon the natives of India those vast moral and material blessings which flow from the general diffusion of useful knowledge. They hoped by means of education to extend the influ ence which the Government was exerting for the sup pression of demoralizing practices, by enlisting in its favour the general sympathy of the native mind. They also sought to crenie supplii of puhlic servants to whose prohit if offices of timst mitjht with increased confidence he committed and to promote the material interests of the country by stimulating its inhabitants to develop its vast resources. The italics are mine. This policy appears to have been faithfully carried up to 1882, by which time the out turn of the educational activity in the land had come to be immensely in excess of the requirements of the ad ministration merely.

To quote the resolution again the growth of schools and colleges proceeded most rapidly between 1871 and 1882, and was furthur aug mented by the development of the Municipal system, and by the Acts which were passed from 1865 onwards pro viding for the imposition of local cesses which might be applied to the establishment of schools. By the year 1882, there were more than two million and a quarter of pupils under instruction in public institutions.

The Commission of 1882-83 furnished a most copious and valuable report upon the state of education as then exist ing, made a careful enquiry into the measures which had been taken in pursuance of the Despatch of 1854, and submitted furthur detailed principles of that Despatch. They reliance upon, and sjisteinatic encourarfement of private effort and their recommendations were approved by the Government of India.

The italics are again mine. This was the first step towards reaction. The Anglo-Indian bureaucracy raised a cry against high education and bitterly complained that the Government was entirely wrong in spending large sums out of their resources on high education. It was thus laid down as a principle of policy to gradually withdraw from the work of secondary and high education and confine the energies of the State to the task of extending Primary Education. In pursuance of this policy some Government Colleges were abolished, a few transfer red to private management, and the fees in all Govern ment and aided colleges were greatly raised.

To the great misfortune of those provinces which had only recently come under the British rule and where education had only very recently been introduced, as the Punjab, the policy formulated by the Government of India in 1882 affected them most injuriously and was very effectual in retarding high education therein.

As a natural result of this policy, however, the people of the country began to look up for themselves, and systematic efforts were made by them to provide against the loss likely to follow from the partial withdrawal of Government from the field. This withdrawal of Government, or the contraction of Government expenditure on high education, and the raising of fees, have had different effects in different provinces, but so far it has had only a most disastrous effect in the Punjab. The truth of this remark will appear from a glance at the following table in which the 5 large provinces range themselves according to fee incidence; —

Punjab

... 5-4

Bengal

.-. 3-9

Madras

... 3-5

Bombay

... 3-0

United Provinces...

... 3-0

The following figures show that of all the 5 important provinces into which British India proper is divided, the Punjab is only next to the most backward of them in the matter of University education.

The following table gives the number of boys of school-going age of which one is an Arts College, in the

5 University provinces of India: —

Bengal.............. 711

Madras............... 755

Bombay............ 1,029

Punjab............... 1,319

The following table shows the increase in all British India in the total number of collegiate students in the 3 quinquenniums that have elapsed since 1882 :-

1887-88 to 1891-92......... 4,364

1891-92 to 1896-97......... 1,509

1896 97 to 1901-02.........3,215

Thus it took full 10 years for the private colleges to develop in order to reduce the decrease that was so marked and startling in the second quinquennium of this reactionary period.

During the last quinquennium while Bengal gained 1,768 pupils (collegiates)

Bombay............ 877

Madras............... 239

Punjab with the N. W. F. P. only gained 160 while the U. P. fared still worse and only gained 44. in 1896 97 the number of scholars receving education in Arts Colleges in the Punjab was 1,101. In 1899-00 it rose to 1,180 and in 1900-01 it was only 1,152.

The following figures show that but for the private colleges, the collegiate education in India would have fared disastrously, as in 1901-02 there were only 4,000 students in Government Colleges and 12,000 in privately managed colleges, 54 per cent, of the latter only being in aided institutions — the unaided colleges of Bengal alone educating no less than 4,541 of them. The figures of increase in the number of students in different classes of institutions show to what extent, during the last quin quennium alone, private enterprise in education has come to the rescue of high education in this country. This increase is divided as follows : —

Government Colleges......... 448

Aided Colleges............ 998

Unaided Colleges......... 1,695

With the exception of Bengal, where the average annual cost of educating a college student is the lowest because of the very large numbers receiving education in cheap private colleges, the cost is the lowest in the. Pun jab, as shown by the following table : —

Bombay............ 188

Punjab............... 136

Bengal............... 97

hile the total expenditure on collegiate education stands thus : —

Bengal............ 8 lacs.

Madras............ 6 lacs.

Bombay......... 3 lacs.

Punjab............ If lacs.

Of these 25 lacs, only 8,96,000 are furnished by Provincial Revenues while fees contribute 9f lacs, i, e., :80,000 over and above the conirilmtion of Government, During the last quinquennium the expenditure from public

Revenues has actually diminished by Rs. 67,000 while that from fees has increased by Rs. 231,000. Compare with the above the amount of money-contributed by the Government of Great Britain and Ireland on University education alone, viz. £ 1,55,600.

The University of London alone gets a grant of £8,000 (see Contemporary Review of December 1903, P. 838);the University of Berlin gets a grant of £1,68,780 from its Government and the University of Tokio (in 1895) £ 1,30,000.

SECONDARY EDUCATION

Descending a step lower and looking at secondary education we shall find that altogether a sum of Rs. 126,84,000 is spent on secondary schools, of which only Rs. 32,76,000 are contributed by public funds.

In the Punjab the fee ratio in the following quotation from the Review of H. H. the Lieutenant-Governor on the Education report for 1900 01, It is interesting to notice that on the average native parents are called upon to pay Rs. 1-3-0 per annum for the education of a son in a Primary School; Rs. 11-8-6 in a Secondary School; and over Rs. 80 in an Arts College. These figures, hower, do not take into account assistance given in the form of scholarships.

In the Nineleenili Century for Oct. 1903 appeared an article on "London Education "from the pen of the Hon'ble Mr. Sydney L. C. C, in which the writer has noticed the work of the London county council in provid ing improved educational facilities for London boys and suggested desirable reforms and changes. Commenting upon the facilities which exist in London for secondary education the writer remarks that:

Every year about eirjlii hundred of the ablest boys and' girls in the public elementary or lower secondary schools, between eleven and thirteen years of age, are picked by competitive examination for two to five years of higher education. These hvo thousand scholarships provide for the cleverest children of the London wogeeamers a more genuinely occeasihle ladder than is open to the corresponding class in any American, French, or German. In addition to these maintenance scholarships there are free places at most of the London secondary schools, from St. Paul's downwards, which are utilised, as is found to be the case with all provision of merely gratutious secondary education, by the lower middle and professional classes.

Above these opportunities stand the intermediate and senior county scholar Aips, and others provided by various trust funds, probabJy iltojeihev about two huudred in each year for candidates between fifteen and nineteen years of age. These serve partly to carry on the best of the junior scholars; partly to admit to the highest secondary schools the ablest children of parents ineligible for the lowest rung of the ladder; and partly to take the very pick of

London' young people to the technical college and the university. This scholarship scheme has now necessarily to be revised, to bring it into accord with the changes lately made in the school-leaving age and the pupil-teacher system. Practically all children now stay at school ntil fourteen, and it is no longer necessary for any substantial payment towards the maintenance of the scho larship to begin before that age.

On the other haad there is a consensus of opinion that, when a child passes from an elementary to a secondary school, it should do so before the age of twelve, and should remain for not less than four years. It looks as if the limit of age for the normal junior scholarship should be reduced from thirteen to twelve, and its duration extended from two to four years, whilst the annual maintenance allowance up to the age of fourteen might be reduced to 51, rising to 1 OZ, and 1 5Z, in the last two years.

And if the need for pupil-teachers causes the number of scholarships to rise to 2,000 a year, it would perhaps be possible to effect the further desirable reform of beginning the selecting jprocess by a preliminary examination, conducted, by-the head-teachers themselves, in their own schools, of 11 the children who had attained the fifth standard before the age of twelve; and of undertaking to award 4:he scholarships, not to any fixed number of wiaaecs but to all who, in the subsequent centralised competitive examination, reached a certain percentage of marks Such a reform would organically connect the scholarship system with all the public elementary schools, instead ofr as at present, only about a third of them; and would bring London's capacity-catching machine' to bear on every promising child.

There must, however, be an adequate supply of eflRcient secondary schools for these picked scholars to attend, not to mention the needs of those who cam afford to keep their boys and girls at school until seventeen or nineteen.

There is a common impression that the public secondary schpols of London are few and inefficient. Yet, including only Foundations, of which the management is essentially public in character, London has today not less than 2500, seven and nineteen in its secondary schools a larger number than either Paris or Berlin.

In the haetc ground and not included in this calculation, stands the hard of private adventure commercial academies and colleges for yoking ladies of the genteel suburbs.

These we may leave gently on one side. The publicly managed schools number about ninety, well dispersed over the whole country ranging from those like Parmiter's School (Bethnal Green) and Addey's School (Deptford), where the leaving age is sixteen or seventeen, through the dozen admirable institutions of the essentially public Girls, Public Day School Company, up to such thoroughly efficient first grade schools as the North London Collegiate, for girls St. Pancrs and Dulwhich College.

London that, with one or two exceptions, the very exis tence of these schools is forgotten by the ordinary citizen and is often ignored by the legislator or administrator. Many a middle class family which could well afford to send its boys and girls to secondary schools is unfamiliar with those which exist within a mile of its home.

Even to the best informed educational administrators the real state and quality of the London secondary schools taken as a whole, are far less accurately known than those of the elementary. All the information points to the conclusion that the efficiency varies immensely from school to school; that nearly all of them have good buildings, mostly well provided with science laboratories and suitable equipment; and that, where any school falls below the mark, the weak point is the staffing.

In at least a third of the Lond&n secondary schools the income from feeM and endoivment is insufficient to provide more than one good salart which goes to the head teacher whilst the atsistants who are to the university graduates ore paid, for the most part, less than is earned by an ordinary certificated teacher in a board school.

Yet even recognising all the shortcomings of these schools, the department of secon dary education is not one which will give the London County Council any serious trouble. About forty of the publicly managed schools are sufficiently well ofP to be independent of its aid, and these, nearly always charg ing high fees, and providing an education of high grade may be left to themselves.

The other fifty, including practically all those in need of help, have already shown by their cordial co-operation Board their willingness of course, be necessary to disturb the present governing bodies, on which the local authorities are already well represented, arid it would he untviae for the Council to interfere in the details of ctdministration. In no department is it so important to maintain variety and independent experiment as in the secondary schools.

But construct what scholarship ladder we will, the secondary schools can be used only by a small fraction of the population. For the secondary education of the masses there has been organised, by the School Board on the one hand, and the Technical Education Board on the other, an extensive assortment of evening classes.

Providing instruction in every imaginable subject of lite, rature, science, art, and technology. The classes of the School Board, which enrol over 1,20,000 students for the winter session and have an average attendance of half that number, are conducted in 410 of its day-school buildings, mainly by the younger and more energetic of its staff of day teachers.

The work of the Technical Education Board, dealing usually with a more advanced stage and older scholars, is concentrated in the forty polytechnics, art schools, and technical institutes under its management or control which have in the aggregate about 50,000 students.

Here the lecturers and teachers are specialists in their respective subjects, teaching in institutions specially equipped for their work. At six of the polytechnics, the highest classes have been included in the faculties of the reorganised London University.

These two schemes of evening instruction have now to be co-ordinated, differentiated, and developed. There cMa b no question of stopping either the one or the Other; on the contrary, both sides of the work will have to be increased.

It ought not to be too much to asJc that every hoy or girl who leaves school at fourteen or fifteen should up to twentji one, he at any rate entailed at some evening-class in titution even if attendance is conjined to an hour per week. Yet there are in London over 6,00,000 young people between fourteen and twenty-one and not a third of these are at present members of any sort of institution, recreational or educational. Out of 84,000 boys and girls between fifteen and sixteen, only 21,000 are on the rolls. What is happening to the others ? We cannot, as yet, compel them to come in, as the Bishop of Hereford proposes, though this is done in various parts [of Germany and Switzerland.

But we might try the experiment of using the school attendance officers to look after those who have not joined an evening school, using the method of persuasion, just as they look after the younger defaulters from the day school. Meanwhile we could bring the whole of the evening instruction in each borough into a single hormonious organisation; we could allocate the work in such a way as to provide appropriately for each-age and each grade, and avoid overlapping; we could take care that each subject is taught under the most effective conditions, and properly co-ordinated with more advanced instruction elsewhere; and we could arrange for the progression of the students from stage to stage, until they reach the highest classes of the nearest poly technic, or the technical college itself.

The italics are everywhere mine and adopted to enable the reader to compare the existing state of things in India with the existing state of this with what in the opinion of the writer in the Nineteenth Century should be the state of things there.

It will thus appear that while the London authori ties are anxious to see that every boy and girl whether rich or poor, is in receipt of some aort of secondary edu cation up to the age of 21, the authorities in India have ruled that the classes in the rural schools be so formed as to exclude the possibilities of scholars reading in them joining the ordinary secondary schools in towns. The statement that in at least a third of the London secondary schools the income from feen and endowment taken together is insufficient to provide more than one good salary which goes to the head teacher whilst the assistants who ought to be university graduates are paid for the most part less than is earned by an ordinary certificated teacher in a Board school, is significant and may with profit be pondered over by the educational authorities in the Punjab who are so strict towards the private schools and are at times inclined to exact higher standards of efficiency than even those ob served by some of the Board and Mission Schools in the province.

If even London tolerates the existence of in efficient secondary schools wherein the income from the fees and endowment together is so meagre, surely there can hardly be a case against similar schools in India which is educationally so backward.

5

The Swadeshi Movement

It is commonly supposed that there are two sides to the Swadeshi movement, one the political and the other the economic. Pure Swadeshi, as some of the Anglo Indians choose to call it, is an economic movement and they profess to have a great sympathy for the same. Boycott of foreign made goods is held to be a political weapon upon the uses and ethics of which there is a £reat divergence of opinion. The Anglo-Indian can see nothing but mischief in it. In their opinion it is morally wrong, politically pernicious and economically unsound And impracticable. But there are a number of Europeans and Americans who see nothing pernicious in it and consider it to be not only a perfectly legitimate weapon but a very powerful and effective one to bring pressure upon any imperial race having commerce as its principal business. Amongst the Indians themselves different.<?lasses of people look at it from different points of view. Firstly, there is that class who can never see differently from their Anglo-Indian patrons.

The opinions of this.class do not count for mnzh anl ned not bt considered-at all. Secondly, there are those, who both by nature :and habit are in favour oi peace at antj cost. They cannot approve of any methods which are calculated to cause the least disturbance in the relations of the different per sons and communities, whether Indians or aliens, who ure in some way or other interested in India. These ood people have great faith in moral persuasion and prayers — prayers addressed to the Great Ruler of the Universe as well as to our rulers in affairs mundane They believe that a combined force of these two is sure to bring about a quiet, bloodless, moral revolution in India which will set matters right and remove all the political disqualifications and disabilities from which the Jndians at present suffer and which result in so much iiardship, oppression and wrong to the people of this country.

Personally I am a believer in the efficacy of prayer as an instrument of religious discipline but it will require a reat stretch of imagination aad atv vucotvvN "wxva\«c of credulity on my part to accept that prayer to the Al mighty coupled with prayers to the ruling nation are likely to lead to any practicable results, in matters political and international. Prayers to the Almighty may be useful in intensifying your desire for political liberty and politi cal privileges. Prayers to the ruling nation may be useful to you in proving the Vftelegsness of appealing to the higher sense of man in matters political, where the interests of one nation clash with those of another and in driving you to the conclusion that human nature, constituted as it is, is extremely selfish and is not likely to change or bend unless :the force of circumstances compels it to do so in spite of [itself. But beyond this I cannot pin my faith on prayers.

The third class of Indians consists of those estimable gentlemen who believe in the righteousness of the British nation as represented by the electors of Great Britain and Ireland and who are afraid of offending them by the boycott of English made goods. If there are any two classes into which the British nation can roughly be divided they are either manufacturers or the working men. Both of them are interested in keeping the Indian market open for the sale and consumption of their manufactures. Any movement aiming at the closing or contracting of this market is sure to offend them. They are said to be our only friends to whom we can appeal against the injustice of the Anglo-Indian bureaucracy.

Offend them, say these friends, and you are undone. You lose the good will of the only class who can help you and who are prepared to listen to your grievances. But these good friends forget that, boycott or no boycott, any move jneijt calculated to iiicrease the manufacturing power of India is likely to incur the displeasure of the British Elector. The latter is a very well educated animal, a keen man of business who can at once see through things that are likely to affect his pocket however cleverly they might be put or arranged by those who hold an interest which is really adverse to his. He is not likely to be hoodwinked by the cry of Swadeshi minus the boycott because really speaking and effectively worked and organised both are one and the same.

The Swadeshi aims at the 'production of those arti cles at home which are at present imported from abroad. The boycott means the discontinuance of the consump tion of those articles not made in this country. So far, then, it is not likely to be of much use to drop the boy cott in order to secure for us the continuation of the friendly attitude of the British Elector. But then we may go a step further and maintain that up till now the alleged friendliness of the British Elector has been of no good to us. Past experience shows that they have more than once stood between the people of India and some of its more nobleminded Anglo-Indian rulers whenever the latter tried to obtain econo.

mic justice for the former. The latter from their knowledge of the growing seriousness of the econo mic situation in India have now and then made a bold stand for Justice to India against the demands of the British manufacturer, but they have almost always had to give in because the latter proved too strong for them. Here then we are on the horns of a dilemma. To our wrongs the British Elector is indifferent, to our rightseven if supported by good they have been opposed. The British Elector has no doubt a sympathetic ear to the tales of wrong and op pression that you may carry to England but unfortunate iy he is too busy and too absorbed in his own aifairs to spare any time, to listen to your tales or to take a seri ous view of them.

The burden of the empire is too heavy to be conveniently shifted from the shoulders of a few — magnificently paid for the work — to those of the English people. The struggle for wealth, for luxury is too keen and too intense to leave the latter any leisure or inclina tion for the study of the ethics of Imperialism. Under the circumstances the sympathy of the British Elector is for the present at least a negligible quantity. The question directly put comes to this — are the British prepared to give us full political privileges in exchange for open markets for their goods? Any attempt to answer this in the affirmative must be put down as chimerical. But even granting that the argument has some force, is it not worth our while to impress upon the Britons at home the enormity of the wrongs inflicted upon us by their representatives here in this country, by supplementing the Swadeshi by boycott ?

Admitting that Englishmen at home have the power to set matters right how are you to force their attention to the state of things in India except by directly threatening their pockets ? The logic of losing business is more likely to impress this nation of shopkeepers than any arguments based on the ethics of justice and fair-play. The British people are not a spiritual people. They are either a fight ing race or a commercial nation. It will be like throw ing pearls before swine to appeal to them in the name of higher morality or justice or on ethical grounds. They are a self-reliant, haughty people, who can appreciate self-respect and self-reliance even in their opponents. It is then for the Indians to decide whether they mean to continue to appeal to them in the name of political justice, fair-play or whether they intend to attract their atten tion to the existing intolerable condition of things in India by inflicting losses in business and by adopting an attitude of retaliatory self-reliance.

But then there is another class of Indians who tread on more solid ground than any of those spoken of above. This is the class who oppose the boycott on Economic grounds. Here we feel we are on more sub stantial ground. Theirs is no plea of expediency, nor does it arise out of fear of the authorities in India or of the British Elector at home. Their warning note has a scientific basis and deserves the most careful and attentive consideration of all patriotic Indians. Whether Free Trader or Protectionist, you cannot dismiss them off hand nor treat their reasoning with contempt. They may be fadists (a term which in their turn they apply to Swadeshists) but they are neither cowards nor traitors. Speaking for myself I am an out and out Swadeshist and have been so for the last 25 years, in fact ever since I learnt for the first time the true meaning of the word patriotism.

For me the words Swadeshi and patriotism are synonymous though I do not maintain or insinuate that those who are freetraders are not patriots. I advised ly do not say "not Swadeshists, "because I am not prepared to say that those Indians who are free-traders are not necessarily Swadeshists, Be it as personally inclined to attach the greatest importance possible to the Swadeshi Movement. I look upon it as the remedy upon the right and continued use of which depends the alleviation of the sufiFerings of our country.

I regard it as the salvation of my country. The Swadesh I ought to make us self-respecting, self reliant, self sup porting, self sacrificing, and last, but not least, manly. The Swadeshi ought to teach us how to organise our capital, our resources, our labour, our energies and our talents to the greatest good of all Indians, irrespective of creed, colour or caste. It ought to unite us — our religious and denominational differences notwithstanding. It ought to furnish us with an altar before which we can all stand in the fullest sincerity of our he;rts and in the deepest strength of faith to pray for the good of our common motherland, with a determination to stand to gether and work together.

In my opinion the Swadeshi ought to be the common religion of United India, But all this notwithstanding, as a practical Swadeshist, I want a better understanding of the economic needs and requirements of the country and a practical programme of industrial development based on scientific calculations. As an indication of the lines upon which I shall like this programme to be framed, I cannot do better than quote from a very famed paper from the journal of the Royal Economic Society of London for the month of March 1903, under the heading of Protection of infant Indus tries.' Discussing the economic effects of a protective tBnff the writer remarks :

"We see that when the import of good exchanges sure affected in a way prices at home; and that this rise continues until impor tation is again possible, unless such heavy duties are im posed that the country can be cut off both from impor tation and from exportation, and so become entirely self contained. We find also in this process the explanation of the fact that the relief afforded by a protective tariff is frequently of a somewhat temporary character. For a few months the home producer has the field to himself: then his costs of production gradually rise : at last he finds foreijn competition pressing on him once more; and finally he falls back upon the fatal demand for more Protection.

But this — the common course of protection in both the new and the old countries — is not the only possible course in theory. It is caused, so far as I can see, princi pally by the attempt to do too much at once. Your new country is inclined to be generous to its home manufacturers, and to start manufacturing in all lines at once : by so doing it fritters away energy, and spreads expenditure over a wide field which if concentrated might produce im posing results.

For, supposing that a"new country would consent to do one or two things at a time, its difficulties would probably be far less. If it started, for instance, by at tempting to found one textile or one branch of metallurgi cal industry, it could afford to give to its infant for a few years a genuine and important assistance. Gold prices would, of course, still be to some extent affected, but in an infinitely smaller degree than when a dead sat v made against all manufactured concentrating the money which instead of dividing it among several hundreds, more real progress would indubitably be made. After all, under modern conditions, no industry ought to remain an infant for more than five years : during those years it probably needs more assistance than can easily be given it under a general Protective System; later on, the less help it has, the better.

Other important gains could be made — both political and economic — by this system of concentration. In the first place, the opportunities for log-rolling would certainly be diminished. If the system were once esta blished, a most salutary division of the Protectionist forces would assuredly take place: as it is, the tendency in many countries is for everybody to favour protection on the off-chance that he may make more by it than he loses : on the system proposed everybody would know that only one or two industries were to be protected at a time, and those only for a few years. Again the present certainty that a protective system will last much longer than there is any need for it would be removed. For as only one or two industries would receive help at any one time, all the other industries would combine to reduce that time to a minimum in the hope that their turn would come next.

In my opinion, the leaders of the Swadeshi move ment including men actually engaged in business ought to put their heads together and promulgate an indus trial pronouncement for the next five years, prepared on the lines indicated in the above extract.

MEANING OF SWADESHI

Spirit of Swadeshi: Swadeshi is that spirit in us which restricts us to the use and service of our immediate surroundings to the exclusion of the more remote. Thus, as for religion, in order to satisfy the requirements of the definition, I must restrict myself to my ancestral religion. That is, the use of my immediate religious surrounding. If I find it defective, I should serve it by purging it of its defects.

In the domain of politics, I should make use of the indigenous institutions and sere them by curing them of their proved defects. In that of economics I should use only things that are produced by my immediate neighbours and serve those industries by making them efficient and complete where they might be found wanting. It is suggested that such Swadeshi, if reduced to practice, will lead to the millennium.....

Religion: ...Hinduism has become a conservative religion and, therefore, a mighty force because of the Swadeshi spirit underlying it. It is the most tolerant because it is non-proselytizing and it is as capable of expansion today as it has been found to be in the past. It has succeeded not in driving out, as I think it has been erroneously held, but in absorbing Buddhism. By reason of the Swadeshi spirit, a Hindu refuses to change his religion, not necessarily because he considers it to be the best, but because he knows that he can complement it by introducing reforms. And what I have said about Hinduism is, I suppose, true of the other great faiths of the world, only it is held that it is specially so in the case of Hinduism.

Education: We have laboured under a terrible handicap owing to an almost fatal departure from the Swadeshi spirit. We, the educated classes, have received our education through a foreign tongue. We have, therefore, not reacted upon the masses. We want to represent the masses, but we fail. They recognize us not much more than they recognize the English officers. Their hearts are an open book to neither. Their aspirations are not ours. Hence there is a break. And you witness not, in reality, failure to organize but want of correspondence between the representatives and the represented.

If during the last fifty years we had been educated through the vernaculars, our elders and our servant and our neighbours would have partaken of our knowledge; the discoveries of Bose or a Ray would have been household treasures as are the RAMAYAN and the MAHABHARAT. As it is, so far as the masses are concerned, those great discoveries might as well have been made by foreigners. Had instruction in all the branches of learning been given through the vernaculars, I make bold to say that they would have enriched wonderfully.....

Economic Life: Much of the deep poverty of the masses is due to the ruinous departure from Swadeshi in the economic and industrial life. If not an article of commerce had been brought from outside India, she would be today a land flowing with milk and honey. But that was not to be. We were greedy and so was England. The connection between England and India was based clearly upon an error....

If we follow the Swadeshi doctrine, it would be your duty and mine to find out neighbours who can supply our wants and to teach them to supply them where they do not know how to proceed, assuming that there are neighbours who are in want of healthy occupation. Then every village of India will almost be a self-supporting and self-contained unit, exchanging only such necessary commodities with other villages as are not locally producible.

This may all sound nonsensical. Well, India is a country of nonsense. It is nonsensical to parch one's throat with thirst when a kindly Mohammedan is ready to offer pure water to drink. And yet thousands of Hindus would rather die of thirst than drink water from a Mohammedan household. These nonsensical men can also, once they are convinced that their religion demands that they should wear garments manufactured in India only clothing or eat any other food...

Religious Discipline: It has often been urged that India cannot adopt Swadeshi, in the economic life at any rate. Those who advance this objection do not look upon Swadeshi, as a rule of life. With them it is a mere patriotic effort-not to be made if it involved any self-denial. Swadeshi, as defined here, is a religious discipline to be undergone in utter disregard of the physical discomfort it may cause to individuals. Under its spell the deprivation of a pin or a needle, because these are not manufactured in India, need cause no terror. A Swadeshist will learn to do without hundreds of things which today he considers necessary....

I would urge that Swadeshi is the only doctrine consistent with the law of humility and love. It is arrogance to think of launching out to serve the whole of India when I am hardly able to serve even my own family. It were better to concentrate my effort upon the family and consider that through them I was serving the whole nation and, if you will, the whole of humanity. This is humility and it is love. The motive will determine the quality of the act. I may serve my family regardless of the sufferings I may cause to theirs. As, for instance, I may accept an employment which enables me to extort money from people. I enrich myself thereby and then satisfy many unlawful demands of the family. Here I am neither serving the family nor the State.

Or I may recognize that God has given me hands and feet only to work with for my sustenance and for that of those who may be dependent upon me. I would then at once simplify my life and that of those whom I can directly reach. In this instance, I would have served the family without causing injury to anyone else. Supposing that every one followed this mode of life, we should have at once an ideal state. All will no reach that state at the same time. But those of us who, realizing its truth, enforce it in practice, will clearly anticipate and accelerate the coming of that happy day. (SW, pp.336-44)

Service of Neighbours: My definition of Swadeshi is well known. I must not serve my distant neighbour at the expense of the nearest. It is never vindictive or punitive. It is in no sense narrow, for I buy from every part of the world what is needed for my growth. I refuse to buy from anybody anything, however nice or beautiful, if it interferes with my growth or injures those whom Nature has made my first care.

I buy useful healthy literature from every part of the world. I buy surgical instruments from England, pins and pencils from Austria and watches from Switzerland. But I will not buy and inch of the finest cotton fabric from England or Japan or any other part of the world because it has injured and increasingly injures the million of the inhabitants of India.

I hold it to be sinful for me to refuse to buy the cloth spun and woven by the needy million of India's paupers and to buy foreign cloth although it may be superior in quality to the Indian hand-spun. My Swadeshi, therefore, chiefly centres round the hand-spun Khaddar and extends to everything that can be and is produced in India. (YI. 12-3-1925, p. 88)

[The votary of Swadeshi will,] as a first duty, dedicate himself to the service of his immediate neighbours. This involves exclusion or even sacrifice of the interests of the rest, but the exclusion or the sacrifice would be only in appearance. Pure service of our neighbours can never, from its very nature, result in disservice to those who are far away, but rather the contrary.

'As with the individual, so with the universe' is an unfailing principle which we would do well to lay to heart. On the other hand, a man who allows himself to be lured by 'the distant scene', and runs to the ends of the earth for service, is not only foiled in his ambition, but also fails in his duty towards his neighbours..... (FYM, pp. 62-63)

I believe in the truth implicitly that a man can serve his neighbours and humanity at the same time, the condition being that the service of the neighbours is in no way selfish or exclusive, *i.e.*, does not in any way involve the exploitation of any other human being. The neighbours will then understand the spirit in which such service is given. They will also know that they will be expected to give their services to their neighbours. Thus considered, it will spread like the proverbial snowball gathering strength n geometrical progression, encircling the whole earth. It follows that Swadeshi is that spirit which dictates man to serve his next-door neighbour to the exclusion of any other. The condition that I have already mentioned is that the neighbour, thus served, has, in his turn, to serve his own neighbour. In this sense, Swadeshi is never exclusive. It recognizes the scientific limitation of human capacity for service. (H, 23-7-1947, p. 79)

No Chauvinism: Under this plan of life, in seeming to serve India to the exclusion of every other country, I do not harm any other country. My patriotism is both exclusive and inclusive. It is exclusive in the sense that, in all humility, I confine my attention to the land of my birth, but is inclusive in the sense that my service is not of a competitive or antagonistic nature. SIC UTERE TUO UT ALIENUM NON LAEDAS is not merely a legal maxim, but it is a grand doctrine of life. It is the key to proper practice of ahimsa or love. (SW, p. 344)

I have never considered the exclusion of everything foreign under every conceivable circumstance as a part of Swadeshi. The broad definition of Swadeshi is the use of all home-made things to the exclusion of foreign things, in so far as such use is necessary for the protection of home industry, more especially those industries without which India will become pauperized. In my opinion, therefore, Swadeshi which excludes the use of everything foreign, no matter how beneficial it may be, and irrespective of the fact that it impoverishes nobody, is a narrow interpretation of Swadeshi. (YI, 17-6-1926, p. 218)

Even Swadeshi, like any other good thing, can be ridden to death if it is made a fetish. That is a danger that must be guarded against. To reject foreign manufactures, merely because they are foreign and to go on wasting national time and money in the promotion in one's country of manufactures for which it is not suited would be criminal folly and a negation of the Swadeshi spirit. A true votary of Swadeshi will never harbour ill-will towards the foreigner; he will not be actuated by antagonism towards anybody on earth. Swadeshism is not a cult of hatred. It is a doctrine of selfless service that has its roots in the purest AHIMSA, *i.e.*, love. (FYM, p. 66)

PRINCIPLES OF SWADESHI

Gandhi's vision of a free India was not a nation-state but a confederation of self-governing, self-reliant, self-employed people living in village communities, deriving their right livelihood from the products of their homesteads. Maximum economic and political power - including the power to decide what could be imported into or exported from the village - would remain in the hands of the village assemblies. In India, people have lived for thousands of years in a relative harmony with their surroundings: living in their homesteads, weaving homespun clothes, eating homegrown food, using homemade goods; caring for their animals, forests, and lands; celebrating the fertility of the soil with feasts; performing the stories of great epics, and building temples.

Every region of India has developed its own distinctive culture, to which travelling storytellers, wandering 'saddhus', and constantly flowing streams of pilgrims have traditionally made their contribution. According to the principle of swadeshi, whatever is made or produced in the village must be used first and foremost by the members of the village. Trading among villages and between villages and towns should be minimal, like icing on the cake.

Goods and services that cannot be generated within the community can be bought from elsewhere. Swadeshi avoids economic dependence on external market forces that could make the village community vulnerable.

It also avoids unnecessary, unhealthy, wasteful, and therefore environmentally destructive transportation. The village must build a strong economic base to satisfy most of its needs, and all members of the village community should give priority to local goods and services. Every village community of free India should have its own carpenters, shoemakers, potters, builders, mechanics, farmers, engineers, weavers, teachers, bankers, merchants, traders, musicians, artists, and priests. In other words, each village should be a microcosm of India - a web of loosely inter-connected communities. Gandhi considered these villages so important that he thought they should be given the status of "village republics". The village community should embody the spirit of the home - an extension of the family rather than a collection of competing individuals.

Gandhi's dream was not of personal self-sufficiency, not even family self-sufficiency, but the self-sufficiency of the village community. The British believed in centralized, industrialized, and mechanized modes of production. Gandhi turned this principle on its head and envisioned a decentralized, homegrown, hand-crafted mode of production. In his words, "Not mass production, but production by the masses." By adopting the principle of production by the masses, village communities would be able to restore dignity to the work done by human hands. There is an intrinsic value in anything we do with our hands, and in handing over work to machines we lose not only the material benefits but also the spiritual benefits, for work by hand brings with it a mediative mind and self-fulfilment. Gandhi wrote, "Its a tragedy of the first magnitude that millions of people have ceased to use their hands as hands. Nature has bestowed upon us this great gift which is our hands. If the craze for machinery methods continues, it is highly likely that a time will come when we shall be so incapacitated and weak that we shall begin to curse ourselves for having forgotten the use of the living machines given to us by God. Millions cannot keep fit by games and athletics and why should they exchange the useful productive hardy occupations for the useless, unproductive and expensive sports and games." Mass production is only concerned with the product, whereas production by the masses is concerned with the product, the producers, and the process.

The driving force behind mass production is a cult of the individual. What motive can there be for the expansion of the economy on a global scale, other than the desire for personal and corporate profit? In contrast, a locally based economy enhances community spirit, community relationships, and community well-being. Such an economy encourages mutual aid. Members of the village take care of themselves, their families, their neighbours, their animals, lands, forestry, and all the natural resources for the benefit of present and future generations.

Mass production leads people to leave their villages, their land, their crafts, and their homesteads and go to work in the factories. Instead of dignified human beings and members of a self-respecting village community, people become cogs in the machine, standing at the conveyor belt, living in shanty towns, and depending of the mercy of the bosses. Then fewer and fewer people are needed to work, because the industrialists want greater productivity. The masters of the money economy want more and more efficient machines working faster and faster, and the result would be that men and women would be thrown on the scrap heap of unemployment. Such a society generates rootless and jobless millions living as dependants of the state or begging in the streets. In swadeshi, the machine would be subordinated to the worker; it would not be allowed to become the master, dictating the pace of human activity. Similarly, market forces would serve the community rather than forcing people to fit the market.

Gandhi knew that with the globalization of the economy, every nation would wish to export more and import less to keep the balance of payments in its favour. There would be perpetual economic crisis, perpetual unemployment, and perpetually discontented, disgruntled human beings. In communities practising swadeshi, economics would have a place but would not dominate society. Beyond a certain limit, economic growth becomes detrimental to human well-being. The modern worldview is that the more material goods

you have, the better your life will be. But Gandhi said, "A certain degree of physical comfort is necessary but above a certain level it becomes a hindrance instead of a help; therefore the ideal of creating an unlimited number of wants and satisfying them, seems to be a delusion and a trap. The satisfaction of one's physical needs must come at a certain point to a dead stop before it degenerates into physical decadence. Europeans will have to remodel their outlook if they are not to perish under the weight of the comforts to which they are becoming slaves."

In order to protect their economic interests, countries go to war - military war as well as economic war. Gandhi said, "People have to live in villages communities and simple homes rather than desire to live in palaces." Millions of people will never be able to live at peace with each other if they are constantly fighting for a higher living standard.

We cannot have real peace in the world if we look at each other's countries as sources for raw materials or as markets for finished industrial goods. The seeds of war are sown with economic greed. If we analyse the causes of war throughout history, we find that the pursuit of economic expansion consistently leads to military adventures. "There is enough for everybody's need, but not enough for anybody's greed," said Gandhi. Swadeshi is thus a prerequisite for peace. The economists and industrialists of our time fail to see when enough is enough. Even when countries reach a very high material standard of living, they are still caught up with the idea of economic growth. Those who do not know when enough is enough will never have enough, but those who know when enough is enough already have enough.

Swadeshi is the way to comprehensive peace: peace with oneself, peace between peoples, and peace with nature. The global economy drives people toward high performance, high achievement, and high ambition for materialistic success. This results in stress, loss of meaning, loss of inner peace, loss of space for personal and family relationships, and loss of spiritual life. Gandhi realized that in the past, life in India was not only prosperous but also conducive to philosophical and spiritual development. Swadeshi for Gandhi was the spiritual imperative.

The Rise of English Colonialism

Historically, the Indian local economy was dependent upon the most productive and sustainable agriculture and horticulture and on pottery, furniture making, metal work, jewelry, leather work, and many other economic activities. But its basis had traditionally been in textiles. Each village had its spinners, carders, dyers, and weavers who were the heart of the village economy.

However, when India was flooded with machine-made, inexpensive, mass-produced textiles from Lancashire, the local textile artists were rapidly put out of business, and the village economy suffered terribly. Gandhi thought it essential that the industry be restored, and started a campaign to stem the influx of British cloth. Due to his efforts, hundreds of thousands of untouchables and caste Hindus joined together to discard the mill-made clothes imported from England or from city factories and learned to spin their own yarn and weave their own cloth. The spinning wheel became the symbol of economic freedom, political independence, and cohesive and classless communities. The weaving and wearing of homespun cloth became marks of distinction for all social groups.

Also responsible for the destruction of India's home economy in the eighteenth century was the introduction of British education under colonial rule. Lord Macaulay, introducing the Indian Education Act in the British Parliament, said, "A single shelf of a good European library was worth the whole native literature of India... Neither as a language of the law, nor as a language of religion has the Sanskrit any particular claim to our engagement...

We must do our best to form a class of persons, Indian in blood and colour but English in taste, in opinions, in morals and in intellect."

This aim was pursued with the entire might of the British Raj. Traditional schools were replaced by colonial schools and universities. Wealthy Indians were sent to public schools such as Eton and Harrow and universities such as Oxford and Cambridge. Educated Indians increasingly learned English poetry, English law, and English customs to the neglect of their own culture. Reading Shakespeare and the 'London Times' became much more fashionable than reading Indian classics such as the 'Ramayana', the 'Mahabarata', the 'Vedas', and the 'Upanishads'. Educated Indians saw their own culture as backward, uncivilized, and old-fashioned. They wanted to become rulers of India, but they wanted to rule like the British.

If there was any one person who represented this type of Western-educated Indian it was Jawaharlal Nehru, who became the first prime minister after independence. Nehru sought to promote the industrialization of India not via the capitalist route but by centralized planning. His inspiration came from the intellectuals of the London School of Economics and the Fabian Society - the labour Party's think tank.

Gandhi, on the other hand, believed that India's essential contribution to the world was simply het India-ness. He felt that Indians should recognize their own genius and not try to copy Western culture, which was simply a tool of colonization. Economics and politics should not simply be concerned with material things but should be the means to the fulfilment of cultural, spiritual, and religious ends. In fact, economics should not be separated from the deep spiritual foundations of life. This can be best achieved, according to Gandhi, when every individual is an integral part of the community; when the production of goods is on a small scale; when the economy is local; and when homemade handicrafts are given preference. These conditions are conducive to a holistic, spiritual, ecological, and communitarian pattern of society.

In Gandhi's view, spiritual values should not be separated from politics, economics, agriculture, education, and all the other activities of daily life. In this integral design, there is no conflict between spiritual and material.

It is no good for some people to close themselves in a monastic order practising religion and for other people to say that a spiritual life is only for saints and celibates. Such a separation of religion from society will breed corruption, greed, competition, power mania, and the exploitation of the weak and poor. Politics and economics without idealism will be a kind of prostitution, like sex without love.

Someone asked Gandhi, "What do you think of Western civilization?" He simply replied, "It would be a good idea." For Gandhi a machine civilization was no civilization. A society in which workers had to labour at a conveyor belt, in which animals were treated cruelly in factory farms, and in which economic activity necessarily lead to ecological devastation could not be conceived of as a civilization.

Its citizens could only end up as neurotics, the natural world would inevitably be transformed into a desert, and its cities into concrete jungles. In other words, global industrial society, as opposed to society made up of largely autonomous communities committed to the principle of swadeshi, is unsustainable. Swadeshi for Gandhi was a sacred principle - as sacred for him as the principle of truth and nonviolence. Every morning and evening, Gandhi repeated his commitment to swadeshi in his prayers.

Unfortunately, within six months of independence, Gandhi was assassinated, and Nehru gained a free hand in shaping the economy of India. Nehru found Gandhian thinking too idealistic, too philosophical, too slow, and too spiritual. He gathered around him Western-educated bureaucrats, and the enterprise to which they were jointly committed made them the unwitting agents of economic colonization. They pressed ahead with the construction of large dams and big factories, which for them were the temples and cathedrals of the new India. The spirit of dedication, idealism, and self-sacrifice that had been paramount under the leadership of Gandhi was quickly replaced by a lust for power, privilege, comfort, and money. Nehru and his colleagues followed the opposite path to that of swadeshi, and since that time, the history of India has been the history of corruption and political intrigue at the highest level. The political colonization of India might have ended officially with independence in 1947, but her economic colonization continued unabated and at an even greater pace. She has been turned into a playground for global economic forces.

Colonialism without the Colonialists

Now, India continues to be ruled in the English way, but without English rulers. This is the tragedy of India, and there is no end in sight. The industrialists, the intellectuals, and the entrepreneurs in collusion with the government still see the salvation of India in her subordination to the policies of the World Bank and GATT. They see India as part of the global economy working hand in glove with the multinational corporations. However, discontent among the Indian people is growing rapidly. The failures of the Congress Party under Nehru, his daughter, Indira Gandhi, and her son, Rajiv Gandhi, are fully evident to all. As Mahatma Gandhi predicted, the body politic is seething with corruption. The poor are poorer than ever, and the growing middle classes are turning away from the Congress Party. The farmers are agitating against the patenting of their seeds by multinational companies. The global economy of GATT is built on sand. Even though it may appear that its grip is firm, it has no grassroots support, and as its true implications become apparent, the people of India, among whom the teachings of Gandhi are still very much alive, will react against it and will return to swadeshi for the reenchantment of their local culture, their community, and their lives. In fact, the lessons of swadeshi may bring hope for an economics of permanence even among Westerns, once the fraudulent promise of economic growth and industrialism is exposed.

THE IDEA OF SWADESHI

Boycott was after all a negative concept. Its positive counterpart was the Swadeshi, first applied to the economic field involving the use of Swadeshi or indigenous goods 'even at a sacrifice'. Like Boycott, Swadeshi also soon became an all-comprehensive category. The idea of economic Swadeshi was advocated, among other things, in Bengal as early as the days of the Hindu Mela (functioning since 1867). In the seventies of the 19th century a Swadeshi movement was initiated in Gujarat and the Deccan. Almost about the same time, thanks to the enthusiasm of the Arya Samaj, a similar movement came into existence in the Punjab also. So far as Bengal is concerned, it should be clearly borne in mind that the spirit of industrial Swadeshi was abroad for a long time past, particularly since the early nineties of the 19th century. Barrister Jogesh Chandra Chaudhury was 'one of the earliest pioneers' in the field of industrial revival. It was he who 'first started an industrial exhibition of Swadeshi articles as an annex to the Indian National Congress in December 1901.' Early in the 20th century Satis Chandra Mukherjee founded the Dawn Society (July, 1902) in the premises of the present Vidyasagar College and organized a Swadeshi Stores under its auspices for the promotion of indigenous manufactures. The efforts of the Dawn Society to popularize the cause of Swadeshi goods by lectures and exhibitions, organized sale and propaganda through its journal, the Dawn, were remarkable and together served as a prelude to the Swadeshi Movement of 1905.

Rabindra Nath Tagore was deeply impressed by Satischandra's selfless and total dedication to nationbuilding activities. The Swadeshi Movement, observed Satis Mukherjee in 1906, 'is patriotic in the first instance and only economic or industrial in the second. A purely economic movement would not have proved itself to be a whole people's or a nation's business, but its activities would have been confined amongst a comparatively limited class of people with industrial instincts and business capacities. The Swadeshi Movement, it must therefore be understood, is not an industrial movement, in its essence, but is essentially a moral movement, in the larger sense of the word, concerning itself with rousing the moral sense of a whole people in its relations with a bureaucratic power.'

Bipin Chandra Pal, the foremost architect of the Swadeshi Movement of 1905, also characterized the national upsurge as a 'spiritual movement'. In his article on 'The Bed-Rock of Indian Nationalism', he wrote thus in 1908: 'The strength of the new movement in India lies in its supreme idealism. It is not a mere economic movement, though it openly strives for the economic resurrection of the country. It is not a mere political movement, though it has boldly declared itself for absolute political independence. It is an intensely spiritual movement having for its object not simply the development of economic life or the attainment of political freedom but really the emancipation, in every sense of the term, of the Indian manhood and womanhood.'

INDIAN PATRIOTISM TOWARDS THE EMPIRE

In May last (1906) the Director of Public Instruc tion of the Panjab issued a circular order to all the headmasters and managers of Government, aided and unaided, schools in the province, requiring them to celebrate the empire-day in a certain way. One of the items of the programme laid down by him for observance was the recitation of Urdu poems on loyalty to the Crown of England and patriotism towards the empire. We do not know if the head of the Panjab Education Department was responsible for the wording of the above clause. The document seemed to bear on it abundant marks of that jingo statesmanship which has for a number of years, been in ascendancy in the councils of the British empire. One thing, however, is clear. The Government was sensible enough not to declare the empire-day as a public holiday. The compulsory celebra tion of the empire-day in 1906 was therefore confined to the schools, may be, to the schools of the Panjab only. We propose to examine in this paper if the step taken was educationally sound and in any way calculated to improve the moral tone of the schools where it was, by order, enforced.

Till lately the impression was that the British were,, at least, frank by nature and valued frankness and sin cerity on the part of others, however distasteful and unpleasant, at times, they may be to their imperial tem per. The idea was that although introduced into the English language by the presump tuous genius of the jingoes as an antidote towards the sacred sentiment of patriotism, in the development of which amongst the subject races, they see a dangerous enemy to their own despotic rule. The lexicographers, if they can be accepted as reliable guides, in explaining the meaning of English words to us, almost unanimously agree in expressing the general opinion, as to patriotism signifying "love of country."Johnson defines it as "zeal for one's country "and Webster as the passion which aims to serve one's country."The Encyclopaedia Dictionary says that patriotism is devotion to the interest and welfare of one's country and the Century Dictionary, as the passion which moves a person to serve his country either in defending it from invasion or protecting its rights and maintaining its lands and institutions "and so on and so forth. But how can a subject race governed by another be patriotic towards ks rulers passes one's comprehension, unless one accepts the theory that the latter rules solely for the benefit of the former?

Even in this cae it is love of his own country and Certainly not patriotism towards the empire (signi fying love for the empire) which evokes loyalty for the existing Government. Honestly speaking the two senti ments are antagonistic, viz., loyalty to a foreign govern ment and love for one's country, which is patriotism; unless the patriot is to reconcile his patriotism with loyalty by the idea that in loving the foreign ruler he loves his own country. It may be allowable to a patriot to soothe his conscience by identifying his loyalty with patriotism, but to carry it furthur and to extend the new empire is coining a new expression with an entirely new meaning. When, therefore, in the name of the Empire the British appeal to the patriotism of the Indians in stead of to their loyalty, their object is to give a higher pedestal to the shame which every member of a subject race (having the least vestige of self-respect and honour able feeling in him) must feel at his political helpless ness and at the political non-existence of his country The object is to cover the shame of political bondage with the halo of glory that attaches to the word "patriotism"and thus to remove the sting that bites the con sciences of those of the ruling race and puts to shame those among the ruled, as are still open to any sense of honour.

However commendable the motive and however praiseworthy the object may be, one does not require much common sense to see through the device. jThe fact is that human nature with all its inherent disposition towards selfishness is always apt to find excuses for its idiosyncracies and will not allow itself to be denied the pleasure of putting a gloss of high and pure motives on its basest and meanest acts, whereby it deprives others of the simplest rights of humanity and the price less treasure of liberty. No wrong-doer, however edu cated and cultured he may be, can at times help feeling mortification at the wrongs which in the pursuit of self interest he has inflicted or does inflict upon others, and it is then that his guilty conscience runs riot in search of pleas and justifications for his wrongful conduct.

Makers and rulers of empires are no exception to this general rule, which governs human nature everywhere and in every phase of life. Now empires are neither made nor maintained by right. They are made by might, both physical and intellectual, including that diplomacy and cunning without which no supremacy can ever be gained over other peoples and natipnsj "Only by force can empire, as a rule, be created; only by force can empire, as a rule, be maintained,"rightly remarks Mr. Goddard in his excellent book on Racial Supremacyr although instances are not wanting in which wise and sagacious empire-makers and their equally clever suc cessors have maintained empires for a longer period than they otherwise could, by doses of benevolence and justice in the management of its affairs. But racial supremacy is one of those necessary evils of which the world can never be purged. Its roots are deep.

No amount of philosophizing and high thinking will see its complete overthrow from the world, and as long as this necessary evil exists, which is tantamount to saying that it must always exist, you cannot do away with empires and empire-makers. Still that is no reason why those who are the victims of empires and empire-makers should feel grateful to their masters for having extended their empire over them and for having included them in the category of their subjects. As to the ethics of empire making and as to the claims of the British to the grati tude of those included in their empire, we will prefer to quote some English authorities on the subject rather than give expression to our own views.

First, as to what does "empire "signify ? In the language of Mr. J. G. Goddard, a member of the new House of Commons, it "simply means rule, dominion sway."According to Lord Rosebery, empire is "the predominance of rule."According to Herbert Spencer "not the derivation of the word only but all its uses and associations imply the thought of predominance— imply a correlative subordination. Actual or potential coercion of other individuals or communities is necessarily involved in the conception. "In the words of Mr. Goddard then imperialism is the spirit of rule, ascendancy or predominance; the rule of one race of people by another race of people involving — of course, the subjection of the former to the latter.

Mr. J. M Robertson, another member of the House of Commons, also defines empire as "rule over other communities than his own. "Mr. Joseph Chamber lain, the jingo imperialist of modern England, has, how ever, assured us that the new conception of empire is of a voluntary organisation, based on community of inte rests and community of sacrifices, to which all should bring their contribution to the common good. How far this is in accordance with existing facts has been made clear by Mr. Goddard in examining the above statement, in his book referred to above. In the opinion of this writer imperialism tends to demoralise the dominant race, while it is simply the bane of the subject races. Taking the case of India as the most prominent and pertinent instance of the government of one people by another people, he concludes by saying that India is ruled in the interest of the dominant race rather than in hers and endorses the well-known remark of John Ruskin that "every mutiny, every danger, every crime occurring under our Indian legislation arose directly out of our native desire to live on the loot of India.

The writer further coaiemns imperialism on the ground that it is destructive of liberty and applying it to the case of India he pronounces an indictment on imperia lism in this country in the following terms : —

Here we have countless millions denied the rights accorded to the English agricultural labourer, taxed to pay for a Government in which they have no voice, con demned to support an army they cannot control, rack rented for land they cultivate mainly for the benefit of others, compelled to yield interest on an expenditure they did not make, and generally reduced to the condition of hewers of wood and drawers o water, with sufferance as the badge of all their tribe.

Discussing the ethics of empire the same writer examines the claims of the dominant races in placing themselves in quasi loco parentis over subject races, as follows : —

The bond which unites father or mother with son and daughter is one of mutual affection and so far from self-sacrifice on the part of the dominant race being present, the opposite characteristic is manifested, and there is certainly no constant endeavour to promote the welfare of the putative child. The most serious flaw in the analogy, however, has reference to the main purpose of control. For the primary object of the parental rule of children, is to develop their faculties, and that for their own benefit. It is a teniporartj and not a permanent rule, devoted to the purpose of rendering the child a self' governing person, capable as manhood is readied of exercising shn'thir rule. The primary object the faculties of the governed; even if some develop ment takes place, it is not for their own benefit; the rule is regarded not as temporary, but rather as permanent and it is not devoted to the purpose of rendering them capable of exercising similar rule.

No doubt, in point of time, the infancy of man is incomparable to the in fancy of a race, and a far larger period is requisite for development. But a dominant nation does not work for or contemplate the abrogation of its power, even in the distant future; its rooted idea is that of its own supre macy; its constant aim is to secure the maintenance and generally the extension of that supremacy; its funda mental conception of the relations which exist is subjec tive and not objective. Hence, on almost all points the analogy is absolutely false and misleading. One, and one only, of the many parental functions is selected, and the rest are implicitly or explicitly ignored. The maturity of the parent and the immaturity of the child are at the out get assumed to respectively distinguish the two races; and then from a distorted simile an attempt is made to convert the temporary and qualified and specialised control which a parent exercises into a justification for the permanent and unqualified and general control which a nation claims.

Passing to the consideration of the second hypothe sis of the imperialist, viz., that benevolence characterizes despotism, Mr. Goddard points out that in order to make despotism benevolent the one condition essential — that the power should be vested in one individual — is wanting in the case. Thinking on the same line I have often wished that we had been ruled by Queen Victoria or by King Edward, or by any other single individual exercis ing the power of a despotic nxonarch rather than by the Parliament of Great Britain and Ireland representing the British nation, for you can, at times, successfully appeal to the humanity and benevolence of individuals but to hope for justice and benevolence from a nation is hoping against hope.

The rule of a foreign democracy, is in this respect, the most dangerous. The democracy is swayed by so many diverse interests and motives that it is simply impossible to expect anything like unanimity or even a preponderance of opinion in dealing justly with a subject race, because justice to a subject race often 'Clashes or is inconsistent with the interest of some class of the ruling democracy. Whenever an attempt is there fore made to do justice to the former, the latter rise up, raise a storm and prevent the Government from doing the right thing. Looking to the history of the cotton duties in India, every one will see the truth of my re marks. How many times have the Government of India been overruled in the matter, simply because the Home <jovernment can not afford to risk the opposition of Lancashire and incur its displeasure ?

As a matter of fact, we are at present ruled by a <iemocracy which represents the British nation and in the appointing and controlling of which the Sovereign has really no hand. In my opinion the benevolence of :an individual has greater chances of being effective than that of a whole nation. To me the benevolence of a whole nation seems to be nothing more than a myth and :a fiction, as there can never be an absolute unanimity both as to what constitutes benevolence as well as to how it is to be reduced into practice. Applying the benevolence plea to the case pf India and other subject races of Britain, Mr. Goddard concludes (a conclusion in which other eminent authori ties agree) that the plea is simply untenable.

Examining the plea of benevolence in imperial relations in the light of historical facts Mr. Goddard says: "The truth is that whilst it does not necessarily give rise to exalting acts of cruelty, so far from its ever being largely tempered by benevolence, it has invariably one prominent charac teristic, namely, the exploitation of its victims. The primarj' object and result of alien government is not to confer benefits upon the subject races but to obtain bene fits from them". He further says that : —

Perhaps the most striking testimony to the virtues of benevolent despotism is seen in the employ ment of native races to fight our battles for us. Wild animals are sometimes lured to their doom by means of one of their kind trained to act as a decoy, and we occa sionally hear setting of a thief to catch a thief. The process has been adopted with a magnificent effrontry and a grim sense of humour to the needs of aggressive imperialism, and having extended the empire by bringing the "inferior races" under our swaraj', by a master stroke of genius, we utilise them to still further extend and also to defend the empire and convert them into instru ments for bestowing upon their brethren the boons whiqh they themselves have obtainedIt is very largely in this way that our Indian Empire has been built up.

Then let us see what another English author, Mr J. A Hobson, says about the sophistries of imperialism 'The idea' he says "that we are civilising India in the sense of assisting them to industrial, political, and moral progress along the lines either of our own or their civili sation is a complete delusion, based upon a false estimate of the influence of superficial changes brought by Government and the activity of a minute group of aliens. The delusion is only sustained by the sophistr}' of im perialism which weaves these fallacies to cover its nakedness and the advantages which certain interests suck out of empire."Even the late Professor Seeley writes in the same strain where he says : "We are not disposed to be proud of the succession of the Grand Mcgul. We doubt whether with all the merits of our adipinistration the subjects of it are happy.

We may ven doubt whether our rule is preparing them for a happier condition, whether it may not be sinking them lower in misery."But what Professor Seeley states in rather halting language is expressed affirmatively by another great writer on India, Mr. W. S. Lily. "The test of a people's prosperity", says Mr. Lily, "is not the extension of exports, the multiplication of manufactures or other industries, the construction of cities. No. A prosperous country is one in which the great mass of the inhabitants are able to procure with mode rate toil what IS necessary for living human lives, lives of frugal and assured comfort. Judged by this standard can India be called prosperous? His answer, of course, is a positive No. He adds that comfort is a relative term and that in a tropical coun try like India the standard is very low but millions of peasants in India are half an acre. Their existence is a constant struggle with starvation leading too often in defeat. Their difficulty is not to live hutnan lives — lives up to the level of their poor standard of comfort — hut to live at all and not die.

Such then is the verdict of level-headed Hnglishmen on the result of imperial rule in India, which testimony is of hundred times greater value than the interested sayings of stock exchange brokers and speculators, whom the

British System helps in hording up millions upon millions at the cost of the Indian peasant, the Indian labourer and the Indian handicraftsman. I could add the testimony of many more Englishmen as to the bane ful effects of imperialism in India, but the fear of adding to the bulk of this paper prevents me from doing so, and I will conclude this part of the paper by adding one more quotation from the fascinating work of Mr. Goddard, wherein he shows how detrimental benevolent imperia lism is to the interests of the subject races : —

The gravaman of the indictment of "benevolent despotism "is that it tends to perpetuate the despotism Whilst in practice the benevolence, if manifested at alli is relatively small, and whilst even if it were exhibited to the fullest extent circumstances admit, it would be no adequate justification; its supposed or actual existence obscures the facts satisfies the conscience, and leads to acquiescence in the permanent withdrawal of liberty instead of efforts towards its restoration. It will be seen that in saying all this I have only dis cusscithe general effects of imperial rule in India and have not even touched upon particular grievances.

I have made no allusion to the brutal treatment we receive in South Africa, Australia and other parts of the empire, and I have made no mention of the disabilities from which we suffer in India. Is it then right to ask us to celebrate the empire-day ? Is it then likely to improve habits of sincerity and truthfulness amongst our boys, by compelling them to glorify the empire ? Is it then honest on the part of our teachers and professors and directors to flatter us by saying that we are either the sons of the empire or its citizens, while we are neither, but are treated as the subjects of the empire — the victims of the imperial spirit that rules?

Britishers may or may not glory in their empire. Perhaps from the ordinary point of view they have every reason to be proud of it and to glory in it. It tickles their fancy to think of their possessions, their dependencies and their subjects, though the sober-minded amongst them have begun to talk loudly as to the evil effects of the imperialism on the morale of their own people.

The once sturdy and vigorous, both in thought and indeed, the simple but the high-minded, the reserved but solid Britisher is perhaps exchanging his virtues for the comforts, ease and luxuries, which attend an unchecked sway of empire and the bumptiousness and the vulgar pride of unbounded intoxication of uncontrolled power. Be however as it may, we do not and we cannot object to the Britisher at home or in India celebrating his empire-day, but it is nothing short of adding insult to injury to ask us and our boys to do so. Devoted patriots, as the British are, is it fair on their part to ask us to celebrate the empire day in the name of "Patriotism to Leaders— a patriotism which we do not feel, which does not inspire us with noble thoughts and which evokes neither love nor homage in our bosoms ?

As helpless victims of the aggressive imperialism, as servants of the Crown and as students of schools and colleges, we might silently put up with the humiliation, but I dare say I am not wrong in reading the hearts of the bulk of my educated countrymen when I say, that the idea is simply revolting and extremely provoking to their sense of honour and shame. Those Britishers and Indians who thus trade in hypocrisy, and who thus would inoculate the minds of the innocent boys and girls with the serum of hypocrisy, are doing a positive injury to human nature, and to the principles of sound education without doing any good to British rule in India. In the name of loyalty we are prepared to submit to any order which the authorities issue, but we earnestly beg of them not to drag our patriotism into the mire and not to force us to compromise the same. The demands of patriotism are sacred and ennobling, which require no hypocrisy, and which evoke the deepest feelings of love for our country and for our people.

THE NATIONAL OUTLOOK : THE CHEAT NEED OF THE SITUATION

Problems of the gravest import await our solution — problems which need all our nerve, all our determination, all our courage, all our hope.and which affect the life and death of us all, were the words uttered by one of the most popular divines of England, portraying national perils for the consideration of his countrymen.

Well did he say that the conditions of things then or at any time may be looked at in two different ways. There is one set of facts, which when considered exclusively, would make us hopeless pessimists. There is another set of facts which when taken by themselves may furnish good ground for the most sanguine optimism.

The truth, however, generally lies between the two. While pessimism is positively harmful as dispiriting and discouraging, optimism may be misleading as tending to produce a frame of mind which is always sanguine, prone to ignore difficulties and to neglect very necessary precautions. The best and the safest course, therefore, will be to steer clear of extreme views, to weigh the situation as accurately as may be possible in the light of our own history, that of the ruling race, and that of other countries and people similarly situated.

Practical wisdom lies in eschewing, over-estimating as well as under-estimating. While it is no good under-estimating our difficulties and overestimating our capacities, it is perhaps more harmful to have a very low opinion of ourselves and our people. Both are equally bad; though if compelled to make a choice between the two, I would rather choose the former than the latter. Keeping the past history of the Hindus in mind I would rather see them indulge in optimism than in pessimism. We have so long been in doubt about ourselves about the world and about the good in the world that it Is time to exchange this latter attitude of mind for confidence in self, confidence in our people, and hope for a our efforts and the object of all our agitation, has been placed before us in clear, unambiguous and unmistakable terms. In a happy and inspired moment Mr. Naoroji struck upon that noble word — "Swaraj, "which sums up all our political aspirations. Henceforth, "Swaraj "is our war-cry, our all-inspiring and all-absorbing aim in life.

Henceforth, the duty of our earthly existence should be to forget self in this aim prescribed for us by the exigencies of the times and accepted by us after consideration of all the pros and cons. For the first time in the history of political agitation in this country under British rule, the goal of all our political effort has been so clearly laid down before us; and thank God that for that we are indebted to no other but one who is the flesh of our flesh and the bone of our bone — a chip of the old block. We are now no longer groping in the dark as to the final goal of our political ambition.

Swaraj has now been, officially, so to say, and definitely set up as the polestar in the firmament of Indian nationalism, and there it shall stay and shine with ever resplendent glory and splendour as the guiding star of our hopes and aspirations.

So far well and good. The next question that now arises is how to reach that goal and how to realise that aim ? Like practical men, who have every desire to go into the matter in a businesslike spirit, we should first of all make a complete survey of the difficulties in the way of our success and then take stock of our resources, so that we might successfully employ the latter to meet the former. Coming to our difficulties in my opinion must be given to our want of the scepticism that is the ruling doctrine of our life, to the habit of too close an analysis which paralyses both action and thought.

Unfortunately for us, though born in a country dominated by a religious atmosphere of great depth all round we are wanting in that pity of faith and will which neitier counts obstacles nor mea ui'es time. At present, we are nothing more that of doubting Thomases fond of analysis and entirely devoid of synthesis. Per haps we are getting into a habit of destroying rather than that of building. We cm calculate profits and losses to annas and pies, but we are devoid of that spirit of enter prise which can dare and at time play boldly. In a country whose history is brimful of instances of thousands of men and women having willingly and gladly sacrificed their all for the sake of honour and faith, we find that a century of Western domination has so changed the rul ing impulses of life as to convert the people into a set of clay-puppets having no will or faith of their own.

Thank God, the country has not lost all sense of spirituality.. The gold is there. It requires the touch of a magician to find it out and to make it over to them whos3 it is by birthright. The true solution of the problem lies in appealing to the true instincts and tendencies of the Indian heart, mute just now, but revealed to us in the pages of our history. In the words of Mazzini, the first step towards this aim is "to make war against the exist ing idolatry of material interests and substitute for it the worship of the just and the true: and to [Indians] that their sole path to real — constancy in sacrifice.

They make not only an endeavour to create a united nation to make her great and powerful — worthy of her filioUirf glories and conscious of her future mission. India is just now materialistic, benevolence of English Ministers or English Parliament seeking rather the amelioration of the condition of poor classes than to constitute itself a nation.

The couoestflioil and its leaders rather fight shy of high princip stepflf and are ready to accept any compromise, any of a post here or a post there, any tinkering with, their rights, any mode of assistance and last but not the least always ready to accept any maa brought forward with a promise of relieving her immediate sufferings as their Messdah.

Our attitude towards the questions of the day is not determined by its inherent rignteousness, but by the chance of its reception at the hands of the powers that be. We are not always actuated by truth and justice, but by expediency and tactics. Our object is to propitiate our foreign rulers but not to inspire our people. We choose to live in a world of myth and fiction and not in a world of truth, faith and duty. We conceal our sentiments not because they are not true and just but because we cannot afford to offend those whom they might hurt. In trying to deceive others we often deceive ourselves. The result is that we are lacking in that power of faith which alone i can make us men, able to create a nation and win liberty for the same.

Our mortal disease is that unlimited confidence in every thing bearing the outward and tactics, that constant distrust on greatest simultaneous action — three things which sum from witl science of revolution. We wait, study and to be neither seek to dominate nor to are open honour with the name of prudence The latters action, merely mediocrity of intellect, the former bottom smacks of fear, the heads losing in the estimation of those whom we that the hearts believe to be only usurpers; fear of sunshine of the smile of those whom we be lieve to be day and night engaged in the exploitation of our country and the spoliation of our people, fear of offending the false gods that have by fraud or force taken possession of our bodies and souls fear of being shut up in a dungeon or prisibn house, as if the freedom that we enjoy, is not by its own nature, one to be abhorred despised and hated, — a freedom by default or by suffer ance.

In my opinion the problem before us is in the main a religious problem — religious not in the sene of doctrines and dogmas — but religious in so far as to evoke ' the highest devotion and the greatest sacrifice from us. Our first want, then, is to rise our patriotism to the level of religion and to aspire to live or to die for it. We believe i in religion for the sake of the truth in it which is tosecure for our souls communion with God. There in the pre sence of our God we forget our tiny selves, the pettiness of our minds and rising above the same, drink from the pure fountain of bliss and love. In the same way, let the edifice of patriotism be raised on the solid rock of truth and justice.

If we do this, the future of our country kg ijsio oyf hands. There is no power on earth that can iirliairstajid bet ween us and our country as there is no petition Cf odthat can ever come between the conscience of an hCxe coxst,bM worshipper and his Almighty Maker. The political ladder, then, consists in our education people in a school of true politics, of our initiating them into a religion of true patriotism with a creed of Nation, ality, Liberty and Unity, to be believed and striven after with all the sincerity of heart and devotion, worthy of the oriental mind. Let us first renounce all kinds of self interest and class-interest, in favour of a noble and universal patriotism embracing all the people and all the provinces of mother India, irrespective of creed, caste and colour.

All talk of unity is futile unless we succeed in bringing about a unity of purpose in the minds of the people whom we desire to unite. An attempt to base this unity of purpose on material interests, might land us in interminable dissensions and endless controversies — in insuperable friction and unsurmountable irritation. But a sincere effort to give a higher and spiritual basis to our unity of purpose might save the situation and lead us safely to the haven of our hopes. That oneness of purpose is very happily summed up in the sacred salutation Bande Mataram and in the war-cry of Let us aext proceed to examine to oppose us in our propaganda.

To the Government there are only two paths that are open — a system of terror or a system of concessions. The latter possesses more possibilities of success than the former. A system of terror invariably recoils over the heads of those that resort to it, and I am confident that the British are sufficiently wise not to forget that there is a great deal of truth in what is so often quoted by European revolutionists that : —

"Blood calls for Blood, and the dagger of the conspirator is never so terrible as when sharpened on the tomb-stone of a martyr."

A system of small concessions, however, might be more effectual to stem the rising tide of nationality. Therein probably lies a greater danger to the rapid growth of the idea of nationality in the country than in a system of repression. Trivial changes in administrative fnachinery. the reform of the most crying Governmental abuses and a few more ineffectual concessions not involving any fundamental change in the principles of Government or in the constitution of the same, should not satisfy our people, unless the same are accompanied by a guarantee of fixed institutions, and a fundamental contract recognising a right, a power and a sovereignty in the people. That the opposition of the dominant race will be tremendous and terrible, I readily grant; but what I fear most is the opposition from within, the opposition of the classes enjoying the special atco nage of the Government, the opposition of privilege, and opposition of timidity and cowardice. The divine, whom I quoted in the opening lines of the paper, has in one of his essays on social amelioration drawn the following picture of the attitude of his countrymen towards the social evils existing in English society. He says : —

"The attitude of some — let us hope very few — is simply not to care at all to live in pleasure on the earth and be wanton : to have hearts as fat as brawn and cold as ice, and hard as the nether mill-stone; to heap up superfluous and often ill begotton wealth, to be hoarded in acquisition, squandered in luxury, or reserved for the building up of idle families. But to men, whose immense riches are squandered, in all but an insignificant fraction, on their own lust and their own aggrandizement comes the stern strong message of St. James, your riches are corrupted, your garments are moth-eaten. Ye have lived delicately on the earth, and taken your pleasure. Ye have nourished your hearts in a day of slaughter.

The attitude of others is that of a scornful pity, half cynical, half despairing. The attitude of others again is stolid acquiescence. They are weary of the whole thing; sick of hearing anything about it It annoys,.them. Tell them of it and they shrug their shoulders with an impatient "what can we do I "Ask them for help, and they hare "so many claims, "that they practically give to none. Press the claims and they resent it as a personal insult: Suggest a plan and they will call it "Utopian. "Describe a case of anguish and they will call you "sensational." Take part in a public effort and they will sneer at you as self advertising. "The one thing they believe in is selfish laisez faire. Things will last their time and that is all they care about. They grow too indulgent and too selfish to care about anything but their own indulgences and their own ease.

Applying this to Indian society, I am afraid, the pic ture will have to be painted great deal blacker. There are at any rate no traitors iry English society. In our case the chief difficulty does nrft solely lie in the persistent and deliberate discouragement which is held out by a large sec tion of the community to all efforts towards progress. Here it is not the scoffer and the cynic only that stand in the way of advance but even more dangerous are those who insist to be of you, and with you, but whose heart is not with you, and whose interests, as understood by them, lie the other way.

Although they are apt to betray them selves at every other step, they cover their shame by ridiculing the zealous and the earnest, by quietly and philosophically questioning their motives and by poisoning the minds of others against them. Their attitude undergoes no change whether the reform advocated is religious social or political. The first bores them as an affection of the brain; the second annoys them as tending towards puritanism and misanthrophy; the third frightens them. The beauty of the whole thing, however, lies in the fact that large number of them cannot help poking their noses almost everywhere. They enlist as members of societies whose proposed object is to preach religion. They display great interest in social reform so long as it does not interfere with what they call the joys of life. Maintaining an attitude of boldness and defiance to public opinion when the latter propose any way with the "pleasures of life,"they are docile as lambs when their ladies and biradmn (caste) people insist on the celebration of the marriages of their boys and girls at tender ages. As for political associations, these are their special hunting grounds.

They have no objec tion to preside at public meetings or to move or second resolutions or to attend Conferences and Congresses, if it suits their convenience or is likely to be profitable, but all the same they will continue to revel in scoffing at and laughing down those who are seriouaj and earnest about the matter. The general mass of the people are so ignorant of political ideas that it is impossible for them to understand or find out the real game which these gentlemen are playing. Consequently they are often cowed down and persuaded to let matters alone rather than make a bold stand for their rights.

The first necessity of the situation is, therefore, the coming forward of a number of whole-time workers in each province, devoted to the work of giving political education and imparting right ideas, irrespective and regardless of the scoffer and the cynic. Mr. Dadabhai Naoroji exhorts us to agitate, agitate and agitate. I say, Amen ! but on the clear understanding that agitation is an educational duty which has to be performed regard. less of success in the shape of concessions. Let the pupblic be accustomed to agitaiefor the sake of agitation and not in the hope of getting any immediate redress. That is, in my opinion, the only way to ward oflF disap pointments and to prepare the people for more effective methods of political activity.

I say, that is only possible by training the people to a habit of suffering for principles, i.e., to dare and to risk; and by infusing in them a spirit of defiance wherever a question of principle is involved. The way is to be shewn by personal example and not by precept alone. There is the old truth no risk, no gain. The line of least resistance, of empty resolutions on paper, of simple resolutions,-memorials, and not petitions backed up by anything which would place our earnestness be yond the shade of a doubt, is a line of action more worthy of women than of men.

If I may be permitted to question the political leaders of the country, what irresistible proofs have they up to this time given of their earnestness for the political demand made by them ? If the time was not and is not ripe for these proofs then why did they not follow the Japanese in making quiet pre parations at home before coming put openly with fiery speeches and long winded resolutions ? If, however we have not wasted 22 years on political agitation and if the Swadeshi and Boycott are not lipplatitudes to be indulg. ed in for the edification of our audiences, let us now take to it seriously and give incontestable proofs of our earnestness for political privileges.

Hitherto our work has lacked that system and solidity which are the outcome of well thought out and well organised plans. Hitherto the political movement has only been carried out by fits and starts. It has completely depended on the moments of leisure which gentlemen engaged in learned should conveniently spare for labour of love to them, but it has always occupied it secondary position in their thoughts. The country has so far failed to produce a class of men whose chief and. prime business in life will be political agitation and political education. The chief and crying need of the national movement, in the coming forward of a class of earnest, sincere, able and devoted men, who will move about the country freely and preach the Gospel of freedom, both by word of mouth as well as by example— men who will win over the masses to the cause of Truth and Justice, by words of wisdom and lives of service. The non-existence of this class at the present moment, combined with other difficulties makes the national out look very gloomy indeed, but the remedy to change the face of things lies in our own hands.

There is an all round awakening in the land, and if the awakening were to bs properly utilised by the class of men I have spoken of above, I am sure that the dense gloom that prevails now, will soon be thinned by streaks of encouraging and cheering light, crowed by the dawn of hope and the sunrise of national birth. Most of our people are unnerved by the prevailing disunion and other vices which are the neceary outcome of a foreigti domination. It is true that foreign domination is always brought on by disunion but once it has come in, it accen tuates the same and adds to its volume and intensity, as without it, it loses the chief reason for its continuance Some of our people are very angry (and at times rightly) at the narrow, sectarian, denominational spirit that i rampant in the land.

In their eyes, it is the chief obs<st ch in the way of political independence and as a meaiysr to obtain the latter, they set about in all sincerity and earnestness to root out the former. All honour to their sentiments and to their impulses. But a calm considera tion will show that; the task is almost impossible. If the boon of Self-Government is to be denied to us so long as the people of this country do not give up denominationalism and do not take to the religion or nb religion, I am afraid there can be no hope for us. The problem before us is, to accept the facts before us as they are, and then to build up the edifice of nationality on them or in spite of them. I hope I shall not be misunderstood.

I am not opposed to the cultivation of a spirit of catholicity amongst the followers of the different religions that are to be found in the country. By all means carry on your work in this direction as zealously as you can. I wish you all success. But I can not persuade myself to believe that it is possible to uproot denominationalism from this land and for the matter of that, from any land. Our best efforts should then be directed to create a nation in spite of them. I am not quite sure, if it is desirable to do away with religion or with religious denominations altogether, even if it were possible to do so. All these differences in religion serve their own purpose in the general economy of the world, and there are a good many people whose views are entitled to the greatest respect from us, who are inclined to think that the world would be poorer and monotonous by the entire removal of these differences.

Our readers are probably aware of the rebuke administered by Burke to the authors of the French Revolution in their efforts to enforce a universal Reflections on the French Revolution,"addressing the people of France, he questions the wisdom of the sweep ing changes effected by them in their constitution in the following words : —

In your old States you possessed that variety of parts corresponding with the various descriptions of which your community was happily composed, you had all that opposition of interests, you had that action and counteraction which in the natural and in the political world from the reciprocal struggle of discordant powers, draws put the harmony of the universe."

I express no opinion upon the force of the anathemas hurled by Burke on the French Revolution, but I cannot help remarking that there is a great deal of truth in the general observation quoted above. The world is no doubt, good and beautiful only witn its diversity The chief object of human yearning is, has been, and ought to be, to find harmony in diversity. Nations are built and unified by the differences that exist between the various classes of their population. The Apostle of Unity in order to succeed must find a common object to achieve and a common enemy to fight. All differences must be sunk in the presence of the latter and to achieve the former but not necessarily otherwise.

For as this and this only can be the common basis of nationality, I do not think there are insuperable difficulties in the way of Indian Unity, if the denominational and other differences are faced in that spirit. Another evil which often stsersnis, is the illiteracy Bud ignorance of our people. Here are the absolute necessity of educationists to see the soundness of the proposition, that universal education must precede any demand for self-government. In fact it is hopeless to expect anything like universal education without self-government. Over a century and a quarter of British rule has failed to educate more than 5 or 6 percent of the people of India, while Japan has been wholly educated within less than 40 years.

The educational work is one of the most important of our national duties, but by no means should it be made a condition precedent to our demanding self-government. Here, too, the principal question is of men and money. Find out the former and the latter will be forthcoming. That is, therefore the chief thing, for the finding of which, the nation should put forth its best energy and talent.

Give us a dozen men in each province, exclusively devoted to the work of national regeneration, and the situation will at once assume a bright appearance and will promise the most hopeful results. Let us hope that the best talent and the best patriotism of the country are engaged in tapping the resources which are eventually to give us the desired class of men who shall be our national Sannyasis in the present crisis was probably said of times like these that These are the times that try men's souls. The sunshine soldier and the sunshine patriot will, in this crisis, shrink from the service of their country; but he that stands to it now, deserves the thanks of man and woman. Tyranny like hell is not easily conquered; yet we have this consolation with us, that the harder the contest, the more glorious the triumph. What we obtain too cheaply, is dearness only that gives everything knows how to set a proper price upon its goods; and it would have been strange indeed if so celestial an article as Freedom should not be highly rated.

Lajapat Rai

To His Government and Countrymen.

POLITICAL ASPECT OF SWADESHI MOVEMENT

Educated liberal Muslims who came forward and tendered support to the anti-partition agitation and the Swadeshi Movement. Though their number was insignificant, yet their role added a new dimension in the thought process of the Muslims. This broad-minded group supported the Indian National Congress and opposed the partition. The most prominent among this section of the Muslims was Khwaza atiqullah. At the Calcutta session of the Congress

(1906), he moved a resolution denouncing the partition of Bengal Abdur Rasul, Khan Bahadur Muhammad Yusuf (a pleader and a member of the Management Committee of the Central National Muhamedan Association), Mujibur Rahman, AH Abdul Halim Ghaznavi, Ismail Hossain Shiraji, Muhammad Gholam Hossain (a writer and a promoter of Hindu-Muslim unity), Maulvi Liaqat Hussain (a liberal Muslim who vehemently opposed the 'Divide and Rule' policy of the British), Syed Hafizur Rahman Chowdhury of Bogra and Abul Kasem of Burdwan inspired Muslims to join the anti-Partition agitation. There were even a few Muslim preachers of Swadeshi ideas, like Din Muhammad of Mymensingh and Abdul Gaffar of Chittagong. It needs to be mentioned that some of the liberal nationalist Muslims like AH Ghaznavi and Khan Bahadur Muhammad Yusuf supported the Swadeshi Movement but not the Boycott agitation.

A section of the Muslim press tried to promote harmonious relations between the Hindus and the Muslims. Ak Fazlul Huq and Nibaran Chandra Das preached non-communal ideas through their weekly Balaka (1901, Barisal) and monthly Bharat Suhrd (1901, Barisal). Only a small section of Muslim intellectuals could rise above their sectarian outlook and join with the Congress in the anti-partition agitation and constitutional politics.

The general trend of thoughts in the Muslim minds was in favour of partition. The All India Muslim league, founded in 1906, supported the partition. In the meeting of the Imperial Council in 1910 Shamsul Huda of Bengal and Mazhar-ul-Huq from Bihar spoke in favour of the partition.

The traditional and reformist Muslim groups-the Faraizi, Wahabi and Taiyuni-supported the partition. Consequently an orthodox trend was visible in the political attitude of the Muslims. The Bengali Muslim press in general lent support to the partition. The Islam Pracharak described Swadeshi as a Hindu movement and expressed grave concern saying that it would bring hardship to the common people. The Muslim intelligentsia in general felt concerned about the suffering of their co-religionists caused by it. They particularly disliked the movement as it was tied to the anti-partition agitation. Reputed litterateurs like Mir Mosharraf Hossain were virulent critics of the Swadeshi Movement. The greater body of Muslims at all levels remained opposed to the Swadeshi Movement since it was used as a weapon against the partition and a religious tone was added to it.

The economic aspect of the movement was partly responsible for encouraging separatist forces within the Muslim society. The superiority of the Hindus in the sphere of trade and industry alarmed the Muslims. Fear of socioeconomic domination by the Hindus made them alert to safeguard their own interests. These apprehensions brought about a rift in Hindu-Muslims relations. In order to avoid economic exploitation by the Hindus, some wealthy Muslim entrepreneurs came forward to launch new commercial ventures. One good attempt was the founding of steamer companies operating between Chittagong and Rangoon in 1906.

In the context of the partition the pattern of the land system in Bengal played a major role to influence the Muslim mind. The absentee Hindu zamindars made no attempt to improve the lot of the raiyats who were mostly Muslims. The agrarian disputes (between landlords and tenants) already in existence in the province also appeared to take a communal colour. It was alleged that the Hindu landlords had been attempting to enforce Swadeshi ideas on the tenants and induce them to join the anti-partition movement.

In 1906, the Muslims organised an Islamic conference at Keraniganj in Dhaka as a move to emphasise their separate identity as a community. The Swadeshi Movement with its Hindu religious flavour fomented aggressive reaction from the other community. A red pamphlet of a highly inflammatory nature was circulated among the Muslim masses of Eastern Bengal and Assam urging them completely to dissociate from the Hindus. It was published under the auspices of the Anjuman-I-Mufidul Islam under the editorship of a certain Ibrahim Khan. Moreover, such irritating moves as the adoption of the Bande Mataram as the song of inspiration or introduction of the cult of Shivaji as a national hero, and reports of communal violence alienated the Muslims. One inevitable result of such preaching was the riot that broke out at Comilla in March 1907, followed by similar riots in Jamalpur in April of that year. These communal disturbances became a familiar feature in Eastern Bengal and Assam and followed a pattern that was repeated elsewhere. The 1907 riots represent a watershed in the history of modern Bengal.

While Hindu-Muslims relations deteriorated, political changes of great magnitude were taking place in the Government of India's policies, and simultaneously in the relations of Bengali Muslim leaders with their non-Bengali counterparts. Both developments had major repercussions on communal relations in eastern Bengal. The decision to introduce constitutional reforms culminating in the morley-minto reforms of 1909 introducing separate representation for the Muslims marked a turning point in Hindu-Muslim relations.

The early administrators of the new province from the lieutenant governor down to the junior-most officials in general were enthusiastic in carrying out the development works. Bampfylde Fuller was accused by the anti-Partition movement leaders as being extremely partial to Muslims. He, because of a difference with the Government of India, resigned in August 1906. His resignation and its prompt acceptance were considered by the Muslims to be a solid political victory for the Hindus. The general Muslim feeling was that in yielding to the pressure of the anti-Partition agitators the government had revealed its weakness and had overlooked the loyal adherence of the Muslims to the government. Consequently, the antagonism between the Hindus and Muslims became very acute in the new province. The Muslim leaders, now more conscious of their separate communal identity, directed their attention in uniting the different sections of their community to the creation of a counter movement against that of the Hindus. They keenly felt the need for unity and believed that the Hindu agitation against the Partition was in fact a communal movement and as such a threat to the Muslims as a separate community. They decided to faithfully follow the directions of leaders like Salimullah and Nawab Ali Chowdhury and formed organisations like the Mohammedan Provincial Union.

Though communalism had reached its peak in the new province by 1907, there is evidence of a sensible and sincere desire among some of the educated and upper class Muslims and Hindus to put an end to these religious antagonisms. A group of prominent members of both communities met the Viceroy Lord Minto on 15 March 1907 with suggestions to put an end to communal violence and promote religious harmony between the two communities.

The landlord-tenant relationship in the new province had deteriorated and took a communal turn. The Hindu landlords felt alarmed at the acts of terrorism committed by the anti-partition agitators. To prove their unswerving loyalty to the government and give evidence of their negative attitude towards the agitation, they offered their hands of friendship and cooperation to their Muslim counterparts to the effect that they would take a non-communal stand and work unitedly against the anti-government revolutionary movements.

In the meantime the All-India Muslim League had come into being at Dacca on 30 December 1906. Though several factors were responsible for the formation of such an organisation, the Partition of Bengal and the threat to it was, perhaps, the most important factor that hastened its birth. At its very first sitting at Dacca the Muslim League, in one of its resolutions, said: 'That this meeting in view of the clear interest of the Mohammedans of Eastern Bengal consider that Partition is sure to prove beneficial to the Muhammadan community which constitute the vast majority of the populations of the new province and that all such methods of agitation such as boycotting should be strongly condemned and discouraged'. To assuage the resentment of the assertive Bengali Hindus, the British government decided to annul the Partition of Bengal. As regards the Muslims of Eastern Bengal the government stated that in the new province the Muslims were in an overwhelming majority in point of population, under the new arrangement also they would still be in a position of approximate numerical equality or possibly of small superiority over the Hindus. The interests of the Muslims would be safeguarded by special representation in the Legislative Councils and the local bodies.

Lord hardinge succeeded Minto and on 25 August 1911. In a secret despatch the government of India recommended certain changes in the administration of India. According to the suggestion of the Governor-General-in-Council, King George V at his Coronation Darbar in Delhi in December 1911 announced the revocation of the Partition of Bengal and of certain changes in the administration of India. Firstly, the Government of India should have its seat at Delhi instead of Calcutta. By shifting the capital to the site of past Muslim glory, the British hoped to placate Bengal's Muslim community now aggrieved at the loss of provincial power and privilege in eastern Bengal. Secondly, the five Bengali speaking Divisions viz The Presidency, Burdwan, Dacca, Rajshahi and Chittagong were to be united and formed into a Presidency to be administered by a Governor-in-Council. The area of this province would be approximately 70,000 sq. miles with a population of 42 million. Thirdly, a Lieutenant-Governor-in-Council with a Legislative Council was to govern the province comprising of Bihar, Chhota Nagpur and Orissa. Fourthly, Assam was to revert back to the rule of a Chief Commissioner. The date chosen for the formal ending of the partition and reunification of Bengal was I April 1912.

Reunification of Bengal indeed served somewhat to soothe the feeling of the Bengali Hindus, but the down grading of Calcutta from imperial to mere provincial status was simultaneously a blow to 'Bhadralok' egos and to Calcutta real estate values. To deprive Calcutta of its prime position as the nerve centre of political activity necessarily weakened the influence of the Bengali Hindus. The government felt that the main advantage, which could be derived from the move, was that it would remove the seat of the government of India from the agitated atmosphere of Bengal.

Lord Carmichael, a man of liberal sympathies, was chosen as the first Governor of reunified Bengal. The Partition of Bengal and the agitation against it had far-reaching effects on Indian history and national life. The twin weapons of Swadeshi and Boycott adopted by the Bengalis became a creed with the Indian National Congress and were used more effectively in future conflicts. They formed the basis of Gandhi's Non-Cooperation, Satyagraha and Khadi movements. They also learned that organised political agitation and critical public opinion can force the government to accede to public demands.

The annulment of the partition as a result of the agitation against it had a negative effect on the Muslims. The majority of the Muslims did not like the Congress support to the anti-partition agitation. The politically conscious

Muslims felt that the Congress had supported a Hindu agitation against the creation of a Muslim majority province. It reinforced their belief that their interests were not safe in the hands of the Congress. Thus they became more anxious to emphasise their separate communal identity and leaned towards the Muslim League to safeguard their interest against the dominance of the Hindu majority in undivided India. To placate Bengali Muslim feelings Lord Hardinge promised a new University at Dacca on 31 January 1912 to a Muslim deputation led by Salimullah.

The Partition of Bengal of 1905 left a profound impact on the political history of India. From a political angle the measure accentuated Hindu-Muslim differences in the region. One point of view is that by giving the Muslim's a separate territorial identity in 1905 and a communal electorate through the Morley-Minto Reforms of 1909 the British Government in a subtle manner tried to neutralise the possibility of major Muslim participation in the Indian National Congress.

The Partition of Bengal indeed marks a turning point in the history of nationalism in India. It may be said that it was out of the travails of Bengal that Indian nationalism was born. By the same token the agitation against the partition and the terrorism that it generated was one of the main factors which gave birth to Muslim nationalism and encouraged them to engage in separatist politics. The birth of the Muslim League in 1906 at Dacca (Dhaka) bears testimony to this. The annulment of the partition sorely disappointed not only the Bengali Muslims but also the Muslims of the whole of India. They felt that loyalty did not pay but agitation does. Thereafter, the dejected Muslims gradually took an anti-British stanc

Rasul, Abdur (1872-1917) nationalist leader and lawyer. Abdur Rasul was born in 1872 in a landed family of Guniauk, a village in Brahmanbaria district. He lost his father Golam Rasul in his childhood but his mother raised him well. He was sent to England for higher studies after he had passed the Entrance Examination in 1888. He took the BA degree in 1896 and the MA degree in 1898. Abdur Rasul was called to the Bar at the Middle Temple in 1898. While in London, he became acquainted with noted Indians like Ali Imam, Syed Hasan Imam, aurobindo ghosh and others. Returning to India he got himself enrolled at the Calcutta High Court in 1899. Abdur Rasul was made an honorary lecturer in International Law at the university of Calcutta.

Abdur Rasul was opposed to the partition of bengal, 1905. He presided over the Bengal Congress Conference held at Barisal in 1906. In collaboration with Abdul Halim Ghaznavi

Dawn Society, The (1902-1906) was founded in Calcutta by Satish Chandra Mukherjee, a proponent of national education, in 1902. Satish Chandra had earlier established *Bhagabat Chatuspathi* in 1896. This was dedicated to the study of Indian religion and philosophy primarily and to Indology in general. The objective was to satisfy the quest for national identity. Its classes were held in the Metropolitan Institution (Modern Vidyasagar College) in the evening. At the same time, the famous Dawn Magazine was also launched. Many articles on Indology appeared in its pages till 1902 when it became the mouthpiece of the Dawn society.

Satish Chandra Mukherjee was a legendary teacher and a mentor of contemporary young men. Men like Binoy Kumar Sarkar, Radha Kumud Mukherjee, Haran Chandra Chakladar, Rabindranarayan Ghosh, Kishori Mohan Gupta and others flocked around him and became the mainstays of the Dawn Society. The society was critical of the colonial education imparted by the university of Calcutta which, according to it, was "all-too-literary, all-too-academic, unscientific and un-industrial" in nature. The Dawn Society wanted to promote education for man-making and nation-building purpose. In its curriculum, therefore, history, geography, economics, and political science were included in the Arts and Sciences & Technology were introduced. Apart from the above mentioned disciples, stalwarts like J.C. Bose, Nilratan Sarkar, Ramendrasundar Trivedi and even Rabindranath were invited to deliver lectures to the society while Ramakanta Roy and Kunjabehari Sen lectured in the technology section. Students were expected to take notes from lectures and submit their notes to teachers concerned for scrutiny. Then there would be discussion on the subject in which the students were supposed to take part. They were also encouraged to submit their essays to the Dawn magazine for publication. The technology section had an elementary and a secondary course, which was backed up by workshop activities. In the workshop, all types of mechanical work were taught, along with chemical processes such as soap making and oil making. Modern weaving methods were also taught. The products of the students were sold in a *swadeshi* shop in Barabazar. Technical education was one of the main planks of the swadeshi education offered by the Dawn Society. This was advancement upon the curriculum of the Indian association for the cultivation of science, which was solely concerned with scientific pursuits.

Dawn Society, The (1902-1906) was founded in Calcutta by Satish Chandra Mukherjee, a proponent of national education, in 1902. Satish Chandra had earlier established *Bhagabat Chatuspathi* in 1896. This was dedicated to the study of Indian religion and philosophy primarily and to Indology in general. The objective was to satisfy the quest for national identity. Its classes were held in the Metropolitan Institution (Modern Vidyasagar College) in the evening. At the same time, the famous Dawn Magazine was also launched. Many articles on Indology appeared in its pages till 1902 when it became the mouthpiece of the Dawn society. Satish Chandra Mukherjee was a legendary teacher and a mentor of contemporary young men. Men like Binoy Kumar Sarkar, Radha Kumud Mukherjee, Haran Chandra Chakladar, Rabindranarayan Ghosh, Kishori Mohan Gupta and others flocked around him and became the mainstays of the Dawn Society.

The society was critical of the colonial education imparted by the university of Calcutta which, according to it, was "all-too-literary, all-too-academic, unscientific and un-industrial" in nature.

The Dawn Society wanted to promote education for man-making and nation-building purpose. In its curriculum, therefore, history, geography, economics, and political science were included in the Arts and Sciences & Technology were introduced. Apart from the above mentioned disciples, stalwarts like J.C. Bose, Nilratan Sarkar, Ramendrasundar Trivedi and even Rabindranath were invited to deliver lectures to the society while Ramakanta Roy and Kunjabehari Sen lectured in the technology section.

Students were expected to take notes from lectures and submit their notes to teachers concerned for scrutiny. Then there would be discussion on the subject in which the students were supposed to take part. They were also encouraged to submit their essays to the Dawn magazine for publication. The technology section had an elementary and a secondary course, which was backed up by workshop activities.

In the workshop, all types of mechanical work were taught, along with chemical processes such as soap making and oil making. Modern weaving methods were also taught. The products of the students were sold in a *swadeshi* shop in Barabazar. Technical education was one of the main planks of the swadeshi education offered by the Dawn Society. This was advancement upon the curriculum of the Indian association for the cultivation of science, which was solely concerned with scientific pursuits.

The Dawn Magazine was not only the mouthpiece of the Society, it also reflected the ends and objectives of national education. Its purpose was to restore the heritage of India and to analyse its political, social and economic problems and to suggest remedies for them. A special section of the magazine was devoted to Indian subject, and the motto of the magazine was that it was essential to know one's own country to promote nationalism. To this effect Satish Chandra himself and his select band of disciples wrote incessantly on all subjects concerning India. In deed, *Dawn Magazine* became the mirror of the contemporary Bengali mind and Indian nationalism. The journal ran from 1896 to 1913, over-arching the Dawn society, which merged into the National Council of Education in 1906. [Chittabrata Palit]

Mukherjee, Satish Chandra (1865-1948) nationalist writer, was born in a Brahmin family on 5 June 1865 at Bandipur in Hughli district. His father, Krishnanath Banerjee, worked as a translator at the Calcutta High Court. Satish Chandra's early education began at South Suburban School, Bhowanipore. In 1884 he passed BA from Presidency College, Kolkata on a government scholarship. After completing his MA in English in 1886, he began teaching at Metropolitan Institution, Kolkata. In 1887 he joined Berhampore College. After obtaining the BL degree in 1890, he started practising law at the Calcutta High Court. In 1895 he established an educational institution called Bhagavat Chatuspathi Bijoy Krishna Goswami was his spiritual guru.

Asutosh Mookerji was Satish Chandra's classmate. Satish Chandra maintained a close contact with contemporary personalities such as shibnath shastri, Brajendra Nath seal, Rabindranath Tagore, Bipin Chandra Pal, Aswini Kumar datta, and swami vivekananda by whom he was influenced variously. In 1902 he established the dawn society as an example of self-reliance in education and became its secretary. Dawn Society was a non-political cultural organisation founded in protest against the Report of Indian Universities Commission. Its aims included providing Bengali students with an ideal education, imparting religious and moral lessons to them, extending their intellectual capacities and building their character. Moreover, it also believed in imbuing students with a sense of nationalism and patriotism while imparting practical technical education and developing indigenous industries.

Dawn Society contributed to the introduction of nationalism in education. It arranged a meeting on 5 November 1905 to inaugurate national education. Rabindranath Tagore, Satish Chandra and Hirendranath Dutta delivered speeches at this vast gathering. Satish Chandra called upon students to leave Calcutta University and boycott its examinations.

Satish Chandra established the Council of National Education (NEC) in 1906. Aurobindo Ghosh became principal of the newly founded Bengal National College under the NCE and Satish Chandra became its Caretaker. In 1907 Aurobindo resigned and Satish Chandra was appointed principal. But he also resigned the next year because of ill health.

Satish Chandra also protested against the Carlyle Circular of 10 October 1905 the intention of which was to keep students away from the swadeshi movement. Dawn Society worked for the revitalization of indigenous industries long before the formal beginning of the movement in 1905. The monthly *Dawn* (1897), edited by Satish Chandra, served as the mouthpiece of the Society in awakening and propagating nationalism.

Satish Chandra also contributed to the English magazine *Bandemataram*. The non-cooperation movement (1922) of Gandhi influenced him greatly. When

Mahatma Gandhi was arrested, Satish Chandra fled to Sabarmati and for two months assisted in the management and publication of *Young India*. In 1930 he visited Dr. Rajendra Prasad's Vihar Vidyapith and stayed there for some time. Satish Chandra was a profoundly religious man. At the same time he did not believe in religious superstitions and the caste system and was against provincialism. He died on 18 April 1948

Santiniketan began as an *ashram* in 1863. Maharshi Debendranath Tagore founded it on twenty bighas of land purchased from Bhubanmohan Sinha, landlord of Raipur. The *ashram,* located near Bolpur in the Birbhum district of West Bengal, was intended as a retreat for householders, where they could spend their time in prayer, away from their worldly preoccupations. The Santiniketan Trust, established by the Maharshi in 1888, provided for a guest house, a prayer hall, and a library dedicated to religious literature.

The Swadeshi Movement: The partition of Bengal in 1905 had far reaching repercussion and accelerated the pace of freedom movement in India. The event led to the launch of swadeshi movement and boycott of British goods. It also resulted in the split of the Indian National Congress into two factions, the moderates and the extremists and gave birth to revolutionaries clubs and Muslim League.

The Partition of Bengal: The province of Bengal consisted of Bengal proper, Bihar and Orissa, with a population of 78 million people. In East Bengal, Muslims were in a majority while Hindus predominated in West Bengal as well as in Bihar and Orissa. Way back in 1896, William Ward, an official had prepared a scheme of partition of Bengal for administrative convenience.

But due to financial constraints it was abandoned. The scheme attracted the attention of Viceroy Curzon and he decided to implement it. In February 1904, Curzon toured East Bengal and roped in Nawab Salimullah Khan of Dacca by promising him a loan at nominal interest and the latter succeeded in assembling a huge gathering of Muslims to cheer the Viceroy's plan for a Muslim province. But the Bengali intelligentsia and the Indian nationalists opposed the partition on the ground that it undermined the traditions, history and language of the Bengalis and divide them on the basis of religion. Curzon had admitted during his tour of East Bengal that one object of the partition proposal was to create a Mohammedan province where Islam could be predominate.

The Boycott movement: The new province of East Bengal was inaugurated on 16th October 1905. The leaders of the anti-partition movement made a public declaration that the day of inauguration would be observed as a day of national mourning. A detailed programme was drawn up for the day. Food would not be cooked, except for the sick and invalid; business would be suspended and people would walk barefoot and bathe in the Ganga in the morning to purify themselves. To symbolise the unity among the Bengalis, the programme of tying a red band round the wrists of the people was undertaken. Streets was echoed with the cry 'Vande Mataram' and a national fund for carrying on the agitation was started and in a few hours Rs. 10,000 was collected through subscriptions. Earlier in a public meeting held at Ripon College in Calcutta under the leadership of S.N.Banerjee on 17th July 1905, a resolution asking the people to boycott all British goods till partition was undone had been passed.

On the occasion of a religious festival in August 1905, about 50,000 people took a vow before goddess Kali not to buy foreign articles and not to employ foreigners for jobs for which suitable Indians are available. The boycott movement was not a new thing. Way back in 1849, Gopal Rao Deshmukh, better known as 'Lokahitawadi' of Bombay urged the use of indigenous goods. In 1873, Bholanath Chandra preached the establishment of indigenous Banks, Companies, Corporations, Mills and Factories and denounced the practice of preferring foreign goods to home made manufacturers. Swami Dayananda Saraswati also emphasized on swadeshi. Similarly the Tagore family also lent their full support to the use of swadeshi goods. Rabindranath Tagore started the 'Swadeshi Bhandar' in 1897 and 'Sarala Devi Lakshmi Bhandar' in 1903. During the anti-partition agitation, Swadeshi stores sold homemade goods in retail and student volunteers peddled them. In consonance with the boycott call, contents of the ships arriving with foreign goods were dumped; bags of Liverpool salt were pulled out of boats and thrown into the river. The priests refused to perform religious ceremonies with foreign articles. Those found wearing foreign clothes including Europeans were jeered at. So vehement was the public opinion that nobody would think of buying foreign clothes and those who went in for its cheapness would buy only at night. At an examination hall in Rippon College, students refused to touch answer papers of foreign make and country made sheets had to be substituted. A five-year old granddaughter of S.N.Banerjee returned a pair of shoes sent to her by a relative because they were made abroad. Similarly another girl aged six though suffering from fever refused to take any foreign medicine. If any foreign-made presents were given during marriages they were returned. Guests would refuse to participate in festivities in which foreign salt or sugar was used.

Karnataka and Swadeshi movement: Karnataka enthusiastically responded to the call of swadeshi. On 5th May 1905 a public meeting presided by Gurunatha Rao Patak was held in the Victoria Theatre at Dharwad to protest against the partition of Bengal and to encourage swadeshi industries. The meeting resolved that everyone should vow not to use foreign cloth, except in unavoidable circumstances in order to encourage Indian artisans and trade in Indian goods. To spread the message of swadeshi and boycott, Tilak toured

North Karnataka in 1905-06. Alur Venkata Rao, Sakkari Balachar, Krishna Rao Mudvedkar, Anantha Rao Dabade and others undertook extensive tours and delivered speeches on Swarajya, Swadeshi, Boycott and National Education. Swadeshi industries arose in many places.

Vittal Rao Deshpande of Hebbal started a weaving factory at Kittur. Another factory was built in Badami. Cloths made here were sent even to Bengal. Rama Rao Alagvadi opened a Match factory at Dharwad, while in Laxmeswar a Porcelain factory was established. Factories for manufacturing bangles, pencils and many other articles of common use arose in many places. A Karnataka Industrial Conference met at Dharwad in 1907 to chalk out plans to develop Swadeshi industries in Karnataka. New Banks were established to help these industries. Boycott of British goods: Apart from wide support to swadeshi movement, people of Karnataka wholeheartedly participated in the boycott of British goods. Ranibennur witnessed one of the biggest bonfires of foreign cloth. Textile dealers in Belgaum decided not to import foreign cloth and in Dharwad, grocers decided not to purchase Daboti and Johnson sugar.

In Alnavar it was decided to smoke batti's instead of bidis and anyone found breaking the rule was fined. Hoteliers stopped the sale of tea and people poured kerosene into gutters and instead began to use indigenous oil for lighting. In one instance after it was noticed that a bangle seller had sold foreign bangles saying that it was Indian, the bangle seller was not only abused but also had to forego money. In Belgaum, along with swadeshi movement, prohibition was also advocated and toddy contractors had to incur heavy loss.

For picketing liquor shops in Belgaum nine persons were awarded one-week imprisonment and fined Rs. 680 in June 1908. Though a prominent person of Belgaum offered to pay the fine, the youths refused his help and preferred imprisonment. On 8th August 1908 a public meeting was held in Bagalkot, which was addressed by Jayarao Nargund, Jainapur, Yalagurdrao, Dharwadkar and others. It was proposed to establish a Swadeshi Vyaparottejak Samshtha in Bagalkot. The movement also saw the establishment of National Schools in various parts of Karnataka. Alur Venkata Rao started the Nutana Vidyalaya at Dharwad with arts and crafts also as subjects in the curriculum. Another national school arose at Navalgund by the efforts of Dundopanth Sahasrabuddhe.

In Belgaum Kaka Kalelkar established the Ganesh Vidyalaya, while Jaya Rao Nargund started another at Bagalkot. Similar schools were established at Hanagal, Agadi and other places. The government however saw that these schools close down one by one. In South Kanara district, Ammembala Srinivasa Pai was the moving spirit in the boycott of foreign goods and the spread of swadeshi. Men like K.P.Rao and Panje Mangesha Rao assisted him, while

Kolachalam Venkata Rao and Sabhapathi Mudaliar were the leaders of the freedom movement in Bellary.

The Revolutionary Activities: The youth of Bengal had greatly contributed to the success of the anti-partition movement. They organized meetings, arranged demonstrations, roused enthusiasm, and provided volunteers for Swadeshi-Boycott propaganda and for picketing. Many were fined, expelled, beaten and flogged. But the harsher their treatment the more rebellious became their mood. The restriction on their public activities compelled them to form secret societies to achieve their aims.

Moreover the Englishmen in the past had taunted the Bengalis that they were a race of weaklings, cowardly and lacking in manly virtues. By forming revolutionary clubs called 'Samitis', the Bengali youth proved that they did not lack courage. Newspapers like 'Jugnatara', 'Bhawani Mandir', 'Bande Mataram' and 'Sandhya' were launched to preach the cult of revolutionary violence. Some youths of Karnataka like Dr.Handoor, Baburao Gani and Bheema Rao Bevoor kept up a close correspondence with the revolutionaries of Bengal.

Seeds of Separatism sown: Inspired by Muslim revolutionary activities in Egypt, Iran and Turkey, Abul Kalam Azad came into contact with Shyamsunder Chakravarthi of the Bande Mataram, met Aurobindo and joined one of the revolutionary bodies. He not only dissipated the anti-Muslim suspicious of the revolutionaries but helped in extending their activities outside Bengal and Bihar. The above development made Lawrence, the private secretary to Curzon and journalist like Valentine Chirol and Sidney Low to warn the then Viceroy Minto of the danger of the Hindu-Muslim accord. Theodore Morrison, the former principal of the Aligarh College warned the government against the possibility of Muslim sympathies going over to the Congress party. Colonel Dunlop Smith, the Private Secretary to Viceroy Minto wrote to William Archbold the then principal of Aligarh College that the Viceroy would be happy to receive a Muslim deputation.

The principal asked Nawab Mohsinul Mulk, the secretary of the college to act quickly and to press for introducing the system of nomination or granting representation on religious lines. On 1st October 1906 a deputation led by Aga Khan met Viceroy Minto at Shimla and demanded that seats in the Central Legislative Assembly be reserved for the Muslim community not only on the basis of their population but on the basis of their political importance and their services in the defence of the Empire. Minto readily accepted the demand for according them separate electorates. After their successful deputation, the Muslim leaders mooted the idea of forming an association to look exclusively after the interests of the Muslim community. On 30th December 1906 the All

India Muslim League was formed to promote the political and other rights of Indian Muslims and to promote among Indian Muslims the feeling of loyalty towards the British government.

The true political ideas of the Muslim League became apparent from Nawab Waqar-ul-Mulk's speech delivered at Aligarh. He said "God forbid, if the British rule disappears from India, Hindus will lord over it and there will be constant danger to our life, property and honour. The only way for the Muslims to escape this danger is to help in the continuance of the British rule. If the Muslims are heartily with the British, then that rule is bound to endure. Let the Muslims consider themselves as a British army ready to shed blood and sacrifice their lives for the British Crown". The League achieved its first success when the British government introduced separate electorates for Muslims in the 1909 Act.

6

Rai and Political Situation

THE RIGHT PATH FOR THE GOVERNMENT

But there is no denial that this may lead to further and greater disorders if nothing is done to remove the discontent that is at the bottom of it and to sooth the angered, outraged feelings of the people. Repressive measures might cow down the people for a time, but that they are bound to fail in the end, if it is intended to crush the spirit of the people thereby, is certain so long as people believe that their interests and those of the Government clash.

And so long as these two are in conflict, so long the popular feeling is sure to burst out from time to time do what you may to crush or kill it by force. The thing is new just now. After over 50 years of peaceful Govern ment, when the people have quite forgotten the troubles of a disordered state of society, and after they have taken to easy-going modes of life, it shocks them to hear of the arrests such as have taken place in Rawalpindi. It may unnerve them for the time and the political movement in the Punjab may be put down for some time to come. But as soon as the people recover their stunned senses and begin to think how insignificant are individual interests in the struggle for national rights, their sympa thies for the first victims will change into homage for the cause and for those who were the first to suffer for the cause. Fear will give way to the desire for martyr dom and panic will disappear.

This process will be facilitated and dishastened If these arrests become too common, as they are likely to be, in the present state of panic in official circles, but that these arrests will seal the fate of the national movement I decline to believe. The efforts of the Government at repression are only natural, the effect of these measures on the public mind will show how much real political life there is in the country and how far it can be relied on. It will give a fresh starting point to those who desire to devote their lines to this cause. National evolution is bound to proceed on the lines of repulses, defeats, struggles, None need despair. True wisdom is well as the spirit of resignation to the things as they come, therefrom, modifying ways and means in accordance therewith, and then proceeding steadily and surely. In accordance with the resolution passed at the last session of the Congress laying down certain rules of con stitution it is necessary that the Punjab Congressemen should proceed to form a Provincial Congress Committee at once. The questions deserving consideration in con inection therewith may be roughly stated as below : —

(1) Whether the Indian Association of Lahore should be converted into a Provincial Congress Com mittee for the Punjab, with such modifications in its constitution as maybe found necessary or desirable or whe ther a separate Provincial Committee be organised which shall include the members or representatives from District Associations, and such other persons from Districts where the latter have not been organised as yet, who have ever attended a meeting of the Congress as.delegates. This may not necessarily mean the exclusion of persons who may be otherwise qualified and also will ing to become members.

(2) What should be the minimum subscription qualification (a) for ordinary members and (6) for mem bers of the Executive Committee. I would suggest that all such persons as are prepared to pay Re. 1 per month for political work in the Punjab (including Re. 0-8-0 per month charged by the District Association) should be accepted as ordinary members of Committee. This will secure per member to the Provincial Committee and enable the latter to maintain an Office. The number of the Execu tive Committee should not be very large although it should be sufficiently large to allow of proper representa tion being given to the District Associations. One way of securing an effective committee is to fix a fairly high subscription qualification for the membership, say 5 rupees a month, with power to make a few exceptions in favour of deserving-men the total strength of the latter not to exceed 20 per cent of the former. I am very strongly of opinion that there is no use of talking of the want of political activity in the Punjab and throwing the odium of it on certain individuals unless there are at least some 20 people in the Province who are prepared to give time and money to this work.

(3) What to do of the Bradlaugh Hall. I am of opinion that such of the members of the Provincial Congress Committee as have paid Rs. 100 or are now prepared to pay Rs. 100 towards the construction of the Hall should form themselves into a society to rebuild and maintain the Hall. I understand that was the origi nal intention of those who started the movement for a permanent public Hall in Lahore. Before I conclude 1 may add that these are only suggestions for considera tion and discussion; personally I will accept any rules which are after discussion,

agreed to by the majority. I do not know what is the idea about the next meet ing of the Punjab Provincial Conference. If it is likely to meet during the first six months of the year, the mat ter may be finally settled there. If otherwise, a special meeting of delegates of the Indian Association of the several District Associations that have been formed or may be formed by that time, may be convened to settle this matter. The Punjab has all along been very keen about the constitution of the Congress. Now that a ten tative constitution has been obtained it is absolutely necessary for the good name of the Province that we should show our readiness to act up to it and to profit by the same. I propose that the matter may be taken up for early discussion by the Indian Association of Lahore, and the District Associations that have been formed Subject to considerations of health and engagements already made. I am prepared to go to mufassil stations for organising District Associations whenever invited to do so by men who, in my opinion, are likely to do the thing successfully.

DESH BHAKTI

Lala Lajpat Rai delivered a most impressive and eloquent lecture in Anaj Mandi,-Anoia, before a large audience composed of men of all callings and professions in the course of which he said that it is but natural for every man to possess feelings of love; but love is of two kinds, selfish, having the achievement of immediate gain in view, and unselfish — which impels us on to do works of public utility with more or less depending on the extent of the feelings of unselfishness selfless motives. Selfish love cannot however, make our minds peaceful or calm the inner cravings of man for blissfulness; for the attainment of this end we must all needs do some selfless work. No country can prosper until her sons and daughters are imbued with a genuine sense of unselfish devotion towards her and ready to subordinate their personal interests for country's good.

The Japanese have recently shown to what lofty heights patriotic fervour can rise. A mother's stabbing herself in order to free her son from the burden of her maintenance so that he may go to war and die for her beloved country and the readiness of an overwhelmingly large number of sailors to drown themselves with ships in front of Port Arthur are instances which nothing short of a deep love for country's honor — much less lust for gold or glorification of vain self — can prompt Even in European countries, with their long legend of national patriotism, such examples of sublime devotion are rare. A degenerate country, like ours, badly needs for her service such selfless workers as neither wealth nor power could buy. We had a large number of them in our glorious past when our country's towering moral and physical "capabilities had elevated it to the lofty pinnacle of prosperity and happiness.

Not long ago all our requirements were met with by articles of clean manufacture. Woe, however, to our present situation of helpless dependence on foreigners, who drain away most part of the money earned by us with the sweat of our brow.

And this drain is responsible for the oft-recurring famines and pestilence, which mainly victimise the poor owing to the unhealthy state of their habitations and their inability to get sufficient and wholesome food. Lord Curzon's government estimated that the Indian's average income then was Rs, 30 per annum or 2-8 a month.

When this is the average there must be many who live on Rs. 1-8 or, even, Re. 1 a month. It is a mystery how a man can even parsimoniously feed and clothe himself for a month on this paltry income unless he half starves. As a matter of fact there are seven crores of men who get only one meal in a day and there are many more who live on roots and barks of trees. About forty to fifty thousand are devoured by plague and other diseases very week. Any country having such a horrible and heart-rending tale of sorrow and devastation can never have a hopeful future. Europeans are living comfortably. The reason is that they are true to their country, following Swadeshi in its true essence. Plague and pestilence do not touch them because they live in commodious, well-ventilated houses in the healthiest parts of the towns.

They carry most of our corn to their country — even when our own men are starving for want of food and famines are fiercely raging in the land — for maintaining an adequate supply of staple food for their own countrymen. Our raw products find their way to England in order to develop her trade in manufactured articles, which are brought back and sold in India at enormous profits. They do not scruple to provide lucrative employments for their own men in this con try and are always ready to do everything that is calculated to promote their people's welfare. This genuine regard for providing for the good of their whole community is the secret of their prosperity and success all round.

Our countrymen sadly lack in that spirit of patriotism that characterises the citizens of every prosperous country in the world and consequently there is no end to our troubles. Nothing short of true desk which consists in sacrificing the hankering after pelf and power in favour of the unremunerative yet — important and divine — task of working for the welfare of our countrymen, — can save us from the death and destruction that is staring us in the face. Genuine and selfless devotion (Bhakti) for our death ought to be the dharma, the noble mission of life, of every one of us and in the service of our country we should spare neither money nor life.

SGHOLARSRIPS FOR POLITICAL TRAINING

Lala Lajpat Rai's letter

TO

The Editor of Punjabee.

Sir, — You are aware that in 1905 when I was deputed to go to England as a delegate from Punjab, Rs. 3000 were collected by public subscription towards the expenses of my trip. The expenses actually incurred having by far exceeded that amount, I, on my return, promised to repay the said amount by giving half of it in aid of the Foreign Education Fund of the D. A. V. College and by spending the other half in furtherance of the cause of political education in this province. The 1st mentioned promise has already been made good. The other remains yet to be fulfiled though I have never lost sight of the same and have been thinking of the best way to use it.

At one time I proposed to organise a Council consisting of a limited number of members paying Rs. 50 as admission fee and Rd. 100 as annual subscription to start political work in this province on active educational lines. I intended to make over the amount to that council.

The scheme was printed and circulated amongst a limited number of friends. It met with a fair amount of response in so far that over 15 gentlemen promised to join it on those terms. The idea was to have an office and a Library at Lahore in connection with the council.

After a great deal of cogitation over the matter I have now decided to give up the idea of a separate political council (for the present at least) and resolved to utilise the money in my hands in providing for a training to a few Punjabi youths in methods of political work. I have so far decided to offer two scholarships of the value of Rs 50 per mensem each, to two masters of Arts or B.A. LL.B.'s of the Punjab University who promise to devote one year to the exclusive study of politics and political methods. It may be a presumption on my part to assume that I can guide even a novice in political studies but as at present advised I see no better course open to me. The terms of these scholarships are: —

(1) The scholarship shall run for a year.

(2) The candidate selected shall have to live at Lahore or travel to parts of India, at my discretion, its travelling expenses being borne by me.

(3) He shall not aim at a career in Government service and shall give a declaration to that effect.

(4) He shall prepare for no examination during the time he gets the scholarship.

(5) These scholarships are open to all Indians irrespective of caste, creed or colour.

(6) The scholarship will be held during good behaviour and may be discontinued on proof of misconduct or for want of diligence in studies.

(7) In case of qualified M. A/s or B. A., L. L. B.'s not coming forward to take the scholarships one of these may be given to a distinguished B. A., who has read up to the M. A. Standard, in English, History or Philosophy, or has passed the Intermediate in Law Examination of the Punjab University, and the other may be split into two or three, to be given to candidates of lesser qualifications.

(8) Applications shall be considered and elections made by a committee consisting of the following members of the Indian Association, Lahore: —

(a) The undersigned. (Lala Laiput Rai).

(b) Lala Shadi Lai, m. a., Bar-at-Law, Lahore.

(c) Lala Duni Chand, Bar-at-Law, Secretary, Indian Association, Lahore.

(d) Lala Mulkraj Bhalla.

(e) Sardar Gurcharan Singh, b.a., Bar-at-Law, Lahore

(9) Condition (6) shall not be enforced unless a majority of the above mentioned committee agree to do so.

(10) Rs. 1,500 will be deposited in the Punjab Cooperative Bank and the scholarships shall be payable on bills signed by the undersigned(Lala Lajput Rai).

(11) Applications shall be received up to the 15th of April and decision arrived at publications should be addressed to the undersigned.

THE PUNABEE

The following is the full text of Lala Lajpat Rai speech delivered at the Anniversary of the Arya Samaj in November 1905, as published in the PaiaaAhhhar from which the Wafadar made certain extracts. Paisa Akhhar, December 7, 1905 (page 6), We publish below the lecture delivered by Lala Lajpat Rai Sahib, Pleader, and renowned patriot, on the 26th November on the occasion of the anniversary of the Arya Samaj, Lahore, (College party) when a very large number of enthusiastic hearers was present: — "Brethren, — Yon have come here as our guests and I am ashamed to find that we are unable to show the hospitality (of providing you sufficient accommodation here.)

This poverty of ours is an index of the poverty of our country. However, there is no occasion for anyone to complain. We have been doing whatever is in our power, but there can be no help for that which is beyond our means, and we beg to be excused for it. This morning I had begun by saying, that while I was in Europe I tried to find out a solution of the question. What is the secret of the progress of Europe? What are the causes which have raised the sun of prosperity of Europe to its zenith? How is it that, although the Europeans are few in number, yet they reign supreme in the whole world and nobody dare disobey their command? From the day on which I set my foot on European soil I began to ponder over this question.

The East is that he who has his eyes open can clearly see through such things as these. As soon as you set your foot on European soil, you begin to see things working in a way which itself suggests the solution of the question. He, who has his eyes open, can see that they (the Europeans) are more intelligent than ourselves. He sees that in their systems of education, in their arts and industries, and in their commerce there exists organization (i.e., the quality of doing a thing systematically and continuously). Every man, then, is fond of organization, and nobody dare interfere with the law of organization. You find this law working not only in the navies, the armies and other Departments of Western Governments, but you find it also in their hands.

The home of a European is typical of the marvelous system of organization that prevails in West, and from their very childhood they grow under its influence. There is not a single man who is not under (does not belong to) some sort of organization. In short, it is organization which rules supreme in Europe. But, gentlemen, the one thing that forms the backbone of organization is education. If any one wishes to see (an illustration) of the truth that knowledge is power and that even the elements, i.e., air, firewater and the oceans all recognise the Sway of man, let him go and see the ships, the machinery of the factories of Europe.

There he will see how the stupendous power of nature has been enslaved to provide for the comforts of man. But the secret of all this power lies in the system of education which obtains there. All the nations of Europe are not equally great. Some of these are of ordinary position, while others are highly advanced and powerful by virtue of the vastness of their empires and the influence they exercise over the world. The power and influence of the various nations of Europe depends upon their respective systems of education. The people of Switzerland do not busy themselves with taking away the liberty of any other nation. The system of education that obtains there (in Europe) develops the intelligent and makes man active and bold.

In Europe, the prevalent notion about education is that it should make a man fit to meet his personal and national requirements, that, while, on the one hand, it should develop private virtue in him, it should, on the other, help in making him a true and honest lover of his country. The system that is followed there is such that it makes man fit and well equipped for all those requirements. It is necessary that a man be influenced by his surroundings. No one has the power to avoid the influence of his environments. Even plants and trees that grow in the jungle develop by absorbing the elements that are around them. Nothing in nature is free from the effect of the things that are about it, and development of each individual depends to a great extent upon his circumstances.

European children are highly fortunate in that they are born of civilized parents, and, as such, are influenced, to a great degree, by that civilization. As soon as a child attains the school-going age, he, in a way, becomes free from the protection of his parents, and another power with vast and unbounded resources steps in to take upon itself the responsibility of bringing up the child. This power is the Government of the country. In cases, where position to satisfactorily discharge the duty of giving a proper education to their children, the Government takes this task upon itself, the fulfilment of which it considers the very object of its existence.

The Government there represents the people; it is the head of the nation and is composed of delegates chosen by the people. The state is responsible for the prosperity and protection of the nation. The Government takes upon itself the duty of seeing that no child grows up in ignorance and, therefore, legislates that education up to a certain age is compulsory for all children, whether male or female. In the education of their children, parents are relieved of the burden of providing them with books, pen, ink and fees. The children are not required to take these things with them to school, but they are supplied to them in school. The school authorities supply these things free of charge.

Now they have gone a step further, in as much as poor students are supplied with good food on behalf of the school. Seeing that poor children are placed at a disadvantage compared to the children of the rich, and that mental work tells upon the physique of the former and consequently they cannot derive the fullest benefit from their education, it has been decided that those who cannot afford to get substantial food from their parents, are to be provided with it at the cost of the State. When this question came up for consideration before the Governments of the various self-governing countries of Europe, the French Government was the first to solve the difficulty and it laid down that the State should provide proper nourishment for the children whose parents cannot afford it. In England also the London County Council has introduced the same system in schools under its charge. There girls are taught cookery handicrafts, needlework and singing as part of the educational curriculum.

In connection with cookery they are taught Chemistry, and are told the ingredients and properties of various such details as the quantity of oxygen and nitrogen that go to make up a thing. In one room they receive theoretical instruction on the subject, in another arrangements are made for practical demonstration, girls cook food with their own hands. The food us prepared is given to those boys and girls who cannot themselves provide with it.

This would be sufficient to show how keenly the Europeans feel and realise the importance of education, here (in India) wish to provide the cheapest form of education for our children, regardless of the fact whether influence exercised by the institution is for good or evil. And with all this we (Indians) want to imitate id rival those (the Europeans) who are the rulers of e world. In Europe no problem is considered of such paramount importance as the educational one. In India e function of a teacher ends when the school time is, the relation of teacher and the taught also ending with it. But in very European country a large class of eat thinkers is always busy in devising means for improving and perfecting the educational system of the nation. Some of the best intellects of the country are lid high salaries in order that they might go and study le educational system of every country and compare it with their own with a view to find out the defects of the latter and devise means for their removal.

The results of such investigations are published in reports for the information of the people, they are discussed in public and conclusions are drawn therefrom. A large class (of experts) is always busy in thinking over educational matters and seeing that the country does not lag behind in any department of national advancement. Here (in India) it is customary for the teacher to resort to the use of the cane as soon as the boy begins his alphabet. But in Europe the case is entirely different; there the children are given oral instruction for 2 or 3 years when they are instructed in drawing figures and entertaining exercises. They are taught the methods of bringing their hands and feet into play, such as walking, running, &c.

After this, they are taught the alphabet. Drawing (i, e., sketches and figures), singing, physical exercise are considered the essential points of elementary education. Boys brought up in these schools are never morose. No power can keep them back from the service to their country, the sense of and responsibility towards the nation. Neither can anything develop in them feelings of hatred towards their own nation. Through the teaching of music patriotism and love of the nation are impressed upon the mind of the children. They are taught colour painting as soon as they learn the elements of drawing, needle-work and cookery. The minds of the pupils are not unnecessarily burdened with useless information.

They are told the names, colours and numbers of flower, which is intended to teach them the distinction of colours, their mean and also Arithmetic. The teacher places various things upon the table and enquires from the puplis their names, colours and number. In Europe, children have not to read at home after school hours. We think, and it is no doubt true, that the minds of the children, here, are stinted in growth under unnecessary burden. In Europe the number of subjects taught in primary schools is not less than what it is here, but (the method of teaching there is such) that it does not burden the minds of the student. The result is that after an instruction of 5 or 7 years, the child can use his hands, feet and brain to good advantage and he is in a position to adopt any profession he likes. The grounding in education that he has received stands him in good stead everywhere.

On the other hand, we, too, receive theoretical education in Geometry, but in practice we are unable to draw a straight line correctly. An Englishman, who begins his education withdrawing, can draw good pictures with the least effort. In Europe, in one place, a teacher lectures theoretically (say) upon the art of making a table and the things required for it, and in another place the children are afforded the opportunity of translating theory into practice by direct manipulation. After receiving this sort of elementary education up to the 14th year, they have to decide how they are to live in the world. The arrangements for this purpose are wonderful indeed, some boys study for 5 hours and spend the rest of their time in earning their livelihood. Facilities for high education are provided for those who wish to earn in the day and study at night; even the best equipped educational institution in India does not possess the aparatas, which every night school of that London County Council possesses.

There (in England) absence of pecuniary support does not invariably mean the loss of higher education. Here, on the contrary, those who are intelligent but poor have, after a time, to give up their education and find out means for their livelihood, thus hampering their advancement in life. This involves individual as well as national loss, and the nation is deprived of the valuable services which he would have rendered to the nation by occupying, in his after life, an eminent position. In Europe steps have been taken to avert this national and individual loss. The education they receive is, moreover, intended to make the recipients honest, high-minded, religious and patriotic and capable of earning their livelihood by honourable and industrious means.

Some of the officials, here, frequently remark that Indians do not acquire education for its own sake, but as a means of earning livelihood; but if such a remark were made in Europe, people would ask in amazement, what on earth is the object of education, if it is not to make one better able to earn a living? A great struggle for supremacy is going on in Europe, every nation is trying to march ahead of the rest. Every nation fears that if her educational system becomes defective and consequently its members are superseded by others in sending the cheapest and the best things to the markets of the world, she will lose her position in the field of commerce.

The chief object of their education is to keep their people abreast of the others in Commerce and Industry. The competition of Germany and America is at present threatening to weaken the commercial ascendancy of England. It is certain that the educational system of Germany is comparatively much superior (to that of any other country in Europe) but after careful investigation great changes have been introduced into the educational system of England within the last 5 or 6 years. Now every school in England possesses a workshop for practical training The English are seriously thinking that they may not be beaten by the Germans in the race of commerce. Paisa Akbar, I8th December, 1905, (page 6) The object of educating a child is that in addition to being useful to himself and to the society, he should develop partiotic ideas, inferior to those of no other nation. Europeans in general and the English in particular are devoted admirers of Liberty.

They cannot tolerate a single word directed against it. They hate the word Ruler. Although they have got their own King and Parliament yet they do not look upon them as more than advisers, helpers and leaders in national advancement. A recently published book," Struggle Against the Monarchy," forms a part of the scheme of studies for young boys, which is intended to show that the rights of privilege which the English enjoy have been obtained after manifold sacrifices. It has been stated above, music is an essential part of their elementary training. Boys :and girls assemble in the halls of the schools to sing such songs as to impress upon their minds the importance of the fact that the child is the custodian of national interest Here in India physical training is considered a thing of minor importance, there it is a part of the instruction.

The bodily organs are developed by means of physical exercises in such a way that in times of emergency they may be able to be put to the best use in the service of the State. Europeans regard this world as a paradise (i.e., a place worth living in), being the finest specimen of the workmanship of the Almighty Creator. They want to live in this world seeing that it is so fine, and they think it their duty to prolong their lives as far as they can, no matter how. We also daily pray for a life of hundred years, but we regard the world as a place of misery, hence we can achieve little. Unless we look upon this world as a place of bliss we can never be prepared to make any sacrifices for the attainment of happiness.

So long as we do not consider the world as the abode of eternal happiness, our nation can make no progress. Europeans impress upon the minds of their children that the world is vast and is full of happiness, hence they teach them to be prepared for all sorts of struggles that they shall have to undergo in their onward march. They point to the vast world before them and direct them to go and achieve honours for themselves and for their nation. In Europe no mother cares what her son will do in his life. They love their children (as well as we) but they themselves realise and make their sons realise that just as this world is infinite so their courage should be vast and boundless. It is our duty, therefore, to absorb this spirit from Europe. Besides this, there they have established schools for imparting technical education.

Our rulers here are showing signs o€ impatience at the establishment of four or five Universities and the number of boys educated therein, but in the West there exists a University in every big town, and still the Government there are not impatient at all and are not busy devising means for reducing the numbers of students. On the contrary, their chief anxiety is to improve and perfect their educational systems and to remove whatever defects exist therein.

The Universities there are authorised to impart education in all departments of learning and confer degrees in Banking, Commerce and the various branches of industrial and technical education. The question for us is how can we do anything for ourselves (i.e. can we help ourselves in any way)? If you really wish that your industries may improve and you be not dependent for your necessaries upon foreign countries, then you should prepare your youngmen for (the task.)

It is fortunate that there are a number of schools here, but they are not sufficiently efficient for the purpose. It is necessary for us to send our youngmen to foreign countries. The men of means among you should send their children to other countries for receiving industrial training.

Instead of leaving large sums of money and large quantity of gold for your children at the time of death, it is better that you should give them education of the kind which might enable them to earn their living wherever they may happen to be. The vast world is before you. If there are not sufficient manufactories in India to provide (appointments) for those who return after a technical course in foreign countries, then why not go and earn a living in (the factories of) other countries? In America Arabs, Japanese, Chinese and Austrians labour during the day and receive education at night.

Anxious to calculate what work they shall have to do on return to their own country. He who knows an art need not be anxious about the capital to work his schemes with. Indians who go outside think that on their return others should start factories for them. But a trained man should not complain on that score.

When I think of the day when there will be colonies of Indians in all parts of the world who will not only pray for India and the Indians, but at times of need render them assistance I feel immense pleasure. If there be settled in other countries 500 Indians trained in any art, they can at any particular time fully meet at a minute's notice all our requirements with respect to particular art. If the Indians spread themselves into the whole world and learn various arts and industries then what is the thing which they will not be able to achieve? (For instance) what an important thing ship building is for all nations? Now if there be Indians who have learnt the art of ship-building in the great-making factories of the world, they can be helpful to India, to a great extent, in meeting her nautical requirements.

A number of factories exist in the Punjab, but they are not showing satisfactory progress. (The reason is) that those who work these factories do not posses sufficient skill and efficiency for the purpose. If the proprietors of these factories combine and send a number of young men to other countries for industrial training, on condition of the latter working in these factories on their return then both the factories and the student will be benefited.

Such young men should not be married persons. If they do not object to labour, then nothing can stand in the way of receiving necessary training. In America even an unskilled labourer who has not received any Special training in any particular art or industry, gets at least | 1-50 or Rs. 4-8 as daily wages. If a number of youngmen gird up their loins to receive technical education in other countries and support themselves thereby labour and if there be an organisation formed here to find passage money and preliminary expenses for them and to render them other assistance whenever they are ill or out of appointment, a great deal can be done in this direction. The test of our progress, our advancement, our prosperity, aye, our very existence, is education, Twenty years ago the Arya Samaj put forward Swadeshi and National education as the two tests of advancement in the National struggle, you find Bengal demonstrating practically that the programme which the Arya Samaj adopted in this respect was the right one.

The scheme of the Dayanand College, which was framed, after long and careful consideration of the needs of the nation, and taking into account the direction in which events were marching in India (has been shown) to be correct. The ideal of education put forward by the founders of the Dayanand College is the same which Europe has now adopted Japan says that we cannot live so long as we do not appeal to our souls, so long as we do not keep in view our past greatness and do not draw the attention of the people to the grandeur of our ancient literature and civilisation. I do not wish to follow blindly ancient civilisation.

I have pondered over the question and I have come to the conclusion that the ancient civilization was prior to the modern civilisation of Europe and if I were asked to express my opinion (about the two) I would unhesitatingly give it in favour of the former. But, my friends, it is not in our power to save ourselves from the influence of modern Western civilisation. Western civilisation is a gigantic force and we cannot protect ourselves from its advancing march.

We can struggle against this civilization by modern weapons alone. Ancient weapons cannot check its progress in the least. It is absolutely essential that we should brave it with Western methods and Western means. We are only a portion of the world, we do not live beyond the globe, (and) as such cannot live without taking into account the forces that are working in the world. It is, therefore, only meet and proper for us that, while saving ourselves from the vices that prevail in the West, we should adopt Western virtues. In short, in this struggle with Western civilization we can hardly make any progress without adopting the means and methods that are adopted in the West.

The education of females depends upon the education of males. A nation can never be great until its mothers are great also. Our country does not now produce noble yeomen like the mothers of Jaimal, Fatta, and other Rajputs. In these days, we do not suck the same sort of nourishing and invigorating milk from the breasts of our mothers as our ancestors did from theirs. The path of progress is straight, but so long as our country does not possess high-souled and patriotic mothers no advancement can be made. What can the sons of those mothers who do not allow their children to attend it. The four walls of their houses do, as compared with the sons of those high-minded ladies who are not afraid even of the roarings of the oceans? In Europe, women possess both virtU3s and vices; (but) so is the case here. If we wish to make any progress we should try to get rid of the vices and retain the virtues (that are in them) and make the greatness of women the test of our national advancement. Come I Let us all try and make the Dayanand AngloVedic School a model for all other schools. Let this school possess well-equipped apparatus, and well paid teachers. Let us all come and help the cause of the Dayanand Collge because it is the custodian of our honour. This institution is the centre of all our national activities for (educational) advancement. It is the life and soul of our existence as a nation. The Dayanand College is also the head and heart of the Punjab. If the head and heart get weak or palsied how can the body be expected to exist for any length of time? This College is your own property. It can satisfy all your requirements. Others have no hand in its conduct and cannot interfere with it in any way.

I was extremely pleased to learn in England that the number of new admissions in the College this year has been larger than it was last year. The students have in this way given a practical reply to those who are bent upon ruining the College. The (students) have thus shown that the latter cannot succeed in this matter.

If national progress is proceeding on the right line nobody has the power to stop its advance. We value greatly University degrees, and we all are helping our young men to obtain these degrees. But if instructions are placed in your way, in qualifying yourselves for those degrees then you may give out this craving for these degrees.

The Dayanand AngloVedic College is a national institution. If it is a question between University degrees and national honour, you should give up the former for the latter, I wish that the world be filled with young students for the Punjab. There is no other Province in India which can beat the Punjab in determination and intelligence.

Those who possess these qualities (determination and intelligence) will prosper everywhere. Young men I step forward, spread over France, Germany,.Japan and Canada, you will then see how the powers of the material world quake before you. Those who now despise us and trample us under their feet will then respect us. The wide world is before you, the Aryan blood runs in your veins. None can stop your progress.

You are the descendents of persons who imparted knowledge to the whole world. (Have you fallen so low now that you are unfit even to learn at the feet of others ? Those among us, who marry their children at an early age and thus stun their development by putting a heavy load (of family life) round their necks, ruin their children entirely. Keep your children free (from these trammels) and let Aryan young men soar upon their wings, (i.e., grow to the full height of their manhood.) Do not cut off their wings and like featherless birds, cause them to be trampled under feet by others.

Gentlemen May I appeal to you in the name of nationality? Alas, where is nationality ? This congress of sects holding different views cannot but be altogether wanting in the sentiment. Kin have become our enemies, while others (non-Hindus) are bur friends. Our own (kith and kin) are despised by this, while others are worshipped ! Would that in spite of internecine quarrels we could show a united front to the outer (non-Hindu) world I We shall realize the true meaning of nationality when in the name of nationality' we shall become one to face the antagonist. We have entirely lost, the virtue of national self-respect.

The nation gave birth to Rama Bai, and Rama Bai has been declaring in America that no girl of 13 or 14 years of age can boast of her chastity in India I But are there not many even in this assembly who are warm admirers of the same Rama Bai ? Had we possessed any sense of national honour, would it be possible for us to be crushed under the heels of others or to be exposed to such calumnies? How can national honour be said to exist where 70 millions of the nation's children are found starving and where girls are made over to outsiders (Christian Missionaries and Mahomedans) to save them from starvation.

Ye youth of the Panjabee ! There is one thing alone in the name of which I can appeal to you, and, that is that during the last twenty years [referring to the foundation of the D. A. V. College in 1886] you have shown signs of life [by contributing to its success], and I appeal to you in the name of that very life I

Come, let us spurn away all worldly desires and stick to our word. We should not leave undone what we have once taken in hand. A wave of national advancement (in education) has arisen in another province [referring to the Bengal association for the Advancement of formal Education.] There money is pouring in, young men are coming forward. Youngmen, your blood is warm.

The national tree requires your life blood for its watering. Heaven has written in letters of blood the history of the intellectual advancement of a nation, i.e., it has been ordained that a country can advance intellectually only if its members practise the virtue of self-sacrifice. Your sacrifices will leave their mark in the history of the world. Concrete is required to strengthen the foundations of a building. Let us throw ourselves like concrete into the foundations of the national edifice.

Let us forget ourselves in the interests of national progress. Ye student of the Punjab I students have written the history of the world in letters of gold. Old men can never accomplish what young men can do. Come, let us crown our national institutions with the spires of the edifices of our sacrifices, so that a time may come when we may also take our place among the nations of the world. If the young gird up their loins, our existence is insured and no body can destroy us.

CAUSES IN THE PUNJAB

Some people think that the situation in the Punjab has become very serious. The panic in official circles resulting in the arrest of 5 respectable citizens of Rawal pindi no doubt justifies that view. In my opinion, how ever, this panic has beenjartificially created by the Secret Police and the Government has simply played into the hands of its own agents. It is silly to reproach this or that man for having brought about this state of things to suggest that any one or two or three men in this pro vince possess the power or influence to bring about this state of things is both stupid and absurd. It may be highly flattering to his vanity and in a sense compli mentary also, but it cannot stand the test of close examination on the basis of actual facts. Discontent, no doubt, there is and a great deal of it. But this dis content has been brought about by Anglo-Indians them-' selves, and the causes of these may be thus summarised in chronological order.

(a) The prosecution of the Punjahee, coupled with the refusal of the Government to take similar action against the C. and M. Gazette.

(b) The Colonization Bill.

(c) The Land Alienation Act Amendment Bill.

(d) The increase of Canal rates on the Bari-Doab canal.

(e) The abnormal increase of Land Revenue in the Rawalpindi District.

(f) The appalling mortality from plague which has made the people sullen and labour scarce, and raised the wages abnormally.

Now the first 6 causes are directly attributable to Anglo-Indians. The last is a visitation of God. The first two might perhaps have been innocuous but for the four following. Joined however, they have increased the volume of discontent enormously. The sixth has played the most important part. The silent economic revolution caused by the same has acted terribly on the minds of men belonging to the lower strata of Government ser vants, and has very naturally brought about strikes such as would have been incredible a few years before. Under the circumstances can the Government honestly and conscientiously acquit its own officers of want of fore sight and statesmanship in insisting on unpopular mea sures and passing them in the teeth of universal opposi tion, of disregarding the economic changes, and failing to recognise the claims of classes of Government servants to an increase in their salaries improvement crease in the wages of private labour done in time with consideration, all discontent would have been quieted.

AGITATORS RESPONSIBLE AND IRRESPONSIBLE

Are the agitators to be blamed for having pointed out the Government's mistakes and identified themselves with popular grievances ? What have they done ? They have enlisted the sympathies of the masses by standing for their grievances and agitating for the removal of the same. The Government had from time to time reproach ed them for standing alone, aloof from the masses and as, therefore, having no justification to speak in their name. Here was an opportunity for them to remove this re proach. Can any one honestly say that they have done wrong in utilising this opportunity ? Should they have stood aloof from the people and refused to take up their cause and articulate the same ? Had they done so they would have been unworthy of their education and guilty of treason to their own people.

Why should they then be blamed for having espoused the popular cause in a year before they were incomprehensible to the misses. The masses did not and could not ht expected to follow them in their cry for Self-Government. As for the demand for an increased employments of Indians in higher offices under Government, the people were not quite certain if that would immediately help them very much. They said that it made no difference in their lot whether they were governed by a Mister or a Lala or a Maulvi. The recent legislation, however, made them think differently.

They found that the services rendered by them to the empire in the past had nothing and could not support that Government treating them very badly up the class legislation indulged in by Government, so defiantly in the proud consciousness of their unlimited strength has affected class after class iintil there was hardly any class of population left which could honestly display any enthusiasm for the Govern ment. We know that there is a class of Government hangers-on — their contractors, news vendors, title hunters, &c., whose leaders are always enthusiastic for the Government as it pays them so well to do so. But even they cannot honestly lay their hand on their hearts and say that they had no hand in the agitation over the Colonization Bill and the canal water rates resolution.

The difference is this, that they acted behind the purdah, keeping appearances all right, while others acted boldly and openly. These unpopular measures gave an opportunity to some young talkers who utilised it to their heart's content. Their fearless speeches and their readiness to suffer for their convictions went straight to the people's hearts and attracted thousands to their meeting places. Now it is silly to assume that they had any responsible people at their back, for the simple reason that no thoughtful or responsible man could possibly bring himself to believe that the country was at all ready for a political cataclysm. The cry in the Punjab has always been for organised work.

No organisation could be started or perfected in the state in which the Province has been for the last nine months. The tree of organisation requires a cool atmosphere and undisturbed soil to take root and fructify. People have not rushed into print or in the public meet wgs to denounce youthful writers, but they have all the same do not influencc them towards moderation and towards more permanent and solid ways of doing things such as might leave solid and lasting results behind. It is unfortunate that they did not succeed to the extent they wished, but even their failure has its own significance. If amateur orators and others whom nobody knew two or three months before, repulsed the advances of respon sible leaders to control and guide them with impunity, if they have refused to listen to their advice, questioned their moral courage, and have at times denounced them as cowards and still have practically kept the field to themselves, that shows that they could depend upon the sympathies and appreciation of the people in general, ignoring those who wanted to control and guide them They had soiiie thing in them which appealed to the people and which brought them appreciation and en couragement.

Real grievances vioced by the agitators. It is again silly to suppose that their audiences consisted only or mainly of the juvenile population; could any one in his senses maintain that meetings at Lyalpure Multan, Batala, Amritsar, and Delhi consisted of Stu dents only ? Who attended the meetings at the local Bharata Mata office after the schools and colleges had been closed on account of the plague ? What is the total strength of the school population at Lahore or at Rawal pindi or at Delhi compared with the members that have been attending the meetings addressed by Sardar Ajit Singh and Syed Hyder Raza. The fact is, and it cannot honestly be ignored, that the propasiuda carded on by these gentlemen has met with popular approval, it meets the fancy of the masses and their utterances find a ready and appreciative response from the thousands whom they address, and from tens of thousands, more who devour their speeches or writings as reported or published in the Vernacular press.

The irresponsible writer in the Anglo-Indian journal may talk or write what pleases him, but the responsible authorities can no longer shut their eyes to the fact that Sardar Ajit singh and syed Hyder Raz really represent a solid bulk of public opinion which it will be madness to ignore or treat with contempt. I do not, however, believe that the state of things has come to such a pass as to justify the panic which appears to have got hold of Anglo-Indian circles in the Punjab. The discontent in the Punjab has not yet assumed proportions so as to lead people to overt acts of Violence. The stray acts of Violence hitherto in evidence represent the doings of the secret Police, or of Gundas, or of a few frenzied boys or perhaps of all these combined.

7

Lajpat Rai and Hindu Nationalism

I have read with considerable interest the article by a "Hindu Nationalist," on the "creation of a Hindu Nationality, "In the June number of the Samachaar, as also the contribution on the same subject, in the last number of this Journal, by my friend Pandit Madho Ram.

While I heartily join in the "Hindu Nationalist's' appeal to the educated Hindus, yet I do not share his opinion that "the idea of Nationality is an essentially European and modern idea, "nor can I agree with his reading of the facts of history relied upon by him in support of his assertion. In my humble opinion the ideas of "nationality" and "patriotism" are as old as the different countries into which the earth is divided, as ancient as the distinctions of race and religion that have been existing in this world from times immemorial and pre-historic.

They may have been more phenomenal in one epoch than in another. Their hold on different races and nations may have varied in intensity or extent, but that the ideas have always been there, as fixed and immutable as those of truth and falsehood, is my firm belief. It is not, however, my intention to enter into a speculative or an historical controversy with the "Hindu Nationalist' on the origin of the sentiments of nationality and patriotism Suffice it to say that I agree with most of his conclusions and am prepared to generally endorse the remedies suggested. In fact some of the thoughts expressed in his article were, as if, foreshadowed by me in my article on the Congress published in the Samachar for October 1901. This reference has been made not to suggest any borrowing on the part of the "Hindu Nationalist, "but to show that these thoughts are just now uppermost in the minds of all such Hindus as claim to love their people and to think of the means of.their progress. The "Nationalist" begins of the idea of nationality amongst Hindus, and ascribes all our misfortunes pa>t and present to the same fact.

' The Hindus," he says, "offer a curious instance of a people without any feeling of nationality."Having thus laid down the proposition he appeals to the pages of history to support his conclusion and apparently seems to have made out a strong case. But he had evidently missed the fact that his own proposition assumes the existence of a people having a common name, who have made history by that name. Quite unconsciously he assumes the existence of a Hindu nationality when he talks of the unsuccessful efforts of the Rajaputs and the Mahrattas to throw off the foreign yoke and to found a Hindu empire. What he complains of is that these efforts were spasmodic, not supported by the general body of the people and therefore not quite national, but all the time he admits by implication that there was a nation which could and should have made a combined effort Otherwise what can he possibly mean by saying that "the Mahratta were left to fight the last battle of the Hindus alone, unaided by the Sesodia or the Rahtore?"

He admits that "if allowed to grow unchecked the Mahratta confederacy might have developed into a national empire."In the face of these facts we cannot deny the existence of a nation simply because all the members of that nation did not join in the struggle for defense, or that some of them succeeded, or proved traitors, or joined the enemy's camp. Nor can we deny the existence of the sentiment of nationality, because that sentiment was not sufficiently strong and marked to overcome all differences among the different members of that nation, to enable them to stand as one man in defence of national interests. In the next place, why ignore the united front presented by the Hindus of all classes to repel the fourth invasion of Mahmud of Ghazni, and why forget the empires of the Pandavas, of Asoka, of Siladittya, Vikram, bhoja, and others ?

Even the ill-fated Prithwi Raj, the last of the Hindu Emperors, who paid the penalty of the empire in the battle of Thaneswar, could twice command; the united services of almost the whole nation in his noble and valiant defence of the empire and the fatherland. Who knows that but for the treachery of that fratricide of a Jai Chand, history would have been made otherwise ? But the treachery of Jai Chand and the defeat of Prithwi Raj do not detract from the character of the heroic stand which the nation made against the foreigner. Victories and defeats are not solely made by man but are regulated by many a cause some of which may be quite outside the control of the parties at war. If in 1193 Providence decreed the fall of the Hindus that alone is not sufficient to justify us in damning the Hindus of that period as men who were totally bereft of the sentiment of nationality. Then, as I have already hinted, the very fact of our people being known to other peoples by a distinctive name, is a proof of the existence of a Hindu nationality.

I am too old now to continue to believe that the name Hindu, was for the first time given to us as one involving abuse, contempt and reproach by our Mohamedan invaders. Rather, I believe that our fall and degradation helped the fall of the word also, and perhaps ia peep Into the philogical prove that all the bad meanings that are now assigned to the word in the Persian lexicon were of a comparatively later origin, and an outcome of the fall of the Hindu nation. Long before the Mohammedan invasion, and perhaps long before the advent of the Prophet of Islam, we were known to the people of other countries as Hindus. If so, what did this name signify?

Was it a tribal distinction? I say, no, because the Hindus were of many tribes. Was it a racial name? I again, say, no, because the Persians of Iran too, belonged to the same race. Was it then a religious designation? Yes, partly religious no doubt, but mainly national, and in evidence I can produce a number of quotations from the productions of early Greek Historian? and Mohammedan writers. For example, in what other sense does the Homer of Persia, the gifted Firdausi, who has immortalised the struggles for supremacy between the Iranians and the Turanians, use the expression Hindu in the following verses, which I pick at random from his great work, the Sliahnam : Then we find manj' references to our people as Hindus in the sacred books of the Parsis, the Vindklnd and others. So far as the name is concerned, our only difficulty arises when we fail to find any trace of it in our own literature where our people are invariably styled as" Aryas, But here again we find enough traces of the sentiment of nationality in the passages in which the Rishis ordained all Aryas to combine against the attacks of Doatirtx, Chandalas and Mlechhas, Gods are often invoked.

The verses are in urdu characters which we reproduce at the and of the book. For protection against these latter. As for indications of an imperial spirit amongst the Hindus, why the Ramayana and the Mahabharat are full of evidences of the same. What was King Yudhishthira's Rajsuya Yagna and by what name would you style the ambitious scheme of Jarasindhu. The fact is that the best and the most glorious period of Aryan supremacy is yet closed chapter to us. Almost the whole of the pre-Buddhistic period is shrouded in mystery. Even the literature that has reached us is so full of allusions, enigmas, signs, and names and is written in such an archaic language that the whole thing seems to be a mystery. According to the best of European authorities, the language of the Vedas is so full of obsolete and archaic forms and expressions that the whole seems to be a cipher which with the best of efforts might yet take years to decipher.

Still we know and understand enough to be proud of, and to glory in the heritage which has descended to us from our "barbarien "(?) ancestors in the shape of a national literature. And this must be the fulcrum of the lever with which we are to rise as a nation. It will not do to be unjust to our forefathers and to deny the idea of national love in them. No, they were patriots according to the best of their own light. The history of our country, from the standpoint of a Hindu, has yet to be written and till that is done, let us suspend judgement, remembering that the men whom we desire to judge and whom we are sometimes inclined to hastily condemn (often unheard) were master minds, whose productions and teachings are of the loftiest in the whole range of thoughts. We the English educated. Hindus of the present day, who claim to have imbibed the new spirit of nationality and patriotism from the West would really do well to study a few chapters of the Vedic literature with care and thought, and I am confident that this study wiil open a panorama of new ideas to our view.

Such a study will, I am sure, enable us to see that the Ijey-note of the preBuddhistic Vedic religion was the sacrifice of all for all. True that the genius of a jealous and perverted, sometimes corrupt and selfish, priesthood huilt such a vast and stupendous superstructure of con ventionalities and formalities, with an almost intermi nable labyrinth of rituals and ceremonials obscured by which the true spirit of the religion was practically lost :and could no longer be the stay of the nation.

It is this submergence of the true spirit of the ancient Hindu faith under the load of conventional rituals and formal ceremonials, that has since been the bane of. the Hindus and not the entire absence of the idea of nationality. But you might say, that we have been producing martyrs and no one can be a martyr except by the strength of faith. How can a nation destitude of faith produce martyrs ? Is there a nation who have shown more of faith in their religion, in their individuality, in their sacred laws than the Hindus ? How can you other wise explain their tenacity in clinging to their forms of religion, their pertinacity to stick to their customs ? I purposely say, forms of relifjlon became real religion — the religion that guides and moulds a man, or a nation, and that elevates and ennobles them, that raises them to high ideals, that evokes the highest of sacrifices, has long ago disappeared from us.

In fact it was never in the postBuddhistic period restored to its altar in the temple of hearts. True, martyrs we have certainly been producing, ever and anon, and sometimes in numbers, but when I accuse the Hindus of want of faith, I do not mean individual faiths but that social faith which is the parent of victory; the faith that arouses the multitudes of faith in their own destiny, in their own mission and in the mission of the epoch; the faith that leades on to struggle; the faith that enlightens and bids men advance fearlessly in the ways of God and Humanity, with their religion in their heart and their future progress as their goal. It is such a faith that we have been wanting in since the time of Buddha and it is such a faith that we require to become a nation again. I shall now discuss the observations of Mr. Madho Ram and I shall remark at the outset that even admit ting for argument's sake, the absolute accuracy of all his statements and facts, and also the correctness of the inferences he draws therefrom I would beg to differ from him in a matter of princijple. My esteemed friend seems to think that all these internecine quarrels, strifes and sectarian struggles which he records at such great length in the course of his article largely take away "the chance for the progress of Hindu Nationalism in our country,"or to be more accurate in quoting his words, he questions the Hindu Nationalist, if in the face of circumstances stated by him "there is much chance for the progress of Hindu Nationalism in our country."

I answer the question in the affirmative. What is anxious to point out is, that strifes is neither a bar to the progress of Hindu Nationalism nor is it proof sufficient of the absence of the idea of Nationality amongst the Hindus. And this, for the simple reason that the idea of nationality does not necessarily imply a complete union amongst all its members on all matters, social, religious or political; nor does it suggest the existence of a state of perfect concord and harmony among its members or leaders, or the freedom of the latter from all human weaknesses such as lead to personalities or indulgences in strong or even abusive language amongst, and towards each other.

Has there been any nation in the world in the past, or is there any nation now living, which has been or is free from these differences or quarrels? Surely, Roman, Grecian, and Mohammedan histories must be admitted to present splendid and noble types of nationa lity and nationalism, and the present times can not furnish better and nobler types of nationality than the English, the German, and the American and the French, not to speak of others equally noble though not so influential and powerful, such as the Swiss, the Italian, and the Dutch. Religious and social differences have played a prominent part in the histories of these nations and even now they are not free from the same.

A mere glance at the English and Irish papers, a perusal of the speeches in Parliament and out of Parliament by political men, a study of the literature of different religious sects in the West and a perusal of the biographies of public men in these countries, will show that the incidents narrated by my friend, altogether lose in significance and weight in the presence of the more vituperative and sometimes highly abusive difference and quarrels of these magnates of the European world.

The truth is that honest differ ences, controversial discussions, and criticisms of public men by public men, are absolutely necessary for the healthy growth and progress of nationality. Then we inust he prepared to meet with human weaknesses, partialities, jealousies, personalities, insinuations, innu endoes, use of strong language etc., in these discussions, and controversies. Carried beyond a certain degree and limit, they mij.ht retard the growth of nationalism, or might bring down an already completed edifice of natio nality. I am not however prepared to admit that the differences and the disputes amongst the different classes of educated Hindus at the present moment exceed that limit, ht is wrong to suppose that the idea of nationalism or nationality requires a complete union in all details of religious, social, economical, or political life or that it requires a complete freedom from sectarian quarrels or disputes or jealousies.

To expect so, is to expect what is an impossibility and what entirely ignores human nature, in my humble opinion it is sufcient for the growth of nationality, if the different parts that claim the shelter of its ways have a sense of unity, which is sufB<;ient to make them combine against a common enemy and a common danger. Run on a few basal principles in reli gion, on the community of a sacred language, and on the community of interests, the Hindus ought to foster the growth of a national sentiment which should be sufficiently strong to enable them to work for the common good in the different ways and according to the lights vouchsafed to each. Let us keep us. Let our ideal be sufficiently high to cover all, sufficiently broad and extensive to include all, who take pride in ove common name, a common ancestry, a common History, common religion, a common language and a common future.

We will not advance the cause of nationality by one inch, if we decide to preserve an attitude of silent quietude, and non-disturbing peace in all matters religious and social. Such an attitude can only mean stagnation and gradual extinction. Struggle, hard struggle, is the law of progress. Yes struggle we must, both inter se as well others. There must be a struggle between truth and untruth, between vice and virtue, between honesty and dishonesty, betwen expediency and righteousness, bet ween indolence and energy, between enterprise and a spirit of lethargy and between time-seeing selfishness and noble disinterestedness. Without this struggle no nation can ever aspire to be great and iufluential.

This struggle we have just entered upon. We have just emerged out of stagnation, and it is no wonder that we are sometimes apt to exceed the limits of propriety, or to irresistibly throw in more of sectarianism and personality, where more or much less is needed. But national delinquencies or faults are not made up or remedied in a day. Let us not be impatient of what in my humble opinion seems to be a healthy sign of growth. Let us not strangle it by drawing its undesirable concomitants in high colours or by attaching undue importance to the same. Then there are men and men in all public bodies, religious and social. Because there are some violent men, some bad tempered, some dishonest men, some traitors, and limeservers in our public associations, it is no reason to record a wholesale condemnation of the same or to be disappomted with them. Public opinion in this country has yet to grow.

It is a very feeble plant yet. Its growth must cause some unpleasant friction and struggle. Let us not be impatient of it. The country has yet to foster a cold spirit of disinterested, fearless criticism. Few peo ple in this country are guided by purely public interests Fewer still are those who can be moved to take interest in things which do not concern them exclusively and in which they have little at stake. The interests of others do not move them. What little criticism exists in the country, is at once dubbed as sectarian, as interested, or as the outcome of jealousy or personal animosity.

This criticism, that potent weapon, which alone can effectually check the vicious or selfish tendencies of great and power ful men, is discouraged and strangled. What we should aim at is not the silencing of criticism but the purging it out of personalities, jealousies, abuse and vituperation. This will take time, but so long as this is not achieved, let us not discourage, run down and do away with criti cism altogether. At any rate, in my humble opinion im patience at, or silencing of mutual, criticism, or absence of all controversy will not necessarily mean unity, or a healthy progress of nationalism. Having thus disposed to the best of my power the objections of the "Hindu Nationalist "based — to my mind — on a wrong view of our ancient history, and that of Pandit Madho Ram, who has, in my opinion, drawn erroneous inferences from the facts detailed by him and the accuracy of which I have assumed for the sake of argument, with a hope that I may be able to return to the subjects in a latter issue and discuss the present condition and prospects of Hindu Nationalism, the evidence of its pro gress and the chances of its future growth. Lajpat Rai.

HINDU NATIONALISM AND POLITICAL STRATEGY

The Jana Sangh always wavered between two strategies: one, moderate, involved positioning itself as a patriotic party on behalf of national unity, as the protector of both the poor and of small privately-owned businesses, deploying a populist vein. The other line, more militant, was based on the promotion of an aggressive form of 'Hinduness', symbolized by the campaign to raise Hindi to the level of India's national language and protecting of cows (by banning cow slaughter), the cow being sacred for Hindus but not for Muslims. The latter were in fact the implicit target of an agitation against slaughtering cows set off in 1966, in the context of the fourth general elections campaign.

Although the militant strategy was more in keeping with RSS wishes and the feelings of its activists, it ran up against India's constitutional rules of secularism and prevented the Jana Sangh from broadening its base and striking up alliances with other parties. This strategy changed in the 1970s. In 1977 the

Jana Sangh resigned itself to following a moderate line and merged with the Janata Party, which had just defeated Indira Gandhi's Congress Party. However, the former Jana Sangh had not broken with the RSS, to the great displeasure of some of its new partners in power, particularly the socialists. This latter group, associated with the government's second-in-command Charan Singh (who sought to destabilize Prime Minister Morarji Desai—all the better to take his place), drew their argument from an upsurge in Hindu–Muslim riots within which RSS activists were involved, to demand that the former Jana Sanghis break with the RSS. The Jana Sanghis' refusal precipitated the break-up of the Janata Party, paving the way for Indira Gandhi's return.

In 1980 the former Jana Sangh leaders started a new party, the Bharatiya Janata Party (BJP), which remained faithful to the moderate strategy.The BJP, which had Atal Behari Vajpayee as its first president, diluted the original ideology of the Jana Sangh in order to become more acceptable in the Indian party system and to find allies in this arena. This more moderate approach to politics was considerably resented by the rest of the Sangh Parivar.

The RSS kept its distance from the BJP and made greater use of the VHP to rekindle ethno-religious political activism. This more militant strategy found its main expression in the launching of the Ayodhya movement in the mid-1980s. Ayodhya, a town in Uttar Pradesh, is described in the Hindu tradition as the birthplace and capital of the god-king Lord Rama. The site was supposedly once occupied by a Rama temple until destroyed in the sixteenth century on the orders of Babur, the first Mughal emperor, and replaced by mosque, the 'Babri Masjid'. In 1984 the VHP called for this site to be returned to the Hindus. In 1989, throughout the entire summer, with the logistical support of the RSS, the VHP organized Rama Shila Pujan festivals, which involved worshipping bricks (*shila*) printed with Rama's name. These holy bricks were to be used to rebuild the Ayodhya temple.

The BJP rallied to the call of this ethno-religious mobilization strategy and even participated in the processions which took place all over India: the agitation contributed to its success at the polls, taking it from 2 to 88 parliamentary seats and from 7.4 to 11.6 per cent of the votes cast.

In 1990, while the party was a major component of the coalition in power that had just ousted the Congress Party, its president, L.K. Advani, went on a 10,000 km 'chariot-journey' or Rath Yatra that was to culminate in the construction of the Ayodhya temple. Advani was stopped before entering Uttar Pradesh and during the repression of activists who attacked the mosque some dozen were left dead.

This episode reinforced the champion-of-Hinduism image that the BJP had been trying to acquire among the majority community. The 1991 general elections actually enabled the party to win 20.08 per cent of the vote and 120 seats in the Lok Sabha. Paradoxically, its success in Uttar Pradesh, where the BJP was able to form the state government, did not enable it to solve the Ayodhya issue.

Hindu nationalist militants put an end to this deadlock by demolishing the mosque on 6 December 1992. This operation and the ensuing Hindu–Muslim riots—1200 dead within a few days—prompted New Delhi to take a number of repressive measures, including the dissolution of assemblies in states where the BJP was in power (Uttar Pradesh, Madhya Pradesh, Himachal Pradesh, and Rajasthan), and a ban on the RSS and the VHP. These proved temporary measures and did not affect the Sangh Parivar.

By the mid-1990s the BJP reverted to its moderate line, discarding the manipulation of religious symbols for political ends in favour of touting more legitimate issues such as national unity and economic independence. This was not only because it had lost elections in UP, MP, and HP in 1993—the voters obviously punishing the party for violent excesses related to the Ayodhya affair—but also because Sangh Parivar leaders admitted they could not acquire power unless the BJP formed political alliances with regional parties. Moreover, Advani, the party's president, allowed Vajpayee to take the forefront once again because Vajpayee was less marked by Hindu nationalist activism.

The BJP was able to build a coalition of more than fifteen parties in the late 1990s. This 'National Democratic Alliance' enabled Vajpayee to form a government after the 1998 and 1999 elections. The arrangement forced the BJP to put on the backburner contentious issues— such as the construction of a temple in Ayodhya; restrict Article 30 of the Indian constitution guaranteeing the right of religious and linguistic minorities to establish educational institutions; abolish Article 370 of the constitution granting a partially autonomous status to Jammu and Kashmir; promulgate a uniform civil code, primarily to put an end to the possibility given to Muslims to follow Islamic law (*sharia*).

Once in office, the BJP implemented some of the traditional items of the Hindu nationalist programme. Vajpayee's first major decision was the nuclear test of May 1998. The policy of the minister for human resources and development, Murli Manohar Joshi, was also well in tune with Hindu nationalist leanings: he appointed personalities who had been close to the Sangh Parivar as heads of the directive body of the Indian Council of Historical Research (ICHR),the Indian Council of Social Science Research (ICSSR), and the search committee for faculty appointments in the National Council for Educational Research and Training (NCERT) which was entrusted with the task of designing a new school curriculum.

One of Joshi's priorities was to create new textbooks—including those dealing with Indian history— rewritten in a vein more in line with Hindu nationalist ideology.

But the BJP distanced itself from several other traditional mainstays of its ideology, such as economic nationalism—a notion encapsulated by the word 'swadeshi'.The government in fact opened new sectors to foreign investment. This new, sympathetic approach of 'liberalization' caused some concern within the Sangh Parivar. The Swadeshi Jagaran Manch—a newly created offshoot of RSS—and the Bharatiya Mazdoor Sangh complained to the RSS, whose governing body, the Akhil Bharatiya Pratinidhi Sabha, passed a resolution in March 2000 supporting an 'India-centric and need-specific' model of development.In May 2004, during the parliamentary elections, the NDA government led by the BJP was surprisingly defeated and replaced by a Congress-led coalition.

The defeat was considered by most components of the Sangh Parivar to be that of the Vajpayee moderate line. The VHP leaders were especially vocal. For them the BJP-led government had betrayed the Hindus by not building the Rama temple they longed for in Ayodhya. The compulsions of coalition politics had stymied the Hindutva agenda. Former socialists and other self-proclaimed secularist allies of the BJP-led coalition would not allow Hindutva-oriented objectives such as the building of a Rama Mandir in Ayodhya.The BJP had become adept at coalition-making, to stay in power, but the rules of the coalition game had diluted the agenda.

As a result, Hindutva forces are today deeply divided. The BJP leaders consider that any return to a radical brand of Hindu nationalist politics by the party will alienate its allies and postpone *sine die* its comeback to the helm of political affairs in the country. The RSS and VHP leaders assume that the BJP lost the 2004 elections because the Vajpayee government had disappointed too many Hindus.

They fear that any further dilution of the ideology of the party would widen the gap between the BJP and the rest of the Sangh Parivar. When such differences emerge between the political sector of the Sangh Parivar and the rest, the political wing eventually falls in line. In the late 1980s, for instance, Advani succeeded Vajpayee for the second time and took the party towards the Hindutva direction, as desired by the RSS.

Undoubtedly, Advani departure as president of the BJP on the eve of new year's day 2006 was largely perceived as being at the behest of the RSS. The tensions between the RSS and the BJP cannot be taken lightly anyway. They affect two mainstays of the self-perception—and indeed the identity—of the Hindutva movement. First, while the Sangh Parivar claims to form a 'family', with its members playing complementary parts, the RSS and the BJP (and the VHP and the BJP) appear to be at cross purposes.Second, the experiment of the Vajpayee government has shown that the RSS could not really exert the influence it wanted over power, even when the BJP was in office.

This failure, once again, puts into question a key element of the Sangh Parivar's identity. Certainly, the RSS aspires to reshape society in its own image at the grassroots level, in a long-term perspective. But it also wants to the 'Raj guru', the mentor of goverment.The Vajpayee government episode has demonstrated that such an objective is very difficult to achieve. This realization may force the Sangh Parivar to change its functioning.

THE SOCIAL GENIUS OF HINDUISM

An idea seems to be gaining ground amongst Hindus educated on Western lines that the genius of Hinduism is essentially individualistic and anti-social and that therefore no substantial reform in social life can come out of a revival of the past, and that we can only draw on the West and take light therefrom. They do not place much faith in reform on national lines and would rather go in for wholesale or bodily adoption of most at least, if not all, of the social institutions of the West. Tney would rather build a new social edifice on rationalifii as distinguished from nationalitiy, in religion and in social life. Aain there are a large number of Hindus who, although they are prepared to grant that there is much in our national religion as handed down to us in our sacred literature which may satisfy even the highest cravings of the human mind, whether in the sphere of the spirit, intellect or morals, cannot yet see the existence of a spirit of nationality among the old Hindus, or the old Aryans (as I will prefer to style the pre-Pauranic ancestors of the Hindus).

This current impression of the educated Hindus has very much been strengthened by the utterances of some eminent Hindus of the Western Presidency, whose lear ning, scholarship and devotion to the cause of the coun try entitle them to be heard with respect and admira tion. They are supposed to say that Hinduism was wanting in the social principle, being ostensibly indi vidualistic.

It is very unfortunate to have to differ in any point from men of such vast erudition, deep learning and great reputation. Ordinarily any man will shrink from such an unpleasant and risky task however strong and cogent his reasons may be for that difference of opinion. Still, what sometimes deters men of deep learning and reat reputation, may not stand in the way of a man who, though possessed of lesser qualifications, is pos sessed of a stronger faith in the truth of his cause and believes that the question is of vital importance to the cause of progress and reform amongst his people. It is therefore upon the strength of this faith, though with the greatest possible diffidence and hesitation, that I venture to express an opinion on the question raised in the open ing sentences of this paper. Let me however make it clear that I quite concur in the opinion expressed by so many eminent social reformers, that the question of social reform is one of paramount national importance.

There can be no doubt that the whole future of the nation depends upon the amount of social efficiency we secure and display, but I do not at the same time share the general belief that socially, the ancient Hindus were a very inferior people and had no, or xr Q>ci sKno of social or national responsibilities. In one of my paper on a similar subject, I have already expressed an opinion, giving my reasons and proofs, that the old Hindus were not entirely void of the idea of nationality or patriotism. In this paper I propose to discuss their social ideals and standards. I am prepared to grant that the tendency of the prevailing Hindu beliefs (which are gerierally styled orthodox and Pauraaic) has a greater leaning towards individualism and appeals more to the interest and well-being of the individual than to that of the society to which the believers belong. But beyond this I cannot go. I do not share the commonly accepted opinion that Hinduism as a whole is either essentially or even principally individualistic at the cost of the social obligations. No religion can be worth its name which does not take sufficient care of the individual. The development of the individual soul and its attain ment of spiritual beatitude must be the goal of all reli gions. There can be no religion without this object. A religion without the teaching of spirituality is a misnomer and a lever without a fulcrum.

All purely spiritual deve lopment must, from the very nature of things, be individu alistic, and it should be the ambition of every human being to strive after the elevation and refinement of the spirit in him and thereby secure spiritual perfectioa resulting in perfect bliss, or (as some religions style it) salvation. No religion can, therefore, be condemned as individualistic, because it attaches great importance to the unfolding and developing of the spiritual side of men nor can any religion be extolled as socialistic which either ignores the spirit altogether or gives it only a subordinate or secondary position.

In judging of a religion or of a system of religious beliefs, what has to be seen is whether it gives sufficient importance to the different requirements and the different sides of human nature without sacrific ing one for another. To be a perfect and sound religion, it must make adequate provisipn for the harmonious development of all those sides of human nature which are to form the basis of the upward progress of man. Such a religion cannot afford to neglect even the physical side, much less can it throw into the background the social.

But before we proceed further we should like to clear the ground by first examining the social ideal which our English-educated friends have set up before themselves. The social ideal of Herbert Spencer is stated to be "a state of fhings in which the antagonism between societies having utterly ceased on the one hand and the concilia tion between the interests of the individual and those of the social organism having been perfectly attained to, on the other, the individual also will have reached a stage of development in which it will afford him the highest pleasure to act in a manner conducive to the good of the social organism, and this even where such conduct is to all appearance directly antagonistic to his own material interests. Just as at present the highest happiness is often obtained in parental sacrifice. He expects that this altruistic instinct will, in course of time, "attain a level at which it will be like parental altruism in spontaneity" and so lead the individual to obtaining the highest of all satisfactions in voluntarily sacrificing himself in the in terests of the social organism. In his DiUa of EiK\ Spencer professes to see in the process of social evolu tion going on around us, a reconciliation taking place '•between the interests of each citizen and the interests of citizen at large, tending ever towards a state in which the two become merged in one and in which the feelings answering to them respectively fall into complete con cord."

Leaving out of consideration for the present that social millennium of Spencer in which the antagonism between societies shall entirely cease, we are just now concerned with the internal social efficiency of our own social organism. The point to be seen is whether the religion and the laws that have guided the formation and development of that social organism do or do not contain the germ of that principle by which members may be re quired to sacrifice what to them appear to be their best interests as individuals for the interests of the or ganism to which they belong, or, to put it more accurately, whether Hinduism as a religion, in its teach ings and in its system of laws contemplates that concord between the interests of its individual members and those of the community at large which, according to Spencer, is the key-note of the process of social evolution going on around us and which he so admiringly holds up as affording prospects of that social millennium which, according to him, will soon be established on earth. In the opinion of Mr. Benjamin Kidd the Darwinian science of evolution as it is now understood, does not afford "any warrant for anticipating the arrival of that state of society contemplated by Mr. Herbert Spencer."

Further he rejects his conception of the process of social evolution (quoted above from his Data of Ethics) "as being inconsistent with the teachings of evolutionary science."

Admitting that ' the forces which are at work in the evolution of society, are certainly, on the whole, working out the greatest good of the greatest number in a pro gressive community; he takes care to point out that the earlier utilitarian conception of the greatest number being related merely to the majority of the existing mem bers of society at any time, has now iven way to the greatest number being "comprised of the nvmber of gener afions yet unborn or itn thought of, to ivhofe interefnts the exis ting individuals are absolutely indifferent."And in the pro cess of social evolution which the race is undergoing, says he, it is these latter interests which are always in the ascendent."

Applying the principle to the limited sphere of a particular social organi?m it comes to this, that the social efficiency of the latter depends not only on the subordination or merging of the individual interests of its members to or in the intersts of the whole, but also in looking forward to and guarding the interests of the generations yet unborn. A Social organism can there fore be considered as efficient, only if, beyond requir ing its members to sacrifice what to them seems to tend to their individual good, happiness or prosperity; if the same clashes or is inconsistent with the good of the whole, it also takes sufficient care of the interests of the generations yet unborn so as to guarantee the continu ance of that state of efficiency in the future.

The social system of a nation is perfect or imperfect, complete or incomplete, natural or unnatural, progressive or cetto gressive, according as it does or does not fulfil the require ments set forth above. But before we proceed to examine the social system of the ancient Hindus in the light of these considerations, we prefer to clear two more points. The first is that there must surely be something wrong in a social system from which has developed the modern civilization of Europe, which has evoked strong and sweeping condemnation from so eminent a scholar and scientist as Professor Huxley.

Even the best of modern civilizations,"he says 'appears to me to exhibit a condition of mankind which neither embodies any further ideal nor even possesses the merit of stability. I do not hesitate to express the opinion that, if there is no hope of a large improvement of the condition of the greater part of the human family if it is true that the increase of knowledge, the winning of a greater dominion over nature which is its conse quence, and the wealth which follows upon that dominion are to make no difference in the extent and the inten sity of the want with its concomitant physical and mo ral degradation amongst the masses of the people, I should hail the advent of some kindly comet which would sweep the whole affair away as a desirable consum mation."

What Professor Huxley says about the whole hu man family can more or less be said of the internal state of every great nation of Europe.

The solution of the social p/oblem of India there fore does not necessarily lie in the wholesale imitation of the West to the entire neglec: of its past, with its glorious heredity of laws and principles which might shine even with greater splendour if studied in the light of modern history. We do not mean to say that we should decline to take any light from the West or be prejudiced against it because it is of the West. But what I do maintain is that social reform should only proceed on safe and, as far as possible, on reasonable and national lines. The best and safest social reformer will be he who can read the ancient system of the Hindus in the light of the modern knowledge thrown upon it and who out of this joint study can recommend the line of action which he considers to be likely to lead to true social progress (felicity).

I may at once say that I do not believe in the possibility of a wholesale bringing back or revival of the past such as perhaps some of the Theosophists and also some of the Arya Samajists con template. Such a thing is impossible and it will be a waste of energy to try to achieve what is impossible. It is very important that my co-religionists should realize the impossibility and also the futility of this attempt, and should desist from doing or sying anything which may tend to lead the Hindus astray and make them di rect their energies into unprofitable or doubtful channels. I have already said that the Jirst necessity of the Hindus of to-day is the acquistion of that degree of social effici ency which alone can enable them to hold their own in the stress and strife of this world of competition. No nation can as such be spiritually high or pure which is socially corrupt, degraded or inefficient.

What I aim at in the present paper is to show that there is a great deal in our past which can rightly in spire or guide us in the building up of our future socAai edifice, or in the mending of the existing one and that we should be going equally astray if in our anxiety to copy the West we ignore or neglect our own laws and lessons which a study of our past alone can impress upon us.

The second point which I want to clear up is that it is not by reliance on unguided and uncontrolled reason that we can get at the true principles of social progress. Reason when uncontrolled, is styled by Kid to be "the most profoundly individualistic, anti-social and anti-evo lutionary of all human qualities."In this opinion the central feature of our evolution has always been the sup reme struggle in which the control of this disintegiating influence is being continually effected in the intersts of society first and of the race in the next place; and that the function of the immense and characteristic class of social phenomena which we have in our religious r.ystem is to secure the necessary subordination of the present inte rests of the process of evolution that is in progress. "It would be impossible, "adds he, "to conceive any altruistic feeling of this kind which could exceed in strength the parental instinct.

Let one of the plainest facts of our time and of past history is the perversion of this instinct under the injiiience oj rationalism and the suspension of its operation in furthering the evolution the race is under going. We have discussions proceeding in the literature of the time in which rationalism, with reiterated empha sis, points out, to use the phrase already quoted, that "there is something pathetically absurd in this sacrifice to their children of generation after generation of grown people."No observant person, who has watched the signs of the times, can have the least doubt that in o state of unrestricted raiionalum, the institution of marriage and the familif woidd undergo modijications incompatihle with the continuance of that process of simple self sacrifice with which the interests of the race are bound. We have un mistakable evidence of the perversion of the parental feelings amongst the Greeks and Romans under such rationalistic influences.

Speaking of the decay of the Athenian people, Mr. Francis Galton says, "We know, and may guess something more, of the reason why this marvellously gifted race declined. Social morality grew exceedingly lax; marriage became unfashionable and was avoided; many of the more ambitious and accom plished women were avowed courtesans,and consequently infertile, and the mothers of the incoming population were of a heterogeneous class.' The same state of popular feeling with respect to marriage prevailed during the decline of the Roman Empire.

"The courtesans," says Mr. Lecky, "were raised in popular estimation to an unexampled elevation, and aversion to marriage became very general.' And we have at the present day that striking example,, of the perversion, under similiar circumstances, of the parental feelings amongst the most brilliant and able race amongst the European peoples and the consequent failure of that race to main tain its place amongst others in the evolution which is proceeding under our eyes in the civilization in which we are living.

It will, I hope, be now clearly seen how dangerous it is to give under prominence to "rationalism "in any pr(ramme of social reform and to divorce. We are, in any case, in a position now to judge of the wisdom of the ancient Aryans in developing all the social laws on the basis of religion and in making the latter so comprehensive as to include everything that is necessary for the right progress of man, as a member of a family, as a member of a social organism and last but not least as a member of his race.

With these introductory remarks I proceed to pro duce evidences of the social conception of the Hindus, showing the idea of social unity in their religion and in their rules of life. Firsthjy in my opinion one could hardly come across a more beautiful, a more comprehen sive and a truer view of the unity of the social organism than is expressed in the idea of the division of 'castes, — the much abused, much maligned and much misunder stood idea of the four castes representing the different parts of the creator's body — the Sharir of the Furusha. To take the earliest and the highest authority, first, liig Veda X. 90, verses 11 and 12, literally translated into English by Dr. Griffiths, run as follows : —

11. When they divided Purusha how many por tions did they make ? What do they call his mouth, his arm ? What do they call his thighs and feet ?

12. The Brahman was his mouth, of both his arms was the Rajantfa made. His thighs became the Vaishya from his feet the Shudra was produced.' These Verses give expression to two of the sublimest truths about the social relations of man with man as an individual and with mankind as a whole. They establish the oneness of humanity in the body of the Lord and they explain away the phenomena of differences in the capacities, powers and faculties of individuals. As parts of the same whole, they are to sustain, support, supple ment, help and co-operate with each other. As indi vidual units of one organism they have, each of them their own separate functions to perform. Applying this to a particular social organism as distinguished from general humanity, they form the basis of a complete system of social duties. In no other way could one better express the mutual inter-dependence of all parts of society upon one another, be they high or low, and also the essential oneness of the whole.

Taking it in another and a higher sense, it is a bet ter and more effectual representation of collective Huma nity representing God himself, than any put forward by the Prophets of the Religion of Humanity from Augustus Comte downwards. Read in that light, the verses stand ing by themselves explain only a partial or a relative truth. For the whole truth, you must read the whole hymn together. It was our misfortune that such a grand exposition of the greatest of social truths should have so degenerated in thc hands of an interested priesthood as to be made the basis of the present-day inhumanly, ingenious, corrupt, invidious, and demoralising distinc tions between man and man. But this experience is not so very exceptionally confined to Hinduism only. The evil genius of man has in this and other countries, and in this and other systems of religion, more than occasion ally subverted and distorted some of the sublimest truths taught to him by God and nature with a view to advance the interests of particular individuals co-curricular classes and to oppress others. Take the history of any great religion, be it the humility-professing Christia nity,militant Islam,or Buddhism, you will find similiar dis tortions in abundance, thus showing that the tendencies of priesthood have been almost the same everywhere The same idea of the good of the whole runs through the various duties that the Hindu Shastras assign to the four orders. Manv. Smriti (a treatise on laws, the compilation of which the European scholars fix at about 200 B. C.) is one of those books which lay great stress on caste distinctions, and advo cate vast and rather astounding inequalities of treat ment between the Brahmans and Shudras, verging in some places almost on inhumanity and cruelty. It is a book held in universal esteem by the orthodox Hindus he they of any sect or school. As such we shall be on the safe side in giving quotations from it, supporting the original social conception of the caste system. Verses 88-91 prescribe the duties of the different Varnas : —

88. To Brahmans he assigned teaching and study ing (the Veda), sacrificing for their own benefit and for others, giving and accepting (of alms).

89. The Kshatriya he commanded to protect the people, to bestow gifts, to offer sacrifices, to study (the Veda), and to abstain from attaching himself to worldly pleasures.

90. The Vaishya to tend cattle, to bestow gifts, to offer sacrifices, to study (the Veda), to trade, to lend money, and to cultivate land.

91. One occupation only the Lord prescribed to the Shudra, to serve meekly even these (other) three castes."

The one note that runs throughout these rules is the service of others and the social good and the prosperity of the whole community. The Brahmana is enjoined to study not for the benefit of his soul only, but to teach others, a purely social duty. In the same way, it was'the duty of the Kshatriyas to protect the people, Mark, please, the distinction between ruling and protecting. The same may be said about the duties assigned ±0 the Vishyas and the Shudras, We may, here, for a moment take the liberty of drawing the attention of the promoters of the different caste conferences and caste organisations to these rules of Manu. These rules show that each of these castes was understood to exist and work for the benefit of all, and not for the benefit of their own caste-people only. If it was the duty of a Brahmana to teach all, a Kshatriya to protect all, similar ly the duty of a Vaishya was to produce and to trade for all and that of a Shudra to labour for alL

From the division into varnas (castes) we might proceed to the division of an Aryan life into the four Ashra mas and there also you will find the same idea running through the duties and obligations assigned to each. For instance, wherein can you find such a system of free and compulsory education deeply interwoven with religi ous merit as amongst the Hindus ? Every twice-born Hindu was bound to educate his children unless he intended to degrade them to the level of a Shudra, and every Aryan householder was threatened with severe religious demerit if he refused food or alms to a Vidyarihi.

The various rules laying down the respect that it was the privilege of the teacher to command, importance which the old Aryans attached to the position and the professionof a teacher. Shloka II, 165, lays down the obligation of studying the Veda, for all Aryans: —

"An Arya must study the whole Veda together with the Ra hasyas, performing at the same time various kinds of aus terities and the vows prescribed by the rules of the Veda." Shloka 154 gives precedence to one who has learnt the Veda, over all those whose claim to respect lies either "through years,"i.e., age or. "through white hair," Le,, old age, or through wealth or "through powerful kinsmen."

A householder destitute of the knowldege of the Veda was looked down upon as unfit for social intercourse with the twiceborn. A student was not to accept food from the house of any one who was deficient in the knowledge of the Veda or in performing sacrifices or who were not known as earning their livelihood by lawful means. Similarly at the time of the selection of a wifcr a good man was ordained to "avoid the ten following families, be ihetf ever so great or rich in kine, horses, grain or (other) property.' "(Viz.) One which neglects the sacred rites, one in which no male children (are born) one in luhich the Veda is not studied, one (the members of) which have thick hair on the body, those which are sub ject to hemorrhoids, phthisis, weakness of digestion epilepsy, or white and black leprosy,"The same idea is again prominent in III. 63 :—

"By low marriages, by omitting (the performance of) sacred rites, by neglectiiig the study of the Veda, and by irreverence towards Brah man as, (great) families sink low."

Jn the case of Brahmana it is so very pronounced in the following verses:—

"II, 197. The oblations to gods and manes, made by men ignorant (of the law of gifts), are lost, if the givers in their folly present (shares of them) to Brahma nas who are mere ashes. "III, 168. As a fire of dry grass is (unable to con sume the ofΓeriiigs and is quickly) extinguished, even so (is it with) an unlearned Brahmana; sacrificial food must not be given to him, since it (would be) offered to ashes, " See also 133 and 142.

Texts to this effect, full of similar 'sentiments and breathing the same spirit, can be multiplied by hundreds, not only from the Manu Smriti but from the other Sutras and Smritis as well.

Looking to the life of a Hindu Grihasta (house holder), what ideals of altruistic sentiments are set forth by the texts that describe his daily duties ? Where, on earth, will you find rules such as those which are so explicitly laid down by the epics, the Puranas, and other books containing pictures of ancient Aryan life, and which rules were so scrupulously observed in olden times? The five great daily duties of the Hindus are well known. In English phraseology they are styled sacrifices.' In Sanscrit they are called Maha (great) Yajnas, Tracing back their origin you find the germs and the ideals in the Veda Mantras, but in the Shatapatha BraJi mana, one of the most ancient Hindu Shastras, whose place in antiquity is, by common consent, only next to the Vedas themselves, you see them in a more organised shape.

We quote from the translations of Julius Eggling, published in the Sacred Books of the East series, Vol, XII, pp. 190 and 191.

"1. Verily, whoever exists, he, in being born, is born ar. (owing) a debt to the gods, to the Rishis, to the fathers and to men.
2. For, inasmuch as he is bound to sacrifice, for that reason he is born (owing) a debt to the gods; hence when he sacrifices to them, when he makes offerings to them, he does this (in discharge of his debt) to them.
3. And further, inasmuch as he is bound to study (the Vedas), for that reason he is born as (owing) a debt hence it is to them that he does this; for one who has studied (the Vedas) they call the RisJiis treasure-warden."
4. And further, inasmuch as he is bound to wish for offspring, for that reason he is born (owing) a debt to the fathers; hence when there is (provided by him) a continued, uninterrupted lineage, it is for them that he does this.
5. And further, inasmuch as he is bound to prac tise hospitality, for that reason he is born as (owing) a debt to men; hence when he harbours them, when he offers food to them, it is (in discharge of his debt) to them that he does so. Whoever does all these things has discharged his duties; by him all is obtained, all is conquered.
6. And, accordingly, in that he is born as owing a debt to the gods, in reg.ird to that he satisfies (ava — day) them by sacrificing; and when he makes offering in the fire, he thereby satisfies them in regard to that (debt): hence, whatever they offer up in the fire, is called avadanam (sacrificial portion)."

This quotation speaks only of the four Indians. But the Sutras and the Smrities which are mostly of later date, speak of five, adding as fifth the debt which man owes to the animals and plants, &c. The Smriti which goes after the name of Manu and is by European scholars believed to be a compilation of about 200 B C, also speaks of five and ascribes the rule to the necessity of expiating the sins committed by each householder, in the use of hearth, the grinding stone, the broom, the pestle and mortar.

Below I give all the verses bearing on the subject, a comparison of which with the quotation given from the Saiapatha will give the reader a very clear idea of the difference between the ideals of the pre-Buddhistic and post-Buddhistic periods of Aryan civilization. "III.—

67. With the sacred fire, kindled at the wedding, a householder shall perform according to the law the domestic ceremonies and the five (great) sacrir flees and (with that) he shall daily cook his food.

68. A householder has Jive slaughter-hovses (as it were), viz,, the hearth, the grinding stone, the broom, the pestle and mortar, the water vessel, by using which he is bound (with the fetters of sin.)

69. In order to successively expiate (the offence com' mitted hif means of all these {Uve) the great sages have prescribed for householders the daily (performance of the five) great sacrifices.

70. Teaching (and studying) is the sacrifice (offer ed) to Brahmana, the (offerings of water and food called) Tarpana the sacrifice to the manes, the burnt oblation, the sacrifice offered to the gods, the bali offering that offered to the Bhutas, and the life. They represent a high state of national righteous ness.

"IV. 2. A Brahmana must seek a means of sub sistence which either causes no, or at least little, pain (to others), and live by that except in times of distress.'

"IV. 17. Let him avoid all (means of acquiring) wealth which impede the study of the Veda; (let him maintain himself anyhow, but study (because that) devotion to the Veda-study secures the realisation of his aims.

"IV. 18. Let him walk here (on earth), bringing his dress, speech, and thought to a conformity with his age, his occupation, his wealth, his sacred learning and HIS RACE.'

"IV. 170-174. Neither a man who (lives) un righteously nor he who (acquires) wealth (by telling) falsehoods, nor he who always delights in doing injury ever attains happiness in this world. Let him, though suffering in consequence of his righteousness, never turn his heart to unrighteousness; for he will see the speedy overthrow of the unrighteous, wicked men.

Unrighteousness, practised in this world, does not at once produce its fruit, like a cow; but advancing slowly, it cuts off the roots of him who committed it. If (the punishment falls) not on (the offender) him self, (it falls) on his sons, if not on sons, (at least) on his grandsons, but an iniquity once committed never fails to produce fruit to him who wrought it.

He prospers for a while through unrighteousness, then he gains great good fortune, next he conquers his enemies, but (at last) he perishes (branch and) root." "IV. 176. Let him avoid the acquisition of wealth and the gratification of his desires if they are opposed to the sacred law, and even lawful acts which may cause pain in the future or are offensive to men." The following lay down a perfect standard of chari ty :-~

"IV. 120, A Brahmana who neither performs austerities nor studies the Veda, yet delights in accept ing the gifts, sinks (with the donor) into hell just as (he who attempts to cross over in) a boat made of stones {is submerged) in the water.

191. Hence an ignorant (man) should be afraid of accepting any presents; for by reason of a very small (gift) even a fool sinks (into hell) as low into a morass. 192. (A man) who knows the law should not offer even water to a Brahmana who acts like a cat, nor to a Brahmana who acts like a heron, nor to one who is un acquainted with the Veda."(For a definition of cats and herons see 195 and 196).

"193. For property, though earned in accordance with prescribed rules, which is given to these three (persons), causes in the next world misery both to THE GIVER AND THE RECIPIENT.

194. As he who (attempts to) cross water m a boat of stone sinks (to the bottom), even so AN ignorant donor and AN IGNORANT DONEE SINK LOW.

195. (A man) who, ever covetous, displays the flag of virtue, (who is) a hypocrite, a deceiver of the people, in tent on doing injury, (and) a detractor (from the merits) of all men, one must know to be one who acts like a cat.

90 THE SOCIAL GENIUS OF HINDUISM.

196. That Brahmana, who with downcast look, of a cruel disposition, is solely intent on attaining his own ends, dishonest and falsely gentle, is one who acts like a heron.

197. Thos2 Bramans who act like herons, and those who display the characteristics of cats, fall in con sequence of that wicked mode of acting into (the hell called) Andhaiamisra,

The following shlolcas will show how the social and national interests of the community were guarded against an undue and unseasoned desire towaids abnega tion and ascetic life.

"VI. 35-37. When he has paid the three debts, let him apply his mind to the attainment of final liberation; HE WHO SEEKS IT WITHOUT HAVING PAID (HIS DEBTS) SINKS DOWNWARDS.

36. Having studied the Vedas in accordance with the rule, having begat sons according to the sacred law,, and having offered sacrifices according to his ability, he may direct his mind to (the attainment of) final liberation.

37. A TWICE BORN MAN WHO SEEKS LIBERATION WITH OUT HAVING STUDIED THE VeDAS, WITHOUT HAVING BEGOTT EN SONS, AND WITHOUT HAVING OFFERED SACRIFICES SINKS DOWNWARDS.

The following extracts will show how strongly the ancient Aryas felt and believed in the unity of a political or social organism.

In their opinion the safety and welfare of all con sisted in the righteousness of all. Any failure of duty by individuals operated to corrupt the whole society, and if ever the number of those who failed to fulfil their obligations or act in accordance with law, increased, it was considered a sure sign of the decay of the nationa power, strength and virtue. The king representing the commonwealth was required to protect his people, always to keep their interests in view, to see that all orders and classes and individuals performed their res. pective obligations properly. His neglect or failure to secure the due performance of every one's duty was (Calculated to result in disaster to the whole community. There are numerous texts in Manu and other Shastras which can be quoted in support of the above position, but I am afraid, I will be only increasing the length and size of the paper if I did so. I will therefore confine myself only to a few, by way of example, in which the Mea stated by me seems to be sufficiently prominent. VIII. 22.

Foretells the ruin of a commonwealth by famine and disease in which the number of the twice born decreases and which principally consists of Shudras (i. «. labourers and menial classes). How can a nation continue to exist which has no brain to guide the or ganism, no arms to protect it, and no traders and manufacturers to maintain and increase its wealth ? No one can conceive of a self-governed community consist ing of labourers only. An increase of the labouring classes with a corresponding decrease of the learned, the fight ing and the producing classes, is a sure index of decay and coming ruin.

"That Kingdom"says Manu, "where Shudras are very numerous, which is infested by atheists, and desti tute of twice-born (inhabitants), sootv iB.tVKE\x t'v. afFected by famine and disease.

Being "destitute of twice-born"is equivalent to being destitute of knowledge, power and wealth. A nation not possessing these cannot exist as a nation and is bound to lose its position as such. Famine and disease are sure to follow in the train of ignorance, weakness and poverty. Let my countrymen ponder over the sub lime truth preached in this verse and it shall at once dawn on them as to why they are such frequent victims of famine and disease. The true course then to be followed in order to uproot them is to increase the stock of national knowledge, national strength and national wealth. That is the best, the safest, the most effective, and the only cure of these national afflictions of ours. Here is a remedy, an unfailing remedy, pointed out by the son of Swayambhuva"himself, the great Manu. Let us apply it with faith, and it is sure to drive away the diseases with which we, each and all of us (both individually and socially), are at the present moment afflicted.

The idea of the ruling class being only a part of the whole social organism and of its earning merit or de merit by the actions of the whole is beautifully and with characteristic force expressed in the following four Molcafi which we quote from chapter VIII : — 304. A king who (duly) protects (his subjects), receives from each and all the sixth part of their spiritual merit, if he does not protect them, the sixth part of their demerit also (will fall on him).

Whatever (merit a man gains by) reading the Vedas by sacrificing, by charitable gifts, (or by) worship ping (Gurus and Gods), the king obtains a sixth part of that in consequence of his duly protecting (his kingdom). 306. A king who protects the created beings in accordance with the sacred law and smites those worthy of corporal punishment, daily offers (as it were) sacri fices at which hundred-thousands (are given as) fees. 307. A king who does not afford protection, yet takes his share in kind, in taxes, tolls and duties, daily presents and fines, will after death, soon sink into hell."

There are many more texts which similarly tell us of an advanced political science including political econo my, having been developed by the Hindus. Elaborate rules and provisions are laid down for the appointment of state officials, the imposition of taxes, tolls and fines, the regulating of state expenditure, the administra tion of civil and criminal justice, the control of Revenue for the necessity of paying special attention to agriculture, trade, commerce and manufactures, &c., &c. These all give one an idea of the social position of the HindusThere are among them some rules which undoubtedly appear to be very invidious, childish, and grotesque but they form only the exceptions even if we were to grant that they are not subsequent interpolations or additions by interested priests. That they are later interpolations can be proved in many ways and by the testimony of the best scholars. However, this is only by the way.

Before I have done with the laws of Manu, I should like to point out that there are various texts in Manu which bespeak an anxiety for the welfare of the unborn generations. Amongst Hindus, marriage is a sacred duty and a sacrament, and as such strictly and with the greatest regard for the interests of the unborn generations. The rules as to Brahmacharya, marriage, and its consummation are all framed with that express object in view. It is the procreation of good, virtuous and strong progeny whch is the object of an Aryan marriage according to the Aryan laws. Hence all marriages are regulated accordingly.

Let him, "says Manu, "who desires to raise his race, even form connec tions with the most excellent (men) and shun all low ones." With these laws before us, it is surely unjust to say that the genius of Hinduism is essentially individualistic. I have given these quotations from Manu-Smriti alone, although most of these rules and many more simi lar to these are also to be found in other books on the laws of the Aryas. Some of the rules are to be found expressed in almost the same language in every book on Hindu law.

From the laws of Manu, we proceed to examine the Vedic literature for traces of the social idea therein. Taking the Rigveda first, which is (according to Euro pean scholars) the most ancient of all the Vedas or for the matter of thajt, the oldest book in the Library of the Aryan race, we find the following exhortations in the 10th Mandala, Hymn CXCI.

Assemble, speak together : let your minds be all of one accord. As ancient Gods unanimous sit down to their appointed share.

The place is common, common the assembly, common the mind; be so their thoughts united. A com men purpose do I lay before you, and worship with your general oblation.

One and the same be your resolve, and be your minds of one accord. United be the thoughts of all that may happily agree.

The translation is that by Dr. Griffiths, but that there is a mistake or a misprint is clear from a compari son of the third stanza as given above with the original Sanscrit.

The word (mantrah) means scripture or vedic hymns — "A portion of the Veda including the Samhita and distinguished from the Brahmana, "— a charm, a prayer, a revolution or plan or policy (see Dr. Aptes Dictionary, p. 842). I fail to find any authority for its being trans lated by ''place''

The 1st stanza, which we have not reproduced, is a prayer to God (Agni) in which the Lord is asked to bring about the gathering of all friendly creatures round the common altar.

The translation of the second stanza, 2nd line, seems to imply that none should encroach upon other's rights and all should peaceably enjoy their shares. In the second line of the third stanza again, the original gives the idea of a common worship. The teaching of the hymn is reproduced in Atharva Veda, Book VI. 64, which Dr. Griffiths translates as below : —

"1. Agree and be united: let your minds be all of one accord. We reproduce the stanzas at the end. Even as the Gods of ancient days, unanimous, await their share.

2. The rede is common, common the assembly common the law, so be their thoughts united. I offer up your general oblation : together entertain one common purpose.

3. One and the same be your resolve, be all your hearts in harmony : one and the same be all your minds that all may happily consent." In this translation the word manirah" is rendered into "rede and the idea of a "common law "is express ly given out. In my opinion these two Mantras inculcate the conditions of an effective social organisation which is thus made to depend upon —

(a) community of language "Speak together or speak alike."

(b) Respect for individual rights.

(c) Common scriptures, common social life and com mon laws.

(d) A common (national) purpose or mission. The same idea is more clearly and still more beau tifully expressed in Atharva Veda, III. 30, which, as translated by Dr. Griffiths, runs as follows : —

1. Freedom from hate I bring to you, concord and unanimity. Love one another as the cow loveth the calf that she hath borne.
2. One-minded with his mother, let the son be loyal to his sire. Let the wife, calm and gentle, speak words sweet as honey to her lord.
3. No brother hate his brother, no sister to sister be unkind. Unanimous, with one intent, speak ye your speech in friendliness.
4. That spell through which Gods sever not, nor «ver hear each other hate, that spell we lay upon your tiome, a bond of union for the men.

5. Intelligent, submissive, rest united, friendly and Icind, bearing the yoke together. Come, speaking sweetly-each one to the other, I make you one-intentioned nd one-minded.
6. Let what you drink, your share of food be com mon: together, with one common bond I bind you. Serve Agni, gathered round him like the spokes about the chariot nave.
7. With binding charm I make you all united, •obeying one sole leader and one-minded even as the Gods who watch and guard the Amrita, at morn and ever may ye be kindly-hearted."

The same spirit runs through Atharva, VI, 73 and 74.

1. Let Varun come hither. Soma, Agni, Brihas yati come hither with the Vasus. Unanimous, ye kins men, come united, come to the glory of this mighty guardian.
2. The inclination, which your hearts have harbour, ed, the purpose which hath occupied your spirits, Bloomfield's translation (Sacred Books of the East, Vol. XVII, P. 134): stanza 5 is translated as follows: ' Following your leader, of (the same) mind, do ye not hold yourselves apart. Do ye come here, co-operating, going along the same waggon-pole, speaking agreeably to one another i render you of the same aim, of the same mind.'' This annul with sacrifice and butter. In me be your sweet resting place, O kinsmen.
3. Stand even here; forsake me not. Before us may Pushan make your path unfit to travel. Vastoshpati incessantly recall you ! In me be your sweet resting place, O kinsmen I"

"I. Close gathered be your bodies : be your minds and vows in union !

1. Here present Brahmanspati and Bhoga have assem bled you.
2. Let there be union of your minds, let there be union of your hearts; All that is troubled in your lot, with this I mend and harmonise.
3. As, free from jealousy, the strong Adityas have been the Vishnu's and the Rudra's fellows. So free from jealousy. Lord of three titles ! cause thou these people here to be one-minded."

Passages like these are to be found in abundance in the Vedic literature (Sacred Books of the East, VoL XIII., P. 360) and can be multiplied at pleasure. For the actual working of this spirit of unity you may study the Ramayana and the Mahabharata. In the latter you find a Devayani being appealed to sacrifice all her kshatriya pride, anger anddignity for the welfare of all of her race with success.

In its pages you find many interesting and instruc tive sermons on political science, the most noteworthy of which are those given by Bhisma on his death-bed. Then the celebrated Chanakya also says in his Niil "Sacrifice a member for the sake of the family, a family for the sake of a village, a village for the sake of a district, and even the earth for the welfare of the soul." There are other treatises on political science which promulgate the same truth. These quotations are only relied on to show that the sacred books of the Hindus contain the germs and the foundations of the highest social ideals and testify to the prevalence of a very high standard of social life amongst them with all the duties and obligations that such a life involves and implies./It is not my intention to suggest that we can or need learn nothing from the Europeans, but my object is only to show that there is sufficient in our sacred books round which we can rally for social strength and reform, and that with all our eagerness to sit at the feet of European savants and scholars we need neither des credit our ancestors nor indulge in general lamentations for want of social ideals in our past."

Lajpat Rat.

THE RELIGIOUS UNITY OF HINDUISM

It is often said that Hinduism is not the name of a particular religion, nor that of a religious nationality, and that it does not represent one set of beliefs, common to In the above article I have relied upon the English transla tion of Sanskrit Texts by European scholars so that there may be no occasion for a charge of straining the words or of extorting meanings or of inventing theories of my own; altliough I do not believe that these translations are the who call themselves Hindus, and that therefore it is perfectly idle to appeal to the Hindus in the name of a common nationality.

It has become almost a fashion to insist that the term Hinduism is too vague to be proper ly deRned, and that there is hardly anything substantially common which binds one Hindu to another in the ties of national brotherhood.

Hinduism, in short, is said to be more of a congeries of different religions, sects holding diverse and not unoften diametrically opposite views on matters of faith and doctrine. Hinduism is said to in clude and cover almost every form of religious faith known to or practised by mankind, from the purest monotheism to the lowest form of animism, polytheism, heno-theism, pantheism, in fact all sorts of isms.

There is a fairly large class of Hindus who suffer from want of faith in the potentialities of their religion to unite them or to inspire them to the lofty ideals of a great religions platform whereupon to bring together a Hindu union. To many the idea of a Hindu union seems to be nothing more than an unrealizable dream.

In their opinion, the talk of a Hindu nationality is a senseless talU, and the attempt to bring about a union amongst Hindus on the basis of religion is extremely impracticable. Some even go further and opine that the religious difficulties of the Hindus cannot be met with, removed or solved by an appeal to the Shastras, and that amongst Hindus religious reform, too, must pro ceed on lines and ideas borrowed from the West. We confess we are unable to subscribe to these views, and are rather inclined to hold just the otherwise. We have substantial reasons to maintain that Hinduism is at least as much a feligious nationality as its sister faiths, Christianity or Islam.

These two latter contain as' many varieties and shades of religious beliefs and doc trines in themselves, if not more, as Hinduism does, of course giving due consideration to the ages of these three religions. If Hindus have got their Vedantists, the Muhammadans have their Sufis and the Christians have those who have raised the banner of higher Christianity, If Hindus have their Trinity in Brahma, Vishnu and Shiva, the Christians havetheirs in Father, Son and Holy ghost. If the Hindus have got their Avatarts, the Chris tians have (besides the great incarnation of God in the body of Christ) their Popes and saints. If the Hindus believe in different deities, there are Muhammadans and Christians who believe in saints, WaHs, Mahdis, &c., &c..

If the Hindus have their sacrifices, the Muhamma dans and Christians have theirs also. If there are Hindus who are steeped in superstitious beliefs and ob serve many gross forms of worship, there are millions and millions of Muhammadans and Christians also, particularly the latter, whose religious practices are as gross as those of the multitude of Hindus. If there are fables in the Puranas, there are equally ridiculous sto ries in the Quran and the Bible. What is, then, that deprives Hinduism of that binding force which knits to gether the different discordant elements in Islam and Christianity ?

What are the special features of the latter that are absent in the former ? Is Hinduism entirely devoid of any basal principles on which the foundations of a church national could be laid ? It is these latter, that, we, at first propose to take in hand and eKamloe. touching upon the former whenever it is relevant to do so. Our first contention is, that, like the general mass of Muhammadans and Christians, the Hindus, likewise, directly or indirectly profess to accept the Vedas as their religious scripture. The great bulk of the latter, like the great bulk of the former, believe that their scriptures are the word of God, and are infallible. There are learned Muhammadans and Christians who cannot go so far and do not believe that the Quran and the Bible are the word of God.

On the question of the exact authority of the scriptures in these great religions of the world there are as many schools and shades of thought with all their varieties and niceties in one as in the other. There are scoffers, agnostics and sceptics everywhere. Everywhere there are men who do not care a jot for the scripture, make no secret of their views, but still cling to the outer form of the religion, the very essence of which they take pleasure in decrying. The number of such Christians is legion who do not believe that Christ was the Son of God or the son of the virgin, or that the Bible is the revealed word of God, but who do not still care to go out of the pale of outward Christianity. For the purpose of reli gious rites and ceremonies, for the purposes of baptism, marriage, etc., they are as much Christians as those who believe that every letter of the Bible was spoken by God Himself.

We have said all this not with the intention of dis paraging either Islam or Christianity but only in support of our contention that in these respects the religious diffi culties of the Hindus are in no way greater in extent, or larger in volume, than those of their fellow subjects, the Muhammadans and the Christians. We know there are some people who are so hepeless of Hindu unity, or who are so much perplexed with the endless variety of religious belief in Hinduism, that in moments of despondency they have been heard to apostrophize if it would not be letter for India if all Hindus were to accept Christianity, But irrespective of spiritual efficiency or inefficiency of Christianity, we are afi-aid even from the unity point of view we will not thereby be nearer the desired millenni um. That such is the opinion of all impartial and dis interested observers will be amply borne out by the following quotations which we cull from a paper written by the late Professor Theodore Goldstucker on the/Religious Difficulties of India.' In the paper under reference were noticed certain (then) recent publications by two learned Hindu converts'to Christianity, criticising Hindu religion and philosophy and exhorting their late co-religionists to solve their religious problem by em bracing Christianity.

After giving copious extracts from these publica tions containing the views of these learned Padries on the inconsistencies and anomalies of Hindu religion and Hindu philosophy, with his own comments there upon, the learned Professor says : —

"There is an other serious perplexity into which our learned authors must be aware that they will throw even those Hindus

(1) Dialogues on Hindu Philosophy.comprising the Niyaya, Sankhya and the Vedanta to which is added a discussion on the authority of the Veda by K. M. Bannerjee of Bishop College, Calcutta.

(2) A Rational Refutation of Hindu Philosophical Systems by Niikanth Shastri Gore. who may be clever enough to overcome all these diffi culties, but it has as little been removed by them as indeed any difficulty which besets the solution of the religious problem in India.

Their object as we have seen, is to persuade their countrymen to embrace the Christian religion, but they have neither explained to them what the Christian religion is, nor where it may be found. Any Hindu, who follows the deductions of Mr. Bannerjee, would simply infer that there is but one Christian religion, which a devout student of the Bible might easily acquire from a perusal of the sacred book. Let him descend, however, from the region of abstrac tion into that of reality, and he will soon discover the' endless variety of opinions which may be founded on the apparently so intelligible scriptural text, and he will soon learn that, so far from this being a mere possibility, hundreds of creeds have sprung up from this same scriptural soil, every one of which claims to be in ex clusive possession of Christanity. Andif he be disposed' to investigate hifdoricalhf the mutual relation of all these creeds he will Jind that their difference is so essential that it tvas strong enough to perpetuate the most inveterate animosi ties and to result in wars the like of which cannot he traced in the history of ang other creed,

We have no desire to enlarge upon this theme,, for we have said enough to explain why we hold the solution proposed by Mr. Bannerjee to be an im possibility. Attempts of conversion are too frequently made without examining the limits within which they are possible and the result in which their momentary suc cess may end. If a man derives his religious views from his own individual information or from sources which are void of authoritative influence, he may yield them to the views which are of a higher range without causing injury to the nobler part of himself.

Bttt if the creed of an individual is founded on texts held sacred and authoritative, it is a national creed; no indiiidual can abandon it without seveHnrj himself from the national stem; no nation can surrender it without latfing the axe to its own root. For religion hated on texts believed sacred, embodies the whole history of the nation which professes it; it is the shortest abbreviation of all that ennobles nations mind, is most dear to its memory aad most essential to its life. No religion has better illustrated this truth than the religion founded on the Bible. It coula be, and was successfully, introduced amongst all nations which possess no texts supposed to be divinely inspired, and therefore of general authority, and whenever a nation possessing merely the semblance of such a text, adopted it, it thereby decreed its own end.

The Romans and Greeks, when becoming Christians, ceased to be the continuation of the classical Romans and Greeks, in history, in literature, in character. Their political im portance based on the conditions of the past, was brought to a close, and they had to grow into another nationality. The conditions under which this religion introduced itself into the countries of Europe was always the absence of a book ascribed to divine authorship. When Mr. Bannerjee speaks of the Jews, he has chosen an exact counter instance which goes far to prove that even a people without land, without any history which can be called their own — that a people exposed to all the horrors of persecution and all the allurements of seduc tion did not and does not espouse that very religion which exercises the most powerful influence on its actual destinies and which it even supports and favours amongst those who profess it. The Jews do not become Christi ans, simply because they believe that their Testament is a sacred book.

Having expressed these views as to the undesirabi lity and impossibility of converting Hindus to Christianity! Professor Goldstucker further addresses the Hindus themselves, and lays down what, in his opinion, is the true key to the solution of their religious difficulty. We cannot do better than once more quote his words which are full of significance and pregnant with great meaning to all educated Hindus : —

"We have been carried, however, with these remarks to the point where we cannot shrink from expressing the views which we entertain of the duties of the Brahma nical Hindus of our own days. We need not empha sise mere than we have already done, that we reject as unwise and unpractical any attempt to persuade them to become Christians or to adopt the Biblical scriptures as their spiritual code. We want them to become a nation worthy of their ancestors and worthy of the great role, which in ancient times they have acted in the history of the human race, and we are satisfied that they cannot regain that position by breaking the spring ties of their life, and by exchanging their own religious uncertainty for that of any other creed.

It is necessary, however, that they should realise the condition in which they are. We need not prove to them that the minds of the en lightened portion of their nation are estranged from the sectarian worship as it is practised now, but who could satisfy them that they are utterly remiss in examining where the root of the evil lies. Every Brahmanical believer, if asked, will tell that the mode of his worship is founded on the Vedas. He refers us, it is true, occa sionally to the Puranas and Tantras, but he himself admits that these works have no authoritative powers unless they can prove that the tenets they contain are drawn from the Vedic source. The pivot, then, on which all religious questions of, India turn, is and remains — the Veda. Philosophers and non-Philosophers, Vishnuits and Sivaits, all echo the word Veda; Forty years have elapsed since these words were written by one of the profoundest Sanskrit scholars and one of the most competent and shrewd students of com parative religions, which Europe produced, but the words hold as good, as true and as forcible to-day as they were ever. In fact, the events of these forty years have, in stead of showing any flaw either in ths arguments or in the sentiments of the learned Professor, proved, if any further proof was needed, how accurately did he grasp the real situation and how truly did he lay down the solution.

We repeat, therefore, before we close, for the pre sent, that the pivot on which all religious questions of Hindu India turn is, and remains — the Veda. To the Veda, therefore, we must go for light and guidance in our religious troubles, and in the Veda we shall find our solace.

Lajpat Rai.

THE ONE PRESSING KEED OF INDIA

(a sense of public duty and a high standard of PUBLIC morality)

A question has often haunted us, asleep or awake,, as to why is it that notwithstanding the presence amongst us of great vigorous and elevating religious truths, and of the very highest conception of morality we have been a subject race, held down for so many cen turies by sets of people who were neither physically nor sprituually nor even intellectually so superior to us as a fortiori to demand our subjection.

We do not require a Herbert Spencer to tell us that the social efficiency of a social organism as such, de pends upon the sense of social responsibility amongst the members of such an organism. The greater and the intenser the sense of responsibility amongst the indivi dual members, regarding the safety and the welfare of the whole, the greater and the stronger the efficiency of the organism.

It is precisely this sense which is wanting in us and which stands in our way as a nation. Physically we are the equals of any people on earth. Barring those high class Hindus who think their glory consists in weak constitutions, delicate limbs and womanly features or who are given to determine their position in society by the amount of fat on their body and by the amount of physi cal inactivity which attends their business in life, the majority of our countrymen possess fine physiques and are able to withstand any amount of hardship and strug gle. Even with the little they get to satisfy their animal wants, with their coarse food, scanty clothing and ill ventilated and excessively crowded homesteads they pro duce a soldiery which ranks amongst the best in the world. Whether it be the Rajput, the Jat, the Sikh, the Gurkha, the Purbia, the Marahtta, or the Punjabi Mussulman the view expressed above holds equally good in the case of all. All of them have by turns, earned the highest praises of military experts under whom they had occasion to serve beneath the British flag. What ever may be said of the many mistakes of head and heart by which they lost their own battles before the ad vent of the British, no one can question their bravery and valour. History is full of their deeds. Intellectually too, given the opportunities, the sons of India have given no occasion to shame their mother country. The Hindu civilization, the Budhistic achievements are standing monuments of their high intellectual calibre.

Under Mohammadan rule as well, when according to the celebrated Alberuni, the elite of the Hindu community sought the safety of the remote and the farthest parts of the country to be secure from the molestation of the fanatically disposed Mohammadans, the country conti nued to produce intellectual giants whose names still shed luster on the country of their birth. Under the British, too, with the few opportunities that are posses sed by the

Indian scholar to distinguish himself, the country has produced a Bose, a Ramchandra, a Paranjpe, a Ranade, and many others whose names are the common property of all Indians.

Then if we look to the domain of religion we stand almost unequalled other country in Europe can show the equals of the un known authors of the Upanishads, Budha, and Shankra charya ? From religion if we come down to the regions of philosophy, where in one country could we find such a galaxy of truth loving, honest and bold thinkers, as the immortal authors of the six Darshanas, and some of their commentators and elucidators ?

Again, glancing at the history of chivalry and noble deeds, does not the history of the Rajputs ifldd like a romance ?IWhy then, are we sa jow in the scale of nations? What is it that keeps us down and does not allow us to raise our head above the waters ?

We are not wanting in flexibility or adaptability. Where on earth will you find another case parallel to Hindu ism ?

Notwithstanding 12 centuries of Islamic propa ganda backed by all the forces of political ascendancy and of that moral superiority which is the ancher sheet of a virgin religion and a conquering creed; notwithstan ding again of 100 years of active evangelical work done in the name of Christ by devoted Missionaries, Hinduism still reigns supreme in the land and baffles all attempts made from time to time, to displace and overthrow it.

How is it then, that with all the education we have re ceived during the one century of British rule, with fran tic professions of patriotism that are the natural result of a knowledge of our degradation and helplessness, with wild cries of nationality in danger, with pathetic appeals for reforms in the administration of the country, we have so far failed to gain anything substantial in our quest after national liberty?

How is it that our cries make no impression, our appeals go unheeded and our professions turn to be of no avail? While sparing no occasion or means of criticising Government measures, very often offering right and sen sible criticism, with that amount of persistency which sometimes we show, we are yet powerless to obtain even the smallest measure of reform either in constitution or in administration, or even of remedial justice ?

Why leaving the political sphere aside, how is it that even in matters of social reform which being in our hands no Government prevents us from giving effect to, we have so far failed to achieve that amount of success which the Herculean efforts of men like Ram Mohan Rai Dayaeand Saraswati, Ishwar Chandra Vidyasagar and Madadeva Gobind Ranade deserved ?

The reply is the same as we have already given above. We are in dividually wanting in that sense of social responsibility which requires each and every member of the organism to place the interests of the community or the nation over and above those of his own. Amongst us selfish ness, greed and calculation reign supreme. Most of us cannot even think of the society or the community or the nation. But even those who can think and do profess to care for them do not care a farthing for the same, when their own individual interests seem to clash with the interests of the society.

Most of us, including some of the very highly educated men, who do not fail to exhibit often an unpardonable pride in the amount of learning locked in their brains who very readily spend hours in finding fault with the commas and semi-colons of less gifted brethren, who do not fail to parade their knowledge of the philosophy of Herbert Spencer, of the Science of Huxley or of the fine or a Tennyson are utterly dovoid of a sense of social responsibility.

We know that men who denounced the institution of child marriage in the vehement language they could "Command, where at the same time conscious of the fact that they had themselves already fixsd a date for the mar riage of their seven years aged g'rl with a boy of a similarly tender age. We have known men whose professions of patriotism were often the most profuse giving a point blank refusal to any demand of help for any na tional institution.

We have known of great patriots roll ing in wealth, possessing palatial residences, enjoying the Wessing of a good fixed income, never moving their finger to reduce misery that was next door to them Wa have seen gresit patriotic Indians passing by in a spirit of per fect indifference, when another countryman of theirs was being cruelly beaten by a European.

No Indian is suppos ed to make any move unless such move pays or benefits him in cash or in kind in any way. If you go to a gen tleman to ask him to join such and such an association or to do such nnd such a thing, the question that he puts to you or if he has not the courage to do so openly, to himself, is what shall he gain thereby ?

We know that people give subscriptions, attend meetings, join Associa tions and Samajes and do a lot of other things that have the look of public spirit or national help but how many of them, may we ask except when moved by religion, db so by a sense of public duty and individual rosponsibi lity for the national cause ?

It is very unpleasant to speak ill of one's own countrymen or to appear to be ungrate to those estimable gentlemen who do keep public movements going but to be truthful we shall be failing in our duty if we were to pretend a belief in their patrio tism.

It is our firm belief that if the country could have claimed the one tenth part of that patriotism which is often paraded and assumed, the state of things would have been different and no Government could have ignor ed the existence or the demands of such patriotism. But. the facts are otherwise; not that the social ideals taught by our religion are low and mean, not that this rank selfish ness and base calculation of self interest is countenanced by the teachings of our greatmen, not that this sense of national and public duty is entirely absent from the teachings of our Shastras.

No Political degradation for so long as practically extinguished the very germs of this noble sentiment from our blood. Our immediate ancestors did not possess it, so we could not inherit it from them. As for its inculcation from without we are sorry that the advantages of Western culture have not been unmixed.

While very few have imbibed its noble sentiments, a large number have taken and adopted in life its materialistic tendencies. We know that we re quire the latter, too, rather badly but we cannot forget that, if we once allow ourselves to be possessed of these only without the other necessary and counteracting ten dncies, we are done for.

The country may grow rich, it may extend its commerce, it might even begin to manufacture for other countries; but unless all this is accompanied by a sense of public duty in the people of this country, all this will not avail us, nay, might be the very foundation of future fall, if further fail is yet possible. Yes, we want, all this..

foremost of all we want the habit and ssnse of sub ordinating our individual interests to end before the in terests of the community at large. In short, what we pre-eminently want is that every Indian may be suffici ently patriotic and dutiful to believe and act up to the belief that the interests of the country are paramount and must override all private considerations. We want this to be regularly taught as the highest religion that will bring about the salvation of India.

To promulgate this we want faithful and true preachers who may be living examples of the truth of their propaganda and who can show the power of their faith in their own persons. Let each province produce a number of such preachers and we are convinced that patriotism will gain firm ground in the country and the cause of nationality will advance with leaps and bounds. Without this we may go on crying for decades and decades but we shall not advance an inch.

REFORM OR REVIVAL?

We thought that with the fall of the old class of Pandits we had done with thdse wars of words which were formerly carried on with all the weight of great learning and accompanied by a demonstrative show of deep erudition, but we had evidently counted without our hosts the great body of Indian reformers that are the products of English education, who owe nothing to the old school of Pandits and for whom the old school of Pandits have incurred no responsibility whatever.

Be fore the spread of English education in this country there were only two classes of public literary or in tellectual entertainments to which the people were treated now and then and which supplied some diversion from the otherwise dull monotonous or in some places extremely hazardous lives which they generally led.

The one was the most popular and useful practice of reciting the mixed and general audiences consisting of all classes of people from old men to boys and from old ladies to young girls. The ancient epics of the land — the chornicles of the life of Rama and his consort, ajid the great Mahabhart — were very often the books that were thus recited.

These were greatly instrumental in keeping the national spark alive through so many vicissitudes of national fortune, when on occasions it had almost reach ed the point of total extinction. The second were the periodical religious discussions, which in most instances originated with the advent of a learned Pandit from the outside.

Very often the new Pandit's discourses had caught the popular ears and the local Pandit or Pandits thought their dignity, presitige and even emoluments were in danger, to prevent which calamity they considered it their duty to come out and give a challenge to the newly arrived, to prove his superiority in the knowledge of the shastras by an open discussion.

Or it might be that the new-comer thought his success depended on drawing out the local theologian and giving him a defeat. Be it as it may, the invariable result was that the discussvow Vs;a.' with words, the accuracy of one or the other, the applicability or the nonapplicabi lity of certain rules of grammar and ended often if not always in words and sometimes in blows.

I am sorry to observe that the present quarrel over "reform or revival"between the reformers seems to me to resemble, at least in parts, the above mentioned wordy polemics between the Pandits. The reformers claim to be the: leaders of the community.

They have occupied the place of the Pandits and divines of former times. They profess to lay down rules for the guidance of the general mass of people. They are agreed that the state of Hindu society is bad and rotten, that it needs great and radical changes and that without these changes the whole social fabric stands in danger of giving way and burying the nation down in its debris. They have remedies ready, patent and infallible. On most of these they agree, only to differ on the name by which the same is to be styled. Their agreement as to the remedy disap pears in their differences about the wordy habitat to be given to the proposed and contemplated changes. One class of people who have already established a name for themselves do not like to give up the name they have patented and by which they have gained distinction.

These latter gentlemen call themselves reformers and insist upon certain social changes being introduced in the name of "reform "and reform only. The other class who have lately come into prominence call themselves "revivalists ", and they swear that any change in the social customs and institutions of the community can only be introduced under the shadow of revival. They think they cannot tolerate reform.

The result is that while the former taunt the latter as "revivalists and ireactionaries', the latter mock the former as "reformers and revolutionists ". Both classes cont'ain amongst them reat and good men, men with pure motives and noble intentions.

They are generally prominent men — well read and deep in the lore of history. Both classes are to all appearances sincere in their convictions and efforts, but to the great misfortune of the country and the nation rthey cannot join their heads and work amicably.

The wordy weapons are sometimes changed, and while the reformers take their stand on reform on rational lines"-the revivalists plead for "reform on national lines."Here for once at least they seem to agree on reform, as the force of the difference is centred on the words "rational " rand "national".

The result is that much ink and paper are uselessly spent in dilating upon the necessary sound ness of reform and the danger and risk of revival, and vice versa. Unfortunately no one ever sees and deplores the great waste of valuable time and precious energy which this quarrel involves — time and energy which could he usefully employed in, nay, which is imperatively demnanded, by so many other things that are the sine qua non of national progress and that should be done but :are not done from want of working hands.

On both sides are arrayed tough warriors armed with the know Uedge and experience which is gathered by deep study iand growing years. On both sides are arrayed sturdy and stout soldiers possessed of and carried by the enthusiasm of youth, full of ambition, and proud of credentials gained by academical successes and literary achievements.

On both sides the pen and with strength. and vigour not totally devoid of grace. It is very perilous to come between such daring, bold, and determined fights specially for a comparatively ill-provided and poorly circumstanced man like myself who can wield neither the pen with the dexterity that comes of practice, nor the tongue with that skill which is the outcome of discipline. In fact I am rather inclined to think that it is positively dangerous for recruits wha have not had the advantage of regular lessons in drill' or of the discipline that comes out of exercises at the manouevres, to interfere between such veteran combat ants. But the interests at stake are so great, the field' is so vast, the workers in the field are so few and far between, the amount of energy available is so little and the resources are so limited, that on better thought I have decided to take the risk and raise my voice against what to me looks sheer waste of opportunities and mis application of energy.

I will begin by examining into the respective pro grammes of reformers and the revivalists and see if there are any vital and real differences which justify so much contemptuous talk of each other.

On both sides, I be lieve that the social reform programme begins and very rightly too, with the question of early marriage. I con fess I am unaware of any radical difference between the views of the reformers and the revivalists on the point,.

In provinces other than the Panjab Mrs. Besant is be lieved to be the leader of the latter. Now, who does not know that she is opposed to early marriages and de nounces them as unshastraic and disastrous ? She has in fact taken pains not only to definitely pronouncer against this evil custom, but to give force to her utter ances, has shut the doors of a department of her school at Benares against those who might have been or might be by the improvidence have their guardians married at a tender age.

The Arya-samajists also may to a certain extent be called revivalists, but in this matter of early marriage and the marriageable ages of boys and girl they go to a step further than even the most radical re former is prepared to go just now.

They say and preach, and try to enforce their precept, that no girl be married under 16 and no boy under 25. Now let us ask if there is anything irrational in saying that the institution of child-marriage is not only condemnable by reason, but is actually opposed to the letter as well as the spirit of the Shastras.

From the question of child-marriage we may proceed to the great evil of the present divisions and sub-divisions of caste. Mrs. Besant and her school have already pronounced against the sub-divisions in the main castes. Her defence of the original Hindu conception of four castes principally coincides with the views of the Arya-samajists in the matter and practically knocks the present caste system on the; head, though in theory only.

In practice neither the Arya-samajists nor the reformers can go further than denunciation. All of them agree that a beginning should be made with the siib-divisions.

The sub divisions having been swept away (which is not likely to be achieved very soon or very easily) the time will then come to think of the remoulding or the fusion of the main castes on shastraic or rational lines. For the present we are all agreed that the existing arrangement is an unmixed evil, and the sooner it va dowe. tlie better. From castes let us proceed to the question of foreign travel, and here again we find a practical un animity.

Of course, there are and there shall continue to be ultra-orthodox people who will not give up their opposition to any of these measures and will continue to say that they are un-Hindus; but just now we are not concerned with them, as we dare say there is no one who can justly or even contemptuously be called a revivalist who condemns foreign travel on the plea of revival and no reform. Then let us take up the great question of female education. I know of no sensible man in the country, not to speak of the revivalists only, who is a man of culture and education, who is opposed to it.

The school of Mrs. Besant, the Arya-smajists, and the reformers are all pledged to it. There may be and there are practical difficulties in the way of educating our girls and sisters and wives, but nobody questions the desirability, nay the necessity, of giving, if possible, the very highest education to girls.

People may differ on the modus operandi or may have different views about schemes of education to be enforced, in the case of females, but there are no two opinions on the question of principle.

There may be some among the so-called revivalists who are not favourably disposed to an exact copy of European customs and usuges relat ing to females being adopted by the Hindus, but surely there is none who can in the name of revival defend the existing Purdah system or the universal ignorance of women. Similarly we do not think there is much difference of opinion at least so far as practice feasible at present are concerned, on raising the social status and bettering the condition of low castes, if Hinduism is not bent upon social indi fference and mad neglect of vital interests which might Tesult in disastrous consequences.

With the exception of some apparently spurious passages in Manu and other 'Smritis, there is absolutely nothing in the more ancient literature to justify the inhuman and cruel treatment to which the low castes are at present or were till lately subjected. We think we have almost exhausted the list of prominent subjects comprised in the list of reforms advocated by the social reformers, having reserved one important matter to be discussed last, viz. the question of widow remarriege.

On this question there exists undoubtedly real difference of opinion between the so-called reformers and the so-called revivalists. We grant that the ques tion is a very important one; but still we are not pre. pared to admit that a difference on this single question justifies all that bitterness which characterises the writ ings of these two classes about one another. The real and important differences are on questions of religion and worship which the social reformers profess to exclude from their curriculum of school and college education Here in the Punjab, fortunately we have been spared that bitter fight over these words which is going on in the Western and Soutnern Presidencies, although we are not unware that of late attempts have not been wanting to introduce it in collegiate and inter-collegiate debates.

We cannot but deprecate these unwise attempts aad hvII warn our young men from the vortex of this absolutely for fight over words. We may be pardoned for pointing out that to us the fight seems to be generally on the same lines and on the same grounds which marked the polemics of the old class of Pandits.

The real truth is that the so-called reformers are mostly in faith and in religion Brahmos. They were the earliest in the field and fought for reform when the revivalists had not yet come into existence. The revivalists are the products of a wider diffusion of Sanskrit literature whcih has taken place principally within the last quarter of a century.

This study has afforded them sufficient and strong evi' dence of their ancestors having enjoyed a great and glorious civilization from which most of the present evil practices and customs that are the bane of modern Hinduism were absent.

They therefore naturally look to the past for light and guidance and plead that a revival might lead them into that haven of progress which is the object of all. They have found that most of the social evils existing in their society were not to be found in ancient Hindu race and they have therefore begun to appeal to the authority of the past and the shastras for the introductions of these very reforms for which re formers had been pleading with much force though with scanty success on grounds of utility and natural justice.

The revivalists are naturally popular in Hindu society as they take their stand on the authority of the Hindu Shastras and thus threaten to oust the reformers from their hard earned position.

Then to add insult to injury, their ex position of the popular religious beliefs of the Hindus is so injurious and cunning as to justify it in the minds of the reformers that nation back to superstitions and low and debased forms of worship from which English education, contract with Western religion, and a study of the master-minds of the West was just extracting them with so de sirable a success. The reformers had thus based their religious propaganda on the same basis on which their social programme rested, viz., grounds of ration ality.

The revivalists having taken to the defence of the so-called national, have extended the same base ta the removal of social evils and thus the fight began between "reform on national lines"and reform on ra tional lines."But, as I have pointed out above, so far as real social reform is considered, both lines of work lead to a common conclusion.

It is not therefore fair to entangle social reform in this quarrel which is really based on differences in religious views. Let the reformers by all means if they like, ridicule the religious views of "the revivalists" and criticise or hold them to derision, but it is not, to say the least, graceful and fair to talk of them contemptuously in matters of social re form. The same should we say to the revivalists.

Happily here in the Punjab, are we have already said, there is not much difference between reform and revival. By far the strongest reforming agency in the Panjab ap pears to accept both.

To them reform is revival and revival is reform. It is true they attach much importance to nationality or to national lines, but subject to the im portant proviso that then irrational.

In for things national if only they are not irrational; but no further. According to them nothing can be either national or rational which is against the letter or the spirit of the Vedas. So far there seems to be no danger of the Panjab being involved in this meaningless distinc tion between reform and revival, but we think it is better to take time by the forelock and sound this note of war ning to guard against any contemplated or impending jnischief.

But over and above that, it is our earnest request to the leaders of the Hindu community in the AVestern and the Southern provinces to abjure this absurd distinction and to work harmoniously for social reform, to least so far as all are agreed upon.

Lately I had occa rsion to listen to an address on social progress by an esteemed friend of mine who is a pronounced social re former. In the course of his remarks he treated the revivalists with scant respect, and in support of his views read the following quotation from the Amraoti speech of-that great reformer — the late Mr. Justice Ranade:—

On the other side, some of our orthodox friends find fault with us, not because of the particular roforms we have in view, but on account of the methods we follow. While the new religious sects condemn us for being too orthodox, the extreme orthodox section denounce us for being too revolutionary in our methods.

According to these last, our efforts should be directed to revive and not to reform. I have many friends in this camp of ex treme orthodoxy, and their watchword is that revival and not reform should be our motto. They advocate a return to the old ways, and appeal to the old authorities and the old sanctions. Here also, as in the instance quoted above, people speak without realising the full significance of their own words.

When we are asked to revive our institutions and customs, people seem to be very much at sea as to w hat it is they want to revive What purticular period of our history is to be taken as the old?

Whether the period of the Vedas, of the Smritis, of the Puranas, or of the Mahomedan or modern Hindu times ? Our usages have been changed from time to time by a slow process of growth, and, in some cases,. of decay and corruption, and we cannot stop at a parti cular period without breaking the continuity of the whole. When my revivalist friend presses his argument upon me, he has to seek recourse in some subterfuge which really furnishes no reply to the question. What shall we revive? Shall we revive the old habits of our people when the most sacred of our caste indulge in all the abo minations, as we now understand them, animal food and drink which exhausted every section of our country's zoology and botany?

The men and gods of those old days ate and drank forbidden things to excess in a way no revivalist will now venture to recommend. Shall we revive the twelve forms of sons, or eight forms of mar riage which included capture, and recognised mixed and illegitimate intercourse ?

Shall we revive the Niyoga system of procreating sons on our brother's wives when widowed ? Shall we revive the old liberties taken by the Rishis and by the wives of the Rishis with the marital tie? Shall we revive the hecatombs of animals sacrifieed from year's end to year's end, and which human beings were not spared as propitiatory offerings? Shall we revive the ahakti worship of the left indecenies and practical debaucheries?

Shall we revive the sati and infanticide customs, or the flinging of living men into the rivers, or over rocks, or hook-swinging, or the crushing beneath Jagannath car? Shall we revive the internecine wars of the Brahmans and Kshatriyas or the cruel persecution and degradation of the aborigi nal population? Shall we revive the custom of many husbands to one wife or of many wives to one husband? Shall we require our Brahmans to cease to be landlords and gentlemen, and turn into beggars and dependants upon the king as in olden times ?

These instances will suffice to show that the plan of revivmg the ancient usages and customs will not work our salvation, and is not practicable. If these usages were good and beneficial, why were they altered by our wise ancestors ? If they were bad and injurious, how can any claim be put for ward for their restoration after so many ages ?

Besides, it seems to be forgotten that in a living organism as society is, no revival is possible.

The dead and the buried or burnt are dead, buried, and burnt once for all, and the dead past cannot therefore be revived except by a reformation of the old materials into new organised being-"

Now, if it be permissible for a comparatively young and inexperienced man without laying himself open to a charge of disrespect for one of our revered leaders whose great wisdom, deep learning, and general judicial-mindedness are accepted all around, I will, with due deference to the late Mr. Ranade, beg to point out the injustice of the observations quoted above.

Cannot a revivalist, arguing in the same strain, ask the reformers into what they wish to reform us? Whether they want to be reformed on the pattern of the English or the French? Whether they want us to accept the Divorce laws of Christian society or the temporary marriages hat are now so much in favour in France or America?

Whether they want to make men of our women by put ting them into those avocations for which nature never meant them ? Whether they want us to substitute the legal vhjoga of the Mahabarat period with the illegal and immoral nhjoga that is nowadays rampant in European society? Whether they want us to reform into Sunday drinkers of brandy and promiscuous eaters of beef?

In short, whether they want to revolutionise our society by an outlandish imitation of European customs and man ners and an undiminished adoption of European vices ? The revivalists do not admit that the institutions which they want to revive are dead, burnt and gone.

The very fact that they wish to revive them goes to show that they believe that there is still some life left in them and that given the proper remedy, their present unhealthy and abnormal state is sure to disappear and result in the bringing about of the normal and healthy condition of affairs.

In fact, in an earlier part of the same address: Mr. Ranade summed up the position of the revivalists in a few well chosen and apt words when he admitted that. In the case of our soc'ety especially, the usages which at present prevail amongst us are admittedly not those which obtained in the most glorious periods of our his tory.

On most of the points which are included in our programme, our own record of the past shows that there has been a decided change for the worse and it is surely within the range of practical possiblity. Religion as defined in the west.

That we may work up our way back to a better state of things without stirring up the rancorous hostilities which religious differences have a tendency to create and foster. It is exactly this working up our way back, which the revivalists aim at. No revivalist has ever plea ded for the institutions selected by Mr. Justice Ranade as the butt end of his attack against them.

The real significance of these words, — reform and revival — if any, seems to be in the authority or authorities from which the reformers and the revivalists respectively seek their inspiration for guidance in matters social.

The former are bent on relying more upon reason and the experience of European society, while the latter are disposed to primarily look at their shastras and the past history, and the traditions of their people and the ancient institutions of the land which were in vogue when the nation was in the zenith of its glory. On our part we here in the Panjab are prepared to take our in spiration from both these sources, though we prefer to begin with the latter and call in the assistence of the former mainly to understand and explain what is not clear and ambiguous in the latter. But so long as our conclusions are principally the same, I think the fight is not worth beinocontinued and may be dropped for good.

Lajpat Rai.

RELIGION AS DEFINED IN THE WEST

A consideration of the religious problem must be begun with a consideration of the what is religion ? "One would tell us what the idea of religion is, there must not be any differences about its meaning and conception and that everybody, all over the world, must have the same notion about it But, strange to say, there is no other subject upon which there exists a greater want of unanimity than that of religion.

There are great, important, wide and extensive differences in men's conceptions of religion. No two communities understand quite the same thing from it. Professor Max Muller says, "If there is a word that has changed from century to century and has a different as pect in every country in which it is used — nay which conveys peculiar shades of meaning as it is used by every man, woman or child — it is religion."

Still a compara tive study of religions will disclose a fair amount of agreement or at least some salient points which form the fundamental basis of most of the great religions of the world.

Before we come to these common salient points we think we might profitably consider the various definitions of religion, that have from time to time been attempted by those who have discussed the subject and thrown light upon the same. We might begin with the root-meaning of the word and its etymological derivation, though perhaps we may not gain much therefrom. Unfortunately even here we fail to find a unanimity. Some amongst them whose derivation has been accepted by Max Muller, derive it from Latin re legere, to gather up again, to take up, to consider, ta ponder — opposed to neglect.

According to this derivation religion originally regard, reverence and audience. reverence for the gods.

Very soon more than more restricted to reverence for the gods and divine beings. People began to speak of a man's religion, meaning his piety, his faith in the gods, his observances of ceremonies till at last an entire system was called religions or religion.

There are others who derive religion from religare, to bind up, to fasten, to moor i.e. what binds or holds us back. But it is quite clear that if religio or religion originally meant attention regard, or reverence it did not continue to retain that simple meaning.

The word has had such a vast and varied use that it is almost hopeless to invent such a comprehensive definition as to cover the meanings of all those who have used it, discussed it and lived by it. With some the word has been synonymous with all that is good and noble in this world, with others it had nothing to do with the affairs of the world.

With some it was only another name for morality; with others it overlapped morality and expressed a sense of spiritual ecstasy. With some it expressed the relationship of the spirit of man with that Universal Spirit, God. With others it directed a number of ideas in which God had no place at all, while there were others whose conception of religion even directed the existence of what we call human soul or spirit. By way of illustration we will notice a few of these attempts at defining religion.

Kant, for instance, one of the greatest European savants, says, "religion is morality."According to him, looking upon all our moral duties as divine commands is religion.

To the question whence originates the building force of those moral duties, Kant has no satisfactory reply. Having no faith in revelation, he-cannot ascribe this authorship to God. Wnat then does he mean by asking us to look upon moral duties as divine commands ?

He calls them divine because in his opinion we are directly conscious of them. In the words of Professor Max Muller, any outward divine authority is in the eyes of a Kantiah philosopher mere phenomenal or as we should say a mere confession of human weak ness. Fichte, however, an equally great name in European philosophy, takes an exactly opposite view.

He denies that religion is morality because he says religion is never practical and was never intended to influence life.

In his opinion pure morality serves the latter purpose and religion is knowledge which gives man a clear insight into himself, answers the highest questions and thus imparts to us a complete harmony with our selves and a thoroujh satisfaction to our mind. Appa rently this seems to be very much like the arya of the Indian Vedanti of the school of Swami Shankaracharya.

Then there are the two definitions of Schleier Macher and Hegel expessing two opposite views. Ac cording to the former, religion consists in our conscious ness of absolute dependence on something which though it determines us we cannot determine in turn.

The latter, however, declares that "the feeling of depen cdence is the very opposite of religion."According to Hegel, "religion is or ought to be perfect freedom,"for it,is, according to him, nothing more nor less than the Divine Spirit becoming conscious of himself through the finite spirit. This again sounds like Vedantism.

The next step from this was taken by Comte who has tauht that man is not only the object of religion and religious worship. We are told that man cannot know any thing higher than man; that man therefore is the only true object of religious know ledge and worship, only not man as an individual but man as a class.

This last qualification is the keynote of Comte's philosophy and no doubt reaJs very solemn,, even sublime. But it was reserved to Fenerbach to give the last of the brush and remove even "this last mystic hold off the brow of religion. According to him "self love is a necessary, indestructible, universal law and principle and inseparable from every kind of love.

Reli gion must and does confirm this on every page of its history. Wherever man tries to resist that humaa egoism, in the sense in which we explained it, whether in religion, philosophy or politics he sinks into pure nonsense and insanity, for the sense which forms the foundation of all human instincts, desires and actions is the satisfaction of the human being, the satisfaction of human egoism.' Hegel's rough but curt criticism of this definition is so pertinent that we cannot resist the temp tation of quoting it. He says that if the feeling of depen dence were the sole test of religion then a dog would be the most religious of all creatures.

Thus if universal philanthropy or humanity is reli gion according to Comte, pure selfishness is religion according to Fenerbach. To the same school belongs the definition of Gruppe who says that "religious belief is a doctrine professing to be able to produce union witb a being or the attainment of a state which, properly speaking, lies beyond the sphere.

According to him, "religion of some body's imagination, the acceptance of which is ue to the unconscious vanity of its founders, a belief in-the happiness which it procures to its believers and the-substantial advantages which society derives from it."

From the philosophers definitions of religion we ifiext proceed to the definitions of European theologians. Martineau describes it as a belief in an ever-living God, i.e. a Divine Mind and Will ruling the universe, and holding moral relations with mankind. Professor Flint defines it as man's belief in a being or beings, mightier than himself, and accessible to his senses, but not lindifferent to his sentiments and actions, with the feelings and practices which flow from such a belief.

Spinoza says, "religion is the love of God founded on a knowledge of his divine perfections." Reville : — Religion is the determination of human life by the sentiment of a bond uniting the human mind to that mysterious mind whose dominations of the world and of itself it recognises and to whom it delights in feeling itself united.

These definitions are objected to because they exclude certain systems of belief and practice which, although univer sally recognised as religious yet ignore the existence of God or gods (such as Budhism).

Consequently an attempt has been made by Professor Max Muller and some other writers to invent definitions of religion which may be sufficiently wide and comprehensive to include :all that has till now been known or styled as religion.

He defines it to be "a mental faculty which independent, ay, in spite, of sense and reason, enables man to.apprehend the Infinite, under different names, and under varying disguises. With great difference to these great names we cannot help remarking that we have quite failed to realize the necessity of finding such a definition of religion as may cover all those forms of belief or faith that have to this day bien, whether rightly or wrongly, described or styled as religions. This, in our humble opinion, is not the correct way of teaching what is religion? It may be a suitable definition for historical purposes but certainly not for theological or ethical or moral.

LAJPAT RAI.

MODERN AGE AND THE HINDU RENAISSANCE IN THE 19TH CENTURY

Many Hindu reform movements originated in the nineteenth century. These movements led to the fresh interpretations of the ancient scriptures of Upanishads and Vedanta and also emphasised on social reform. The marked feature of these movements was that they countered the notion of western superiority and white supremacy propounded by the colonizers as a justification for British colonialism in India. This led to the upsurge of patriotic ideas that formed the cultural and an ideological basis for the independence movement in India.

Brahmo Samaj

The Brahmo Samaj was started by a Bengali scholar, Ram Mohan Roy in 1828. Ram Mohan Roy endeavoured to create from the ancient Upanishadic texts, a vision of rationalist 'modern' India. Socially, he criticized the ongoing superstitions, and believed in a monotheistic Vedic religion. His major emphasis was social reform.

He fought against Caste discrimination and advocated equal rights for women. Although the Brahmos found favourable response from the British Government and the Westernized Indians, they were largely isolated from the larger Hindu society due to their intellectual Vedantic and Unitarian views. But their efforts to systematise Hindu spirituality based on rational and logical interpretation of the ancient Indian texts would be carried forward by other movements in Bengal and across India.

Arya Samaj

Arya Samaj is considered one Hindu renaissance movements of the late nineteenth century. Arya Samaj is often considered as a social movement, many revolutionaries and political leaders of the Indian Independence movement like Ramprasad Bismil, Bhagat Singh, Shyamji Krishnavarma, Bhai Paramanand and Lala Lajpat Rai were to be inspired by it.

Swami Vivekananda

Another 19th century Hindu reformer was Swami Vivekananda. Vivekananda as a student was educated in contemporary Western thought. He joined Brahmo Samaj briefly before meeting Ramakrishna, who was a priest in the temple of the goddess Kali in Calcutta and who was to become his guru. Under the influence of Orientalism, Perennialism and Universalism, Vivekananda re-interpreted Advaita Vedanta, presenting it as the essence of Hindu spirituality, and the pinnacle indeed of the development of human's religiosity.

This project started with Ram Mohan Roy of Brahmo Samaj, who collaborated with the Unitarian Church, and propagated a strict monotheism. This reinterpretation produced neo-Vedanta, in which Advaita Vedanta was combined with disciplines such as yoga and the concept of social service to attain perfection from the ascetic traditions in what Vivekananda called the "practical Vedanta". The practical side essentially included participation in social reform.

He made Hindu spirituality, intellectually available to the Westernized audience. His famous speech at the Parliament of the World's Religions at Chicago on 11 September 1893, followed huge reception of his thought in the West and made him a celebrity in the West and subsequently in India too. His influence can still be discerned in popular western spirituality, such as nondualism, New Age and the veneration of Ramana Maharshi.

A major element of Vivekananda's message was nationalist. He saw his effort very much in terms of a revitalisation of the Hindu nation, which carried Hindu spirituality and which could counter Western materialism. The notions of White supremacy and Western superiority, strongly believed by the colonizers, were to be questioned based on Hindu spirituality. This kind of spiritual Hinduism was later carried forward by Mahatma Gandhi and Sarvepalli Radhakrishnan. It also became a main inspiration for the current brand of Hindu nationalism today. One of the most revered leaders of the Rashtriya Swayamsevak Sangh (RSS), Babasaheb Apte's lifelong pet sentence was "Vivekananda is like Gita for the RSS." Historians have observed that this helped the nascent Independence movement with a distinct national identity and kept it from being the simple derivative function of European nationalisms.

Bibliography

Ajeet, Javed: *Secular and Nationalist Jinnah*, JNU Press, Delhi. 1999.

Anand, Som. *Lahore: Portrait of a Lost City*. Lahore: Vanguard Books, 1998.

Athlye, D. V.: *The Life of Lokmanya Tilak*, Pune 1921.

Aziz, K. K.: *Complete Works of Rahmat Ali*, Islamabad, National Commission on Historical and Cultural Research, 1978.

Bapat, S. V.: *Tilak Sukti Sangraha*, A Kesari Prakashan, Pune, 1926.

Barill, C.: *Social and Political Ideas of B.R. Ambedkar*, Aalekh Publishers, Jaipur, 1977.

Benjamin, Joseph: *Scheduled Castes in Indian Politics and Society*, Ess Ess Publications, New Delhi, 1989.

Bhalla, Alok: *Stories about the Partition of India*, New Delhi, HarperCollins, 1994.

Bhat, V. C.: *Lokmanya Tilak*, Prakash Publications, Pune, 1956.

Bhatia, K.L.: *Dr. B.R. Ambedkar: Social Justice and the Indian Constitution*, Deep & Deep, New Delhi, 1994.

Bruce Carlisle Robertson: *Rammohan Ray, The Essential Writings of Raja*, Delhi, 1999.

Burgess, James: *The Chronology of Modern India*, Edinburgh, 1913.

Campbell-Johnson, Alan: *Mission with Mountbatten*, London: Hale, 1982.

Chagla, M. C.: *Roses in December: An Autobiography*, Bombay, Bharatiya Vidya Bhaven, 1974.

Chaudhuri, Nirad: *Thy Hand, Great Anarch! India: 1921-1952*, London, Chatto & Windus, 1987.

Dalton, Dennis : *Gandhi's Power : Nonviolence in Action*, New Delhi, OUP, 2001.

Dasai, M. H.: *Day to Day with Gandhi*, Varanasi, Sarva Sangh Pakistan, 1968.

Erdosy, George: *The Indo-Aryans of Ancient South Asia*, New Delhi, 1955.

Ghosh, Ila : *Rgvedic Rsikas : Life and Philosophy*, Eastern Book Linkers, Delhi, 2007.

Ghosh, Suresh Chandra: *Education Policy in India since Warren Hastings*, Calcutta, Naya Prokash, 1989.

Ghoshal, U. N.: A *History of Indian Political Ideas*. London, 1966.

Gopal, S.: *Selected Works of Jawaharlal Nehru*, New Delhi, Orient longmsn Ltd., 1972-81.

Gupta, S. P. and K. S. Ranchandrau: *The Mahabharata : Myth and Reality*, Delhi, 1976.

Hasan, Mushirul: *India's Partition: Process, Strategy and Mobilization*, New Delhi, Oxford UP, 1993.

Hasan, Syed Shamsul: *Plain Mr. Jinnah*, Karachi, Royal Book Company, 1976.

Jafar, Malik Muhammad: *Jinnah as a Parliamentarian*, Lahore, Afzar Publications, 1977.

Joshi, V.C.: *Rammohun Roy and the Process of Modernization in India*, Delhi, 1975.

Lumby, E. W. R.: *The Transfer of Power*, London, Allen, 1954.

Mahajan, Mehr Chand: *Looking Back*, London, Asia Publishing House, 1963.

Mathur, Y. B.: *Women's Education in India 1813-1966*, Asia Publishing House, 1973.

Memon, M. U.: *An Epic Unwritten: The Penguin Book of Partition Stories*, New Delhi, Penguin, 1998.

Menon, V. P.: *The Transfer of Power in India*, Bombay, Orient Longman, 1957.

Michel, A. A.: *The Indus Rivers: A Study of the Effects of Partition*, New Haven, Yale UP, 1967.

Moore, R. J.: *Escape from Empire: The Atlee Government and the Indian Problem*, Oxford, Oxford UP, 1982.

Mukhtar, Zaman: *Students' Role in the Pakistan Movement*. Karachi, Quaid-iAzam Academy, 1978.

Naidu, Ratna: *Old Cities, New Predicaments: A study of Hyderabad*, New Delhi, Sage Publications, 1990.

Naik, J. P.: *Political Content of Education*, Socio Research Publications Centre, Calcutta, 1917.

Sarkar, J.: *Caste, Occupation and Change*, B. R. Publishing Co., Delhi, 1984.

Sharma, G. S.: *Legislation and Cases of Untouchability and Scheduled Castes in India*, Allied Publishers, Bombay, 1975.

Shashi B.R.: *Ambedkar and Human Rights*, KK Publishers, New Delhi, 1981.

Silverberg, James: *Social Mobility in the Caste System in India*, Mouton Publishers, The Hague, 1968.

Singh, L.P. : *Portrait of Lal Bahadur Shastri*, Delhi: Ravi Dayal Publishers, 1996.

Talib, G. S.: *Muslim League Attack on Sikhs and Hindus in the Punjab 1947*, New Delhi, SGPC, 1991.

Taneja, Anup : *Gandhi, Women, and the National Movement*, 1920-47, New Delhi, Har-Anand Pub., 2005.

Tinker, Hugh: *Experiment with Freedom, India and Pakistan 1947*, London, Oxford UP, 1967.

Wavell, Archibald: *Wavell: the Viceroy's Journal*, Karachi, Oxford University Press, 1974.

Yasin, Mohammad : *Indian Politics : Processes, Issues and Trends*, New Delhi, Kanishka, 2004.

Yogesh, A.: *The Changing Frontiers of Caste*, National Publishing House, Delhi, 1968.

Yong, Tan Tai and Kudaisya, Gyanesh: *The Aftermath of Partition in South Asia*, London, Routledge, 2000.

Zaidi, A. Moin: *Evolution of Muslim political Thought in India*, New Delhi: S. Chand, 1975-79.

Zelliot, Eleanor: *From Untouchable to Dalit: Essays on the Ambedkar Movement*, Manohar, New Delhi, 1992.

Index

R

S

U

V

❑❑❑